**The Nationalizing of
American Life, 1877–1900**

SOURCES IN AMERICAN HISTORY

GENERAL EDITOR: *George H. Knoles*

Professor of History and Director of
the Institute of American History,
Stanford University

The Nationalizing of American Life, 1877-1900

Edited by Ray Ginger

Brandeis University

The Free Press, New York

Collier-Macmillan Limited, London

Preface

THE FREE PRESS SOURCES IN AMERICAN HISTORY series reviews the history of the United States from its beginnings in the seventeenth century to the present. Each of the nine volumes consists of from 15 to 35 carefully chosen contemporary documents illustrating the major themes—political, economic, social, and cultural—of American history and civilization. The volume editors, selected for their specialized knowledge of the periods into which the series is divided, have drawn upon the rich resources of the American past for the materials to be included in their respective books. They have ranged over the principal geographical areas of the United States and have exploited a wide variety of genres—governmental and political party documents, descriptive and analytical accounts, theoretical writings, and literary products. History is a seamless web and one learns about himself and his past by exploring the multivarious experiences of his forebears and their reflections upon those experiences.

The editors have kept the student in mind while selecting the items to be reprinted in each volume. They have not only chosen significant documents, but they have respected the intentions of the original writers to the extent that the materials are offered substantially as the authors produced them with a minimum of cutting and editing. We have, therefore, put together a set of volumes containing a limited number of major documents reproduced in extenso rather than a series containing hundreds of snippets which can suggest, at best, only an impressionistic view of history. To promote thoughtful reading and discussion of these materials we have introduced each selection with headnotes containing biographical and bibliographical data. Moreover, we have included in each headnote four or five suggestions indicating what students should look for in reading the documents; these do not tell the reader what is in the material, but they are useful in directing his attention to the salient points covered. Finally, the editors have added to each note two or three titles of books that might be consulted for further study of the author of the document or of the problem or episode dealt with in the selection.

Each volume contains an extended introductory essay, an interpretive narrative written by the volume editor, which treats the period as a whole and relates the documents to the history under consideration. These essays incorporate both factual and conceptual information obtained from recent historical research; they reflect the new findings of contemporary scholarship.

Professor Ray Ginger, in *The Nationalizing of American Life, 1877-1900,* has addressed himself with great skill and understanding to the task of providing a set of documents to assist the instructor and the student to come to terms with a puzzling era of American history. The years 1877 to 1900 have long baffled the historian as he sought to find some theme or thread to give a sense of direction and unity to the last quarter of the nineteenth century. Other periods of American history seem to offer the scholar built-in dramatic unities or developmental forces, which he can utilize effectively to provide a framework for his narrative or course of study. Examples of this drawn from book and chapter titles crowd our attention: "The Age of Jackson," "The Civil War and Reconstruction," and "The Age of Roosevelt."

The years covered by this volume, however, do not lend themselves to easy synthesis; one finds no neat formula to summarize the period nor a movement that inexorably progresses toward a climax. The skein is tangled and full of knots. History as experience, of course, is much more chaotic than history as conceived by the scholar. The scholar is obliged to attempt an orderly and usable representation of the past; if he can do this without having his readers lose sight of the contingent quality of experience, so much the better.

The period from 1877 to 1900 displays this quality of contingency as the nation expanded in its economic, political, and social features as well as in its outreach beyond the national boundaries. Moreover, as social change accelerated, thoughtful men and women in their reflections upon experience sought to reduce chaos to meaningful reconstructions with which the minds of men could cope.

Professor Ginger has succeeded in giving structure to the period, at the same time conveying to the reader something of the sense of how it felt to be associated with the events and experiences of that particular generation of Americans. The documents he brings us open windows to the past and permit us to see the clash of men and events during those years as people participated in and reflected upon the nationalizing of American life.

Stanford University   GEORGE HARMON KNOLES

Acknowledgments

The directors of several manuscript collections have been very generous in their help. I wish to thank in particular Leslie H. Fishel of the State Historical Society of Wisconsin; Gene M. Gressley of the Western History Research Center, University of Wyoming; Robert W. Lovett of Baker Library, Harvard University; and Clyde C. Walton of the Illinois Historical Library. I am also indebted to three colleagues at Brandeis University: Eugene C. Black, Howard M. Gitelman, and Ramsay MacMullen. Aid of various kinds has been given by Ann Cooper, Barbara MacDonald, and my wife Evelyn.

In the Introduction, the documents that follow have been referred to parenthetically by number. They are arranged chronologically within each of four broad categories. The classifying of a document into one rather than another of these categories was in substantial degree arbitrary. Indeed, the categories themselves are not self-contained, and one of my chief aims was to include documents that would show the interaction of, say, constitutional doctrine with business history, as does No. 27. Items 1 and 4 are political history as well as business and economic; No. 32 reflects intellectual and political history as well as foreign policy. Each of the four categories might appropriately include some part of No. 33.

RAY GINGER

Contents

Part II. Social and Intellectual History]

Part III. Political and Constitutional History]

**The Nationalizing of
American Life, 1877–1900**

As the advent of the steam railway drove deep into American imaginations, diverse aspects of it captured different men. Already in 1851 an exalted soliloquy in *Moby Dick* had Ahab exclaim: "The path to my fixed purpose is laid with iron rails, whereon my soul is grooved to run." The States by 1900 were far more United than when Melville wrote, not just politically but in many other respects, and the chief force behind this unifying process was the creation of a nationwide railroad network. Even before the Civil War the early and essentially local railways were being welded into trunk lines such as the New York Central, which soon was only one of five lines tying the Northeastern seaboard to Chicago. Other great systems were formed in the Southeast. The first road linking the Midwest to the Pacific was finished in 1869, and by 1893 it had several companions. The pace of railroad construction fluctuated violently from year to year, but in general it shot upward. Fewer than 3,000 miles of new track were opened in 1877; a record 13,000 in 1887. The total mileage of the country by 1889 was twice that of twelve years earlier.

The imaginations of businessmen grasped that cheaper, better transportation was opening up unprecedented opportunities to make money. "The fact is that the railroad has revolutionized everything," said *The Commercial and Financial Chronicle* in 1882. Or as Henry Demarest Lloyd wrote [1] *: "The movement

* Numbers in brackets refer to Documents in the present volume.

of the railroad trains of this country is literally the circulation of its blood." When any region was first linked to the national railway network, the ton-mile cost of shipping goods in or out might well fall to a tenth of what it had previously been by wagon. After the railroad was opened, further mechanical improvements and competition often brought further reductions: the average freight charge on the Lake Shore and Michigan Southern fell from 1.5 cents per ton-mile in 1870 to 0.5 cent thirty years later.

The railroad—and the streetcar—facilitated an enormous growth of cities. Not that the late nineteenth century saw a record rate of urbanization, if by that word we mean the percentage growth of towns having 2,500 or more inhabitants; the peak in this respect came from 1840 to 1850 when the urban population of the United States rose more than 90 percent. But in absolute terms urban growth after 1880 was 8 million persons per decade. A Chicago that hardly existed in 1830 had 500,000 residents in 1880, 1,100,000 in 1890, 1,700,000 in 1900. Such mushrooming caused the value of a square foot of land at a preferred site to soar, and probably more fortunes were made by dealing in real estate than in railroading or in manufacturing. Increases in the value of footage merely because it chanced to be in a certain place—near a new streetcar line, for instance [29]—as distinguished from increases due to building or other improvements by the landlord, were obviously the result of the growth of the community. Insisting that it was unjust to let such "unearned increments" go to private owners, the great reformer Henry George wanted the government to confiscate them by taxation and to abolish all other taxes [4].

Foodstuffs and tobacco and other crops poured into urban markets from farm areas that increasingly tended to specialize in one or a few products. The impact of lower freight rates in an agricultural district can be seen vividly in Bell County, Texas, some 115 miles northeast of Houston. Farmers there in 1879, growing all of the breadstuffs they consumed, had them ground into flour at local mills. They grew little cotton, for the cost of hauling it by wagon to the Gulf ports was too high. Then came railroads. Output of wheat in the county fell by 75 percent in a decade, as farmers began buying flour of better quality that had been ground in Minneapolis from wheat grown in the

Dakotas or Kansas. To pay their bills they sold cotton, growing four times as much in 1889 as in 1879. Improved acreage in Bell Cotton in 1889 was thirteen times as large as in 1869.

Wheat farming became highly mechanized on the Great Plains. With the hand methods used before the Civil War, some sixty-one hours of labor were needed to produce an acre of wheat; with the machine methods after 1890 the job could be done in three hours, nineteen minutes. Already by 1879 farm output was half again as great as it had been six years earlier. The upsurges in the cotton and wheat crops were accompanied by better facilities for dealing in wheat and cotton futures—that is, for buying a given quantity of wheat today at a given price, the wheat to be delivered at some future date [9].

In some regions of diversified farming, such as the fertile corn-hog area of northern Illinois, the railroad and the steamship made it possible for middle-sized operators to ship their products to distant markets, and such men sometimes won through to physical comfort [14]. But in wheat farming the small man was likely to go under, while the survivors were giant and highly mechanized bonanza farms of thousands of acres. The same rule held in cattle ranching. Prior to 1878 meat from the West had been shipped eastward after being cured (salted, smoked, or canned); in that year the Chicago packer Gustavus Swift made his first experimental shipment by rail of refrigerated beef. High profits in ranching the next few years brought a rapid increase in herds ranging the lands from Arizona to Montana. Surprisingly, the ranchers in Wyoming came, not from Texas and California and Mexico, but from the East and even from England. Much of the new capital in the industry also came from Great Britain or was put up by wealthy Easterners such as Theodore Roosevelt and his Harvard classmate Richard Trimble, who spent a few years on a Western ranch [3]. Supplies of beef soared; prices tumbled; as a business, ranching hit a corrective in 1886-1887 when a summer drought and winter blizzards left 15 percent of the cattle in Wyoming dead on the plains.

Nowhere else was farm poverty so severe as in the overwhelmingly rural South. There the average wealth per person in 1880 was only $376, compared to $1,086 in the rest of the country. Four years of war had not only disrupted the Southern labor system by freeing the slaves, it had ruined railroads, destroyed factories, left only two horses or mules where three had been before. As farmers paralleled the trends elsewhere toward specialization by concentrating on the single crop of cotton, editor Henry W. Grady of the Atlanta *Constitution* began to project the vision of a New South in which multicrop agriculture would be balanced by industry and commerce [12]. Textile-machinery builders in New England sold increasing numbers of spindles and looms in Georgia and the Carolinas, and even acted in effect as architects by designing the mill buildings and the plant layouts. But the impetus toward manufacturing did not transform the South overnight: in 1900 the labor force of South Carolina was less than 4 percent in manufacturing, 69 percent in farming, while not one person in twenty-five in North Carolina was an urban resident.

Elsewhere the progress of urbanization and industrialization was more rapid, so that the United States by 1890 was no longer a farming country. Total population rose from 47 million in 1877 to 76 million in 1900. In 1870 nearly 7 million persons were employed in agriculture, fewer than 6 million in other pursuits. But the latter categories grew far more rapidly. In 1890 farming had fewer than 10 million workers, while other jobs could claim nearly 13,400,000 persons.

Just as a farmer in Texas or Kansas found himself competing in a world market against cotton from Egypt or wheat from India and Argentina, so did many factories face the alternatives of producing for a widening market area or going out of business. Since accounting at the time was poor the available figures are not satisfactory, but a made-up example can show the forces at work. Assume two iron mills, each small and inefficient and producing for a localized market. Mill A has manufacturing costs (including a satisfactory profit) of $40 a ton; Mill B of $60 a ton; the two are located 40 miles apart. If it costs $1 a ton-mile to ship iron by wagon, the respective markets of the two mills will meet 10 miles from Mill B, for at that point each mill can deliver iron for a selling price of $70 a ton. Now suppose a railroad is built, so that freight charges fall to 10 cents a ton-mile. Mill A can sell iron at the very door of Mill B for $44 a ton. Mill B must shut down. And Mill A, now able to sell more iron, can increase its scale of operation, cut its manufacturing costs below $40, and reach out for still more distant markets. The "nationalizing of American life" was often a brutal affair.

The railroads did make possible many other efficiencies; in factories, as in farming, output per man-hour rose quickly. But science tended to be applied chiefly in those ways that could be made to yield a monetary profit. Public health conditions were ghastly, and in some places doubtless deteriorated. The population might have grown even more rapidly had it not been for lack of sanitation, epidemics, and the high rate of infant mortality. Any town could yield replicas of the New England gravestone:

> Daniel W. 2d, Died 1876, Age 7 Mos.
> Waldo P., Died 1876, Age 7 Mos.
> Franklin A., Died 1880, Age 5 Mos.
> Children of Daniel E. & Fannie S. Hillyer

If twelve or fifteen infants were born into a family, often only three or four grew to adulthood.

Indeed, the deplorable state of medical practice, added to the possibilities of nationwide distribution, actually created opportunities for the makers and peddlers of nostrums. True social pioneers pointing toward our own day—the first manufacturers to advertise directly to consumers and to aim for a national market, the first merchandisers to experiment at manipulating psychology—were the manufacturers of patent medicines [2]. They led other industrialists into pushing brand names: Wrigley's chewing gum, Grape Nuts, Postum, Bayer aspirin, Chase and Sanborn coffee. The railroads, by vastly enlarging the geographical region within which an efficient producer who advertised shrewdly could hope to sell his output, would have revolutionized much of life even if they had acted impartially. But they did not. They discriminated. The most notorious favoritism was that shown to Standard Oil by the Northeastern trunk lines. They paid it rebates; that is, they refunded part of the freight charges they collected from it. At times they even paid rebates to Standard Oil on oil shipped by its competitors. Thus they played a major role in creating monopoly in other industries [1].

What possible motive could they have for such erratic behavior? A good sound business motive. The root of the trouble
was that there was not enough traffic to enable all of the railroads to make a profit; the president of the New York Central
wailed: "five great railroads to New York, with only business
enough for two." To make matters worse, much of the expense
of running a railroad was in "fixed costs." The interest due on
a railroad's bonds, for instance, was fixed at so many dollars;
it did not change whether the line hauled one ton of freight or
a million tons. Standard Oil could play one trunk line against
another in bargaining for concessions because the road that got
its business by cutting prices would in fact benefit thereby. But
only if its rivals did not retaliate by cutting their own rates.
They were not so foolish; they did retaliate; the rate wars were
ruinous to one railroad after another.

This dilemma of the railroads, like the overproduction of wheat
and cotton, points to a most significant feature of the period:
chronic and general excess capacity. Doubtless temporary over-
capacity in specific industries is a price that must be paid for
any economic progress. But by the 1870s technological advance
and the mechanization of production had made it possible to
make more of everything than the American market would
absorb at profitable prices. (The one important exception that I
have found—raw wool—is a special case that can be explained,
but not in the confines of this Introduction.) Railroad capacity,
farm staples, steel ingots, kerosene, coal, copper, textiles, live
steers and dressed meat—all were fighting desperately to maintain their profit margins. The president of Standard Oil, John D.
Rockefeller, later recalled: "All the fortune I have made has
not compensated for the anxiety of that period. Work by day
and worry by night, week in and week out, month after month.
If I had foreseen the future I doubt whether I would have had
the courage to go on."

By the very nature of the problem, not all businessmen could
solve it, and many companies were forced out of business. But
men did find a wide range of solutions that enabled them as
individual firms to operate at a profit. Some resorted to advertising to capture a larger share of a market not large enough for
all. Others turned to vertical integration, reaching back to an

earlier state of production to acquire their sources of raw material, as Standard Oil did when it began to produce crude oil in the Lima-Indiana field, or reaching forward to a later stage, as Gustavus Swift did when he set up a national sales apparatus to push his meat products. The growth of vertically integrated companies to giant size was often the result of vastly enhanced efficiency that benefited the entire economy: integrated plants in the steel industry such as Carnegie's Homestead mill meant huge savings in fuel costs because the material could be moved without cooling from blast furnace to Bessemer converter to rolling mill.

But Andrew Carnegie knew as well as anybody that another type of integration—the horizontal kind, involving the combination of firms at the same stage of production which formerly had competed with each other—might bring no gains in efficiency, might even, indeed, bring losses. The aim here was less to reduce costs of production than to raise to profitable levels the price at which output could be sold. This might be done by setting quotas to reduce production; it might be done by dividing the market geographically. It might be done all too well to be good for the companies that did it. Thus the Distillers' and Cattle Feeders' Trust for a while kept the price of whiskey so high that distilling attracted a swarm of new competitors; the price of whiskey fell; the Trust went bankrupt in 1896.

Such competition, so Carnegie argued in 1889 in an article that superbly described the genesis of a typical business combination or "trust" [7], would undermine any monopoly that might be achieved. But the voters were not convinced, and they put increasing pressure on Congress to adopt remedial legislation. Already in 1883 the Interstate Commerce Commission had been established, supposedly to regulate the railroads. In 1890 came the Sherman Anti-Trust Act [24], banning all contracts and combinations in restraint of interstate or foreign commerce. Congress, to the superficial view at least, had yielded to public antipathy to the trusts. But the courts did not yield. By ruling that the I.C.C. had no power to fix rates and by weakening its powers in other respects, they made it virtually impotent until the Hepburn Act of 1906. The Anti-Trust Act fared rather better, but similarly the courts construed much of it away. In a brilliant speech during the Senate debates that led to the law, Senator Orville H. Platt of Connecticut pointed to "this deadly, brutal warfare which is called competition" as a justification of combinations to raise prices to remunerative levels. More, he suggested two of the more important constitutional doctrines later applied by the courts: that manufacturing is not part of interstate commerce, and that only "unreasonable" combinations are illegal [23].

The Supreme Court also revised, indeed almost reversed, the meanings of "liberty" and "property" in the Fourteenth Amendment. In the Slaughterhouse Cases (1872) the Court held to the common law meaning of "property" as use value; that is, as the right of physical possession and the right of legal title. A violation of property rights must deprive a man of one or the other. But the minority of justices were already urging a new definition, which was unanimously embraced by the Court twenty-five years later in *Allgeyer* v. *Louisiana* [27]. The rights of property were expanded to include exchange value:

. . . his enjoyment upon terms of equality with all others in similar circumstances of the privilege of pursuing an ordinary calling or trade, and of acquiring, holding, and selling property, is an essential part of his rights of liberty and property, as guaranteed by the 14th Amendment.

So long as "property" meant use value it was a right to produce in order to increase the supply of goods; if it meant exchange value it was a right to limit production in order to gain bargaining power and raise prices.

The rights of property also found defenders in the executive branch, and none was stronger than Grover Cleveland. Laissez-faire—the notion that government should limit itself to police matters and leave the economy alone—had many consistent adherents in England, but not in the United States, where Cleveland would be as close as anybody to this point of view: he stood for personal honesty, tariff reduction, inexpensive government [22]. As governor of New York he vetoed a bill that would have set a maximum fare of five cents on the New York elevated transit lines, saying that it violated the constitutional ban on laws impairing the obligation of contracts. He also vetoed a bill that would have set a maximum workday of twelve hours for drivers and conductors on horse-drawn streetcars (it did allow longer hours, but at higher pay); Cleveland thought it an inexcusable violation of the freedom of contract of employers and employees.

Not that many trade-union contracts actually existed, but a few did, most of them in the building or printing trades or among the skilled crafts on railroads; some too were signed with factories by affiliates of the Knights of Labor [5] or of the league that in 1886 became the American Federation of Labor. It was the latter organization which, during the depression year 1884, urged a campaign to reduce the working day to eight hours, beginning May 1, 1886. This step was essential, said its advocates, because mechanization had created widespread unemployment and chronic excess capacity, so that it had become necessary to share the work [6]. The national unions that pressed the campaign grew swiftly; the Carpenters' and the Cigarmakers' unions, for instance, each doubled its membership.

The agitation produced one of the social crises of the period, in Chicago, where a series of strikes and much violent language led citizens to fear civil war. The climax came on May 4, 1886, when a phalanx of police marched to break up a peaceful but anarchist-sponsored meeting at Haymarket Square. A bomb was hurled into the ranks of the police. Seven were killed. Although the identity of the bomb-thrower was never established, four men were hanged for the crime, and three others served long terms in prison. The defendants' cause was prejudiced, not just by their radical ideas but also by the foreign birth of most of them. And if the German origins of several Haymarket defendants evoked fear and hostility in American nativists, those qualities burst forth even more violently as New Immigrants (still stranger than Germans) began to appear. Repeated efforts were made to impose some barrier against arrivals from eastern or southern Europe, often illiterate, many of them dark-skinned, most of them Catholic or Jewish rather than Protestant. All such efforts before 1900 failed. Bohemians became farmers in Nebraska or factory hands in Des Moines; Italians found work on railroad construction gangs or in the mining districts of Pennsylvania; Greeks operating restaurants or Jewish peddlers and storekeepers could be found across the country; but most of the New Immigrants clustered in the cities and industrial towns of the North-east [8].

Immigration from 1880 to 1893 averaged more than 500,000 persons a year; then financial panic and depression cut the figure in half until 1900 when it surged to new highs. This inflow contributed a great deal to the economic growth of the United States, and especially so since an abnormal percentage of the immigrants were adult males between the ages of 15 and 40 who had been nurtured to a productive age in Europe. Material progress was in some respects unbelievably rapid. Steel production rose nearly 20 times, from 570,000 tons in 1877 to 10,200,000 tons in 1900. Output of bituminous coal and of crude oil each rose about seven times. The tangible assets of the country were perhaps two and a half times as great in 1900 as in 1877.

The gains, however, were distributed very unequally to the population [4, 6, 8, 25], and the startling pace of change itself helped to produce desperate labor struggles. Significantly, the biggest and most violent strikes began on railroads—the upheavals of 1877 [1], the Pullman boycott of 1894—for it was there that large-scale organizations for private profit reached their ultimate in the nineteenth century. But these sensational disputes should not bemuse us, for the organization of trade unions advanced very slowly, and radical ideologies spread hardly at all among wage earners. As early as 1871 the leaders in the United States of the First International Workingmen's Association tried to explain to a world congress in London why Americans were not class-conscious [10].

The sustained and bitter rebellion of the period was made, not by industrial workers, but by farmers. They had excellent cause to become angry and to stay angry. As competition among railroads prompted them to build into unoccupied territory in the West and South for fear some rival might seize it first, it became imperative to them that the lands should be developed quickly so as to provide freight and passengers. Their propaganda to attract settlers was reinforced by that of steamship lines seeking immigrants, of state and territorial and local governments, of real estate dealers. The results were often fantasy: "One good lung here is worth a pair in the damp heavy air of the older states," said a land pamphlet about Kansas. "Western Kansas is pre-eminently 'THE PARADISE OF THE LUNGS.' " Perhaps so, but its low rainfall made it perdition for farmers. Or there was the formula evolved by a land speculator and the state geologist of Nebraska who sought to convince prospective immigrants that rainfall would increase after an area was settled: "Rain follows the plow."

Lured by such propaganda and by their greed for quick wealth, men by the scores of thousands poured into new districts of the Great Plains. But even if they got their land free from the government under the Homestead Act or some other law, they could not establish themselves cheaply. It cost more than $1,000, even on free land, to get a 160-acre farm into operation and to support a family until the first crops were garnered. Many farmers had to borrow a large part of these initial outlays of capital. Even those who had the required $1,000 often borrowed more to buy additional land or equipment: a thresher, a twine binder, a large reaper, another wagon. The typical farmer was in debt.

Present evidence suggests that he was not exploited by the lenders as much as was formerly thought. The supply of liquid capital in the East and in Europe was increasing rapidly; throughout the period, interest rates sagged. This trend was intensified because the Federal government was running a chronic surplus; that is, it was taking out of the economy in taxes each year more than it was spending for goods and services. From 1881 to 1890 Federal debt was being paid off at an annual average rate of $100 million, perhaps 1 percent of the Gross National Product. There can be little doubt that these Federal surpluses had a deflationary effect on the entire economy. The general level of prices in 1896 was only about half of what it had been three decades earlier.

The tendency for prices to fall was especially severe for farm staples. Mechanization and the enormous increases in acreage under cultivation caused supplies of agricultural products to grow far more rapidly than demand. The number of acres in farms doubled between 1870 and 1900. The output of wheat and cotton in other countries was also growing, and staple farmers everywhere threw their crops onto a fiercely competitive world market. American cotton output in 1894 broke the record, but farmers actually got less for their crop than in the panic year 1873, even though they had planted nearly 2½ times as many acres in cotton. Cotton in 1869 had sold for 16.5 cents a pound; in 1894, a mere 4.6 cents. Corn in 1866 brought 65.7 cents a bushel; in 1896, only 21.4 cents. Wheat, at $2.06 a bushel in 1866, was down to 48.9 cents in 1894.

Prices of many things the farmers bought were also falling, but the semimonopolistic manufacturer of farm equipment, for instance, was in a far better position than any farmer to maintain the price of his output. And some of the farmer's important expenses did not fall at all. For him, as for a railroad, the interest and principal of a debt was a "fixed cost"; having borrowed money, it cost him so many dollars a year and so many at its maturity. A wheat farmer who mortgaged his land for ten years in 1866 for $1,000 was borrowing the equivalent of 500 bushels of wheat. But in 1876, with wheat down to $1.03, he had to pay back the equivalent of 1,000 bushels. By 1894, a thousand dollars would buy two thousand bushels of wheat.

Reasoning that an increase in the volume of money would raise the prices of their crops, farmers became convinced inflationists. During the Civil War the government had issued over $400 million in Greenbacks, paper money that could not be redeemed in gold or silver. By 1878 farmers were demanding the issue of even more, and Greenback candidates polled more than a million votes in the congressional elections. But the movement collapsed the next year when poor crops in Europe and bumper crops in the United States sent wheat prices soaring. That same year the United States returned to the gold standard, and thenceforth all American money had to be redeemed by the Treasury in gold at the legal rate. Redemption in gold seemed essential to bankers and many businessmen especially in order to stabilize the relation between American money and British; without such stability it would have been much more difficult to borrow in Britain the capital needed by American railroads and mines and other industries. These groups came into head-on conflict with the demand of debtor-farmers for a greater quantity of money in circulation.

Already another inflationary device was being urged: the free coinage of silver. By the "Crime of '73" Congress had stricken the silver dollar from the official list of coins. Then a great increase in the production of silver from Western mines sent the price of silver on the free market tumbling below the former legal ratio—sixteen ounces of silver equal in value one ounce of gold. Mine owners and miners wanted to compel the government by law to buy unlimited quantities of silver in order to drive its price up. They scored a modest success in 1878 when the Bland-Allison Act required the government to coin not less than $2 million nor more than $4 million in silver bullion each month. But output of silver continued to mount, and the price went on falling. It partially recovered for a time after the Sherman Silver Purchase Act of 1890 increased the amount of silver that the government was required to coin. President Cleveland forced the complete demonetization of silver in 1893, and the next year the price of silver was less than half what it had been at the time of the Crime of '73. Wealthy mine owners gave liberal subsidies to the American Bimetallic League, which hired William Jennings Bryan and other lecturers to agitate the cause [26].

Their words struck ready ears in wheat and cotton regions. In 1890 a farm mortgage existed for every farm family in the states of North and South Dakota, Nebraska, Kansas, and Minnesota. Conditions in the South, which held nearly four times as many farmers as the Northern Plains, were even worse. A letter from Burke County, Georgia, reported that only 14 out of 1,500 customers at one store could settle up their debts after they had sold their crops. By 1891 the Farmers' Alliance was reported to have 35,000 lecturers active in the South, and men supported by it formed the majorities in eight Southern legislatures. The following year rural elements, especially in the South, took the lead at the convention of the People's Party of America. Although the new party was primarily "agricultural interest politics" rather than a class movement, some of its demands were quite radical. In addition to calling for free coinage of silver and for an increase in the quantity of money to $50 per person, it demanded government ownership and operation of railways and telegraph lines. It also advanced an ingenious "subtreasury plan" for short-term loans to farmers at very low interest, with their staple crops serving as collateral [25].

Much of the political ground seemingly won by the Alliances in 1890 was lost by the Populists in 1892. But in 1893 came a financial panic, followed by the worst depression that had ever hit the United States. Tramps appeared on railroads and in small towns; every city held thousands of unemployed; and disaster befell rural areas that had long been depressed. Inflationary agitation was stepped up, and President Cleveland goaded its advocates on by, first, forcing repeal of the Silver Purchase Act, and then undertaking through private bankers a series of loans aimed at bolstering the gold standard. For more than three years the issue was fought in the country at large and within both major parties.

The climax came in 1896, when the Democratic national convention at Chicago virtually repudiated the head of their own party and came out for free coinage and several other radical planks. The most powerful man in this action was Governor John Peter Altgeld of Illinois, but his foreign birth made him ineligible for the Presidency. The nomination went to young William Jennings Bryan after he delivered what is probably the most famous convention speech in American history [26], and he also was endorsed by the Populists. Bryan paid little heed to most of his platform, and based his strenuous and eloquent campaign almost solely on the issue of free silver. He failed to win a single state north of the Ohio and east of the Mississippi; his vote was limited to the regions of wheat, cotton, and silver mining; he was decisively beaten by William McKinley.

Farmers soon found relief in economics rather than in politics. The price of wheat turned upward in 1896, and the next year most rural areas began to share in the general economic recovery, spurred on by war and by gold discoveries. As the century ended, farm interests were better off materially than at any time since the Civil War. But they remained impoverished culturally [19]. The United States was being "nationalized"; it was becoming more integrated and homogeneous in many respects, but it still had a long way to go in others.

In spite of the monotony and desolation of the typical farm, few Americans were willing to acknowledge it. Although good books later described it—Willa Cather told about Nebraska in *My Ántonia;* Edith Wharton about Massachusetts in *Ethan*

Frome; Ellen Glasgow about Tidewater Virginia in *Barren Ground*—even they took an affirmative stance toward farm life. As for the average American, he was content with stereotypes about the virtues of the sturdy yeoman, and he was likely to love any mawkish melodrama about a farmer's daughter who was pure as the driven snow [11] But she must not be, of course, literally driven; she must be sane as well as pure; this contrary to a minister in Indiana in 1879 that farm wives were "not much better off than slaves. It is a weary monotonous round of cooking and washing and mending and as a result the insane aslylum is 1/3d filled with wives of farmers."

Farmers and city folk, native-born Americans and immigrants —all groups contained men willing to sell their votes and to follow a boss. Overwhelmingly rural New Hampshire was run by a machine. Rural districts in Rhode Island were openly corrupt. Rural and native-born Adams County, Ohio, provided one of the worst examples of vote-selling. Immigrant farmers in North Dakota consistently backed a Republican boss who was friendly to banking and milling and railroad interests. But the notion persisted that political machines and bosses and corruption were peculiarly the product of cities and of immigrants. A man who knew that this was not true was journalist Lincoln Steffens, who in 1903 published a detailed account of the methods by which a Republican machine had for a generation dominated the native-born Americans of Philadelphia [28].

A marvelous review of Steffens' *The Shame of the Cities* was given orally by Tammany ward leader George Washington Plunkitt and printed by a reporter [29]. Admitting that politics for him as for hundreds of thousands of others was a way to make money, Plunkitt complained that Steffens failed to appreciate the distinction between dishonest graft and honest graft. The latter might consist, for instance, in the secret purchase by politicians of cheap real estate in a district where they knew, before anybody else did, that a streetcar line was going to be built. They thus grabbed the unearned increment [4]. But dishonest graft aplenty went on. The city council and mayor of Philadelphia in 1897 leased the municipal gas works to a private company under very suspicious circumstances. In Chicago a member of the Chamber of Commerce explained in 1882: "If you want to get anything out of council, the quickest way is to pay for it—not to the city, but to the aldermen."

Political machines kept their power by flattering and doing favors for their constituents [29]; close knowledge of poor districts in Chicago led Jane Addams to estimate that "approximately one out of every five voters in the Nineteenth Ward held a job dependent on the good will of the alderman." Far more lucrative to politicians were the favors done to corporations: a franchise for some public utility firm [16], contracts to pave streets, license for a railroad to violate the safety code, immunity from the building code or the fire laws. The Chicago *Record* charged that aldermen had received $5,000 each for voting for one franchise—at a time when the average laborer made a dollar a day. Intimate acquaintance with such episodes led Lincoln Steffens to charge that the worst fault of the politicians was not corruption but disloyalty, that they accepted the votes of ordinary citizens and then betrayed them to businessmen who wanted favors: "hence our American government is no longer a democracy, but a plutocracy."

Sometimes the boodlers went too far in extorting payment and set off a movement for good government. These movements also caught the ardor of citizens who still held to the old Puritan morality. A result was the first important Federal civil-service law: the Pendleton Act of 1883 [20]. As it worked out, perhaps the most important feature of the law was the fact that it applied only to applicants for Federal jobs, not to incumbents. Because of this, and because the White House passed from one major party to the other every four years from 1880 to 1896, each outgoing President extended the merit system to thousands of additional jobs as a means of preventing his successor from ousting his appointees.

The campaign for civil service reform was only an instance of widespread moral and esthetic repulsion from many traits of American life. Men felt that the United States was becoming too bureaucratic, or too conformist, or too dull, or too thin-spirited, or too materialistic, or simply too competitive. Lawyers found that more and more of their customary business was taken from them by trust companies, by abstract and title-insurance firms, by collection bureaus, by casualty companies. They lost their wonted independence as they found themselves driven, or drawn, to work for wealthy corporations that could pay big fees. The deeds they did on behalf of those corporations often stank in their own nostrils, but they did them anyway. A remarkably honest, scathingly honest, picture of the moral contradictions in which he practiced law was written by Chicago attorney Clarence Darrow [16]. That standards of ethics had declined from antebellum days was remarked by writers as various as Walt Whitman, Henry Adams, Henry James, Willa Cather, Edith Wharton, Mark Twain, and William Dean Howells.

Howells protested also against the literary tastes of the American people [17]. While he was urging upon them great European and American realists, he sadly realized that nearly all readers of books were women who wanted sentimentality and romance, and he referred to "these days, when a man, likely enough, only reaches for a book when he wishes to be fanned, so to speak, after the heat of the daily struggle." Insisting that serious writers were not mere entertainers, Howells declared that a novel "is a perspective made for the benefit of people who have no true use of their eyes. The novel, in its real meaning, adjusts the proportion. It preserves the balances."

This demanding standard was within the reach of the best American writers, including Howells himself. In 1885 *Century Magazine* was simultaneously serializing three novels, one of which may well be the greatest ever written in the United States: Howells' *The Rise of Silas Lapham; The Bostonians,* by Henry James; and Mark Twain's *The Adventures of Huckleberry Finn.* Outside of France, Thomas Eakins of Philadelphia would have ranked at that time with any painter in the world, and Winslow Homer and Albert P. Ryder were not too far behind. A decade later a young man in Maine, Edwin Arlington Robinson, published privately a little book that can be counted as the birth of modern American poetry [18]. John Dewey and C. S. Peirce in philosophy, Thornstein Veblen in historical sociology, William James in psychology, Oliver Wendell Holmes in jurisprudence—all these were Americans of world importance by 1900. But with evidence of prodigious imaginations all around him, noted English observer James Bryce in his *The American Commonwealth* offered an explanation of why the creative intelligence had to be inferior in this country.

A more searching commentary was made by another English visitor here, Matthew Arnold, who admired American equality and thought that life for the common man was better than anywhere in Europe. But the United States was less *interesting* as a place to live than any other civilized country [13]. "Now the great sources of the *interesting* are distinction and beauty: that which is elevated, and that which is beautiful." The United States was weak in both. It was too young and changed too fast to be beautiful. "The glorification of 'the average man'" ate away distinction and leveled everything: ". . . if there be a discipline in which the Americans are wanting, it is the discipline of awe and respect." For this, the ghastly American newspapers were largely responsible.

Although the dominant middle class pretended to a strict puritanism in sexual matters, although it was maudlin over the purity of women and over motherhood, the newspapers it read were filled with salacious stories about white slavery and divorce trials, and in New York a divorce could be had for the asking. While the crusade against liquor scored successes in one community after another, the alcoholic content of patent medicines soared [2]. Many of these nostrums came in decorative bottles intended for the mantlepiece, but buyers almost invariably destroyed the incriminating evidence so that they could buy more. Thus much of the private morality of Americans was characterized by make-believe. In public affairs men were still often brutally frank about what they were doing, but the self-deception typical of private morality early showed itself in attitudes toward a problem of public morality—the denial of the rights of Negroes. Men postured as righteous and high-minded, but in fact they felt less and less ethical *malaise* at injustice to dark-skinned peoples.

The Disputed Election of 1876 was settled by giving the Presidency to Rutherford B. Hayes by one electoral vote, even though he had won 250,000 fewer popular votes than the Democratic nominee, and Hayes in turn pulled United States troops out of Southern states where they had propped up Reconstruction governments. In an 1877 message to Congress the President claimed that the ex-slaves were "now advanced to full and equal citizenship." There was far more truth in his diary entry on election day in 1876, when he thought he was beaten: "I don't care for myself; and the party, yes, and the country, too, can stand it; but I do care for the poor colored men of the South. . . . The result will be that the Southern people will practically treat the constitutional amendments as nullities, and then the colored man's fate will be worse than when he was in slavery."

What new rights could be secured to former slaves under the Thirteenth, Fourteenth, and Fifteenth Amendments? The Civil Rights Act of 1875 forbade discrimination on the basis of race, color, or previous condition of servitude by inns, places of public amusement, or public conveyances. When five suits under the law were combined as the *Civil Rights Cases,* decided by the Supreme Court in 1883, eight justices held that these sections of the act were beyond the powers of Congress. They were not authorized by the Constitution, as amended. Congress could prevent certain discriminations by the states, but not by private individuals. The sole dissenter, Justice John Marshall Harlan, weighed in with a cogent piece of legal reasoning [21], but his colleagues did not listen. Indeed, their decision added humiliation to injury by stating that the ex-slave could no longer be "the special favorite of the laws" but must content himself with the "rank of a mere citizen."

The government even found ways to legalize discriminations by public agencies; segregation was lawful if the facilities available to Negroes were "equal." Lower courts from 1882 to 1888 applied the "separate but equal" doctrine not only in three cases involving common carriers but also in an Ohio school case. The new Interstate Commerce Commission approved the principle in three rulings by 1889. And in 1895 the highest court in the country in *Plessy* v. *Ferguson* upheld a Jim Crow law requiring segregation on railroads. Justice Harlan, again the lone dissenter, declared ringingly: "Our Constitution is color-blind, and neither knows nor tolerates classes among citizens. In respect to civil rights, all citizens are equal before the law."

But in the same opinion Justice Harlan himself wrote: "Every true man has pride of race . . ." To nearly all white Americans,

North or South, this was a white man's country, and should so
remain [33]. A strong pitch to racist thinking was made by
editor Henry W. Grady in his appeals for a Solid South—all
Democratic [12]. Having played to white supremacy, Grady
also played to covetousness. He was a leading advocate of a
New South based on diversified farming with large elements of
industry and commerce. It is symptomatic that Grady bought a
25 percent interest in the Atlanta *Constitution* with $20,000
borrowed from Cyrus H. Field, a native of New England, the
capitalist who promoted the first Atlantic cable, and associate
of Jay Gould in more than one venture. Essential to the New
South was capital from the Rich North, and for it a price had
to be paid in control as well as in money.

Cooperation of Northern whites with Southern whites—in
business and in ideology—and their joint suppression of Negroes,
often conflicted with the needs of Republican politicians. Lincoln had been elected in 1860 as a minority President, and the
Republicans had never had a safe majority in the country. In
1868 they would have lost, even with General Grant heading
their ticket, without Negro votes. In 1876 they did lose the
popular vote. In 1880 they had a national plurality of only
7,368 votes. They carried Connecticut by fewer than 3,000;
Indiana by fewer than 7,000; New York by 21,000. These three
states were the ones to change from one column to the other in
the Presidential elections of the decade; the party that won
them had the White House. In 1884 the Democrats won; of
more than 10 million ballots cast, they had a plurality of 68,299.
They won New York by 1,143 votes. In 1888 the Republicans
lost the election by 90,000 votes, but won in the electoral college.

Faced with a series of hairline verdicts, Republican cam-
paigners repeatedly plugged for Northern votes by waving the
bloody shirt; the Democrats became the party of secession, the
party of treason, the party responsible for the Civil War. The
Grand Old Party also needed every Negro vote it could get, but
90 percent of the Negroes were in the South, where white Democrats made strenuous efforts to keep them away from the polls.
In 1890 the Republicans made their last serious effort to use
Federal power to secure for Negroes the right to vote. Henry
Cabot Lodge of Massachusetts was able to get his Federal

Elections Bill, called by its opponents the Force Bill, through the House of Representatives. But in the Senate a bloc of Republicans from silver-producing states defected in exchange for votes for the Silver Purchase Act. Democrats threatened a filibuster against the McKinley Tariff Bill if the Elections Bill was pushed. Business contributors to Republican coffers were expecting tariff increases, and Lodge's measure was buried. Then, during the next decade, the Republican vote leaped far ahead of the opposition in New England, the Middle Atlantic states, and parts of the Midwest, and the Grand Old Party seemed to have a permanent majority without any Southern votes, Negro or white.

Indeed, the number of Southern voters of both races was sharply reduced. Mississippi in 1890, spurred by the Federal Elections Bill, drew up a new constitution that imposed several barriers against suffrage: residence requirements, payment of a poll tax, literacy tests. The size of the potential electorate by 1892 had fallen from 257,000 to 77,000. South Carolina disfranchised the Negro in 1895, Louisiana in 1898, North Carolina in 1900, other states thereafter, and many of the restrictions also worked against poor white voters.

While they were being stripped of both civil and political rights, nearly all of the nine million Negroes remained terribly poor. The bulk of them were in farming. The typical man worked twenty or thirty acres, as a farm laborer or sharecropper, with no tools except a mule or two, a crude wagon, a wooden plow, a hoe and a spade. He lived in a shack, probably just a room or two, miserably furnished. His life held little consolation except church. But at the same time, some Negroes had bettered themselves materially by prolonged hard work. Spectacular instances of self-help and its rewards were elevated into a conscious program by Booker T. Washington, the most prominent Negro leader in the United States at the end of the century. In his famous speech offering the Atlanta Compromise [15], Washington implied that Negroes, temporarily at least, would yield some political rights and would not even mention social equality if the whites would accord them economic opportunity.

Perhaps one Negro in three was illiterate, and so were many of the New Immigrants. White farmers in many parts of the West had little or no access to literature and art and music [19]. But some urban circles were much excited by the newest cultural developments in Europe. Wagner's music was played in Boston [19]; Harvard-trained Edwin Arlington Robinson wrote a sonnet to Zola [18]; William Dean Howells agitated for European realism [17]. Of all the intellectual tides surging across the Atlantic, none had a greater impact in this country than Darwin's theory of evolution. It revolutionized many fields of science. It posed a devastating challenge to parts of the Bible and to religions based on a literal interpretation of Holy Scripture. A distortion of it joined white supremacy in the ideological armory of complacent upper-class and middle-class Americans.

If the law of tooth and fang ruled in the animal world, why should it not rule in the world of nations? Americans could justify our domination over the Philippines by asserting that we were stronger [33] and more civilized [32]. Businessmen could justify their engrossment of the riches of the earth by calling it an instance of "the survival of the fittest" [7]. But probably most capitalists paid little heed to Social Darwinism, preferring to fight off threats of trade unionism or of government regulation by talking about "the right to manage." More likely still, they could appeal to doctrines known to religion since the sermons of John Wesley and before; they could say that the wealth they owned was merely administered by them as God's stewards. Andrew Carnegie's "The Gospel of Wealth" (1889) was one of the most popular essays of the period, and John D. Rockefeller declared: "I am a trustee of the property of others, through the providence of God committed to my care."

Complacency was a keynote not only in personal affairs and in business but also in politics. President Cleveland's veto of the Texas Seed Bill [22] overflowed with self-righteousness. The message of Secretary of State Olney to Great Britain during the Venezuela boundary dispute [31] was as smug as any document ever written. It seemed that nothing could shake the complacent mood: when a mine disaster at Krebs, Indian Territory, killed sixty-seven miners, Congress did pass a law providing for Federal safety inspection of mines in the territories, but President Harrison a year later plaintively informed Congress that it had not appropriated a penny to enforce the act. While the country drifted toward social crisis, the government did little or nothing. The monetary issue was compromised by the sop of the Bland-Allison Act. Efforts to lower the tariff failed. In the decade after 1880 no important law was passed by Congress save for the Pendleton Act [20] and the Interstate Commerce Act, and the latter exception proved more illusory than real.

Also contributing to the political stalemate was the evenly balanced strength of the two major parties. From 1881 to 1889 neither the Democrats nor the Republicans ever controlled the White House and both branches of Congress. In 1889 the Republicans did achieve that degree of power, and some laws of 1890 did relate to major problems: the McKinley Tariff Act, the Sherman Anti-Trust Act [23, 24], the Sherman Silver Purchase Act. But again, the last two of these were less efforts at solution than attempts to allay the discontent of voters.

After the financial panic of 1893, complacency was battered hard. Unemployment of men and machines mounted. In 1894 the Great Northern strike, a bituminous coal strike, and the Pullman boycott made it seem that society was disintegrating. "It is probably safe to say," wrote *Railway Age*, "that in no civilized country in this century, not actually in the throes of war or open insurrection, has society been so disorganized as it was in the United States during the first half of 1894; never was human life held so cheap; never did the constituted authorities appear so incompetent to enforce respect for the law."

The chasms in society had become so deep that any effort to enforce respect for the law ran the risk of causing some men to become even more disrespectful. This was notably true of three decisions by the Supreme Court in 1895. A Democratic effort to reduce import duties in 1894 came to little, but the new Wilson-Gorman Act did impose a modest income tax on persons and corporations. This tax was declared unconstitutional in *Pollock* v. *Farmers' Loan and Trust Company*. A broadly phrased restraining order against participants in the Pullman boycott was upheld in *In re Debs,* prompting furious attacks on "government by injunction." And the justices, whether aware or not of Senator Platt's earlier contention that excessive competition made it essential to legalize "reasonable" restraints of trade [23], did accept in effect his argument that the powers of Congress to regulate interstate commerce did not give it control over manufacturing. This view was affirmed by the Court in *United States* v. *E. C. Knight Co.*, a case involving the much-hated Sugar Trust.

If courts squirmed to avoid judicial doctrines that might throw large numbers of American companies into bankruptcy, other Federal agencies searched for positive government policies to help business escape from its dilemma: a capacity to produce far more than the American market would buy at profitable prices. The tariff was in part an effort to reserve home markets for American firms, and after the McKinley Act of 1890, which set a record average rate of about 50 percent of the value of imports, duties on many commodities were prohibitive. But import duties do not help an industry that has an export surplus, as many already did in 1877. So businessmen and government officials sought ways, not just to keep imports down, but to boost exports.

One Secretary of State after another stressed the need for markets abroad. In 1878 William M. Evarts told American consuls: "The question which now peremptorily challenges all thinking minds is how to create a foreign demand for those manufactures which are left after supplying our home demands." At the moment in 1881 when President Garfield was shot down, he was listening to schemes from James G. Blaine for increasing our exports to Latin America, and the same goal explains Blaine's plans for the Pan-American Congress eight years later. The need to gain foreign markets for domestic surpluses was believed in strongly by Walter Q. Gresham. When in 1899 American manufacturers became alarmed at threatened Russian expansion into the region that had been taking more than half of our exports of cotton textiles to China, John Hay sent their protest to the American *chargé d'affaires* in St. Petersburg with instructions to "use every opportunity to act energetically" in support of it.

Commercial hopes joined strategic aims in a revamping of the Monroe Doctrine, until at times it became an assertion of American supremacy throughout the Western Hemisphere. This viewpoint found expression in 1895 in the attempt of President Cleveland and Secretary of State Olney to force the English to arbitrate a long-standing dispute over the boundary between their possession British Guiana and Venezuela [31]. Great Britain, without a single important ally, and meeting conflicts in Africa with France that would bring the two nations to the brink of war in 1898, could ill afford to tangle with the United States, and agreed to arbitrate the boundary. This act instituted a series of important concessions she made to us, of which the most important was revision of the Clayton-Bulwer Treaty of 1850. By that document the two powers had agreed that neither would seek "exclusive control" over any Central American canal. When it was replaced in 1901 by the Hay-Pauncefote Treaty permitting the United States alone to build and manage a canal, "the rise of Anglo-American friendship" was in flood.

The proposal for an isthmian canal and the new truculence in foreign policy reinforced, and were reinforced by, the Big Navy Policy. A program for building up the United States Navy and merchant marine, for acquiring overseas bases, for developing foreign trade—such a program had long been urged by Theodore Roosevelt and by his chief mentor in this regard, Alfred Thayer Mahan [30]. Some other businessmen also discovered what the owners of silver mines knew: that the United States Government might be brought to absorb at profitable prices those surpluses that private markets would not take. During the Venezuela boundary crisis, Andrew Carnegie wrote from Europe to the president of his steel company that the time was propitious to seek orders from the Navy.

In the twentieth century the United States Government would prove to be a better customer than all of the foreign markets put together, but before 1900 most businessmen and politicians continued to think that the most promising outlets for American surpluses were abroad. Anxieties were deep and universal. Senator William Frye declared that "we shall have revolution" if we did not capture the markets of China. The president of the newly formed National Association of Manufacturers warned: "Many of our manufacturers have outgrown or are outgrowing their home markets, and the expansion of our foreign trade is our only promise of relief." The conquest of markets abroad seemed certain to benefit idle wage earners and impoverished farmers as well as industrialists.

As Americans faced increasingly outward, they saw grave injustices only "ninety miles from home" in Spanish-ruled Cuba. Germany had built up her output of beet sugar by paying a bounty on exports. The sharp decline in the world price of sugar wrecked the Caribbean economies dependent on sugar cane. Desperate distress in Cuba contributed to a revolt against Spain beginning in 1895. The Spanish occupation responded with a vicious policy of displacing peasants from their lands and herding them into concentration camps. Even Americans usually liberal and pacifistic began to demand that we intervene. On February 15, 1898, a United States battleship, the *Maine*, was sunk in Spanish-controlled Havana harbor, and 250 seamen were killed. The manner of the sinking is still unknown, but Spain was inevitably blamed. The war fever grew. President McKinley, after resisting it for a time, yielded, and war against Spain was declared on April 25. After two Spanish fleets were destroyed, with almost no American naval losses, Spain sued for peace. Spanish authority was ended in Cuba, in Puerto Rico, and in the Philippines.

Profound shifts of opinion had occurred during the brief war. Businessmen who had been cool to the opening of hostilities now urged that we should keep the former Spanish colonies, either as desirable in themselves or as stepping stones to the great markets of China. Liberals and radicals who had called for intervention to free Cuba now denounced any plans for more overseas colonies to join Hawaii, which Congress had declared to be an American territory during the war. Nobody was more incisive in analyzing the militarist passions that had helped carry us into the conflict than psychologist William James, and nobody was more vehement than he in condemning our "piracy" in the Philippines [34]. Former Senator Carl Schurz appealed to many themes, including "government of the people, by the people, and for the people," in arguing that we should not retain the erstwhile Spanish colonies [33]. But the man who had the greatest influence on the American decision thought differently; President McKinley later explained how he had concluded that we must keep the Philippines [32]. Those islands were a base en route to the 400,000,000 potential customers in China, and as the century ended the Department of State sent out the Open Door Notes aimed at forestalling a partition among the powers of that collapsing empire [35].

At the Republican national convention of 1900 Senator Chauncey M. Depew declaimed:

> Why this war in South Africa? Why these hammerings at the gates of Pekin? Why these marching of troops over Asia and Africa? Why this parading of the people and of the empire of other lands? It is because the surplus products of civilized countries in modern times are greater than civilization can consume. It is because this overproduction rolls back to stagnation.
>
> The American people now produce $2,000,000,000 worth more than we can consume, and we have met the emergency, by the providence of God, by the statesmanship of William McKinley, and by the valor of Roosevelt and his associates. (Applause.) We have our market in Cuba, we have our market in Porto Rico, we have our market in Hawaii, we have our market in the Philippines, and we stand in the presence of eight hundred million people, with the Pacific as an American lake and the American artisan producing better and cheaper goods than those of any country in the world.

The American export surplus had continued to grow, and in the autumn of 1899 the President had announced that we were for the first time exporting more manufactured goods than we were importing. But how long could the United States go on selling abroad vastly more than it was buying abroad?

Not much longer, wrote historian and journalist Brooks Adams [36]. As he looked forward in 1901, he foretold an increasingly sharp struggle for the markets of the world. If, he predicted, we continued to force our products into foreign countries without also giving them tariff reciprocity so that they could sell to us, we would compel them to export gold in order to pay for their import surpluses. Such a situation would leave them little choice but to unite and to wage war against us. A new century had opened, but not necessarily a happier one.

> *Unless otherwise noted, all selections reprinted in this volume were taken from the original sources without editorial emendation.*

Part I. Business and Economic History]

1

Standard Oil and the Railroads

H. D. Lloyd's "Story of a Great Monopoly"

Henry Demarest Lloyd (1847-1903) served after 1873 as financial editor of the Chicago *Tribune*, a position that gave him a close view of the revolutionary changes being wrought by the railroads. Becoming incensed at railroad policies that promoted monopoly in other industries, Lloyd made a case study of the favoritism shown to Standard Oil. His "Story of a Great Monopoly" was courageously published by editor William Dean Howells in the *Atlantic Monthly*, and created such a sensation that the issue ran through seven editions. The article is eloquent in its depiction of practices which helped to build Standard Oil into a "great monopoly." In reading the article, note (1) the dependence of the entire economy on railroad transportation; (2) the great strikes of 1877; (3) the significance of kerosene in the nation's economy; (4) some of the measures used to eliminate competition; (5) the magnitude of the rebates that Standard Oil could get by playing the Northeastern trunk lines against each other; and (6) the resulting disaster to independent oil producers and refiners. The charges made here were documented at length by Lloyd in his *Wealth against Commonwealth* (1894), which has been disputed by Allan Nevins, *Study in Power: John D. Rockefeller, Industrialist and Philanthropist* (1953). See also Lee Benson, *Merchants, Farmers, and Railroads: Railroad Regulation and New York Politics, 1850-1887* (1955) and Thomas C. Cochran, *Railroad Leaders, 1845-1890: The Business Mind in Action* (1953).

From H. D. Lloyd, "Story of a Great Monopoly," *Atlantic Monthly*, vol. 47 (March 1881), pp. 317-324.

WHEN COMMODORE VANDERBILT BEGAN THE WORLD
he had nothing, and there were no steamboats or
railroads. He was thirty-five years old when the first locomotive
was put into use in America. When he died, railroads had
become the greatest force in modern industry, and Vanderbilt
was the richest man of Europe or America, and the largest
owner of railroads in the world. He used the finest business
brains of his day and the franchise of the state to build up
a kingdom within the republic, and like a king he bequeathed
his wealth and power to his eldest son. Bancroft's History
of the United States and our railroad system were begun
at the same time. The history is not yet finished, but the railroads owe on stocks and bonds $4,600,000,000, more than twice
our national debt of $2,220,000,000, and tax the people annually
$490,000,000, one and a half times more than the government's
revenue last year of $274,000,000. More than any other class, our
railroad men have developed the country, and tried its institutions. The evasion of almost all taxes by the New York Central
Railroad has thrown upon the people of New York State more
than a fair share of the cost of government, and illustrates some
of the methods by which the rich are making the poor poorer.
Violations of trust by Credit Mobiliers, Jay Gould's wealth and
the poverty of Erie stockholders, such corruption of legislatures
as gave the Pacific Mail its subsidies, and nicknamed New
Jersey "The State of Camden and Amboy," are sins against public
and private faith on a scale impossible in the early days of republics and corporations. A lawsuit still pending, though begun
ten years ago by a citizen of Chicago, to recover the value of
baggage destroyed by the Pennsylvania Railroad; Judge Barnard's
midnight orders for the Erie ring; the surrender of its judicial
integrity by the supreme court of Pennsylvania at the bidding of
the Pennsylvania Railroad, as charged before Congress by
President Gowen, of the Reading Railroad; the veto by the Standard Oil Company of the enactment of a law by the Pennsylvania
legislature to carry out the provision of the constitution of the
State that every one should have equal rights on the railroads,—
these are a few of the many things that have happened to kill the

confidence of our citizens in the laws and the administration of justice. No other system of taxation has borne as heavily on the people as those extortions and inequalities of railroad charges which caused the granger outburst in the West, and the recent uprising in New York. In the actual physical violence with which railroads have taken their rights of way through more than one American city, and in the railroad strikes of 1876 and 1877 with the anarchy that came with them, there are social disorders we hoped never to see in America. These incidents in railroad history show most of the points where we fail, as between man and man, employer and employed, the public and the corporation, the state and the citizen, to maintain the equities of "government"—and employment—"of the people, by the people, for the people."

Our treatment of "the railroad problem" will show the quality and calibre of our political sense. It will go far in foreshadowing the future lines of our social and political growth. It may indicate whether the American democracy, like all the democratic experiments which have preceded it, is to become extinct because the people had not wit enough or virtue enough to make the common good supreme.

The remarkable series of eight railroad strikes, which began during the Centennial Exposition of the prosperity of our first century and the perfection of our institutions, culminated on July 16, 1877, in the strike on the Baltimore and Ohio Railroad at Martinsburg, West Virginia. This spread into the greatest labor disturbance on record. For a fortnight there was an American Reign of Terror. We have forgotten it,—that is, it has taught us nothing; but if Freeman outlives us to finish his History of Federal Government from the Achaian League to the Disruption of the United States, he will give more than one chapter to the labor rising of 1877. The strike at Martinsburg was instantly felt at Chicago and Baltimore in the stoppage of shipments. In a few hours the Baltimore and Ohio, one of the chief commercial arteries of Maryland, Virginia, West Virginia, Ohio, Indiana, and Illinois, was shut up. The strike spread to the Pennsylvania, the Erie and the New York Central railroads, and to the Great Western lines, with their countless branches, as far west as Omaha and Topeka, and as far south as the Ohio River and the

Texas Pacific. The feeling of the railroad employés all over the country was expressed by the address of those of the Pennsylvania Railroad to its stockholders. The stockholders were reminded that "many of the railroad's men did not average wages of more than seventy-five cents a day;" that "the influence of the road had been used to destroy the business of its best customers, the oil producers, for the purpose of building up individual interests." "What is the result? The traffic has almost disappeared from the Pennsylvania Railroad, and in place of $7,000,000 revenue this year, although shipments are in excess of last year, your road will receive scarcely half the amount. This alone would have enabled your company to pay us enough for a living." The address also refers pointedly to the abuses of fast freight lines, rolling-stock companies, and other railroad inventions for switching business into private pockets. Other workingmen followed the example of the railroad employés. At Zanesville, Ohio, fifty manufactories stopped work. Baltimore ceased to export petroleum. The rolling mills, foundries, and refineries of Cleveland were closed. Chicago, St. Louis, Cincinnati, all the cities large and small, had the same experience. At Indianapolis, next to Chicago the largest point for the eastward shipment of produce, all traffic was stopped except on the two roads that were in the hands of the national government. At Erie, Pa., the railroad struck, and notwithstanding the remonstrance of the employés refused to forward passengers or the United States mails. The grain and cattle of the farmer ceased to move to market, and the large centres of population began to calculate the chances of famine. New York's supply of Western cattle and grain was cut off. Meat rose three cents a pound in one day, while Cleveland telegraphed that hogs, sheep, beeves, and poultry billed for New York were dying on the side-tracks there. Merchants could not sell, manufacturers could not work, banks could not lend. The country went to the verge of panic, for the banks, in the absence of remittances, had resolved to close if the blockade lasted a few days longer. President Garrett, of the Baltimore and Ohio Railroad, wrote that his "great national highway could be restored to public use only by the interposition of the United States army." President Scott, of the Pennsylvania Railroad, telegraphed the authorities at Washington, "I fear that unless the general government will assume the responsibility of order throughout the land, the anarchy which is now present will become more terrible than has ever been known in the history of the world." The governors of ten States—West Virginia, Maryland, New Jersey, New York, Pennsylvania, Ohio, Illinois, Wisconsin, Missouri, and Kentucky—issued dispersing proclamations which did not disperse. The governors of four of them—West Virginia, Maryland, Pennsylvania, and Illinois—appealed to the national government for help against domestic insurrection, which the State could not suppress. The president of the United States issued two national proclamations to the insurgents. The state troops were almost useless, as in nearly all cases they fraternized with the strikers. All the national troops that could be spared from the Indian frontier and the South were ordered back to the centres of civilization. The regulars were welcomed by the frightened people of Chicago with cheers which those who heard will never forget. Armed guards were placed at all the public buildings of Washington, and ironclads were ordered up for the protection of the national capital. Cabinet meetings were continuous. General Winfield S. Hancock was sent to Baltimore to take command, General Sherman was called back from the West, and General Schofield was ordered from West Point into active service. Barricades, in the French style, were thrown up by the voters of Baltimore. New York and Philadelphia were heavily garrisoned. In Philadelphia every avenue of approach to the Pennsylvania Railroad was patrolled, and the city was under a guard of six thousand armed men, with eight batteries of artillery. There were encounters between troops and voters, with loss of life, at Martinsburg, Baltimore, Pittsburg, Chicago, Reading, Buffalo, Scranton, and San Francisco. In the scene at Pittsburg, there was every horror of revolution. Citizens and soldiers were killed, the soldiers were put to flight, and the town left at the mercy of the mob. Railroad cars, depots, hotels, stores, elevators, private houses, were gutted and burned. The city has just compromised for $1,810,000 claims for damages to the amount of $2,938,460, and has still heavy claims to settle. The situation was described at this point by a leading newspaper as one of "civil war with the accompanying horrors of murder, conflagration, rapine, and pillage." These were days of greater bloodshed, more actual suffering, and wider alarm in the North than that part of the country experienced at any time during the civil war, except when Lee invaded Pennsylvania. As late as August 3d, the beautiful valley of the Wyoming, in Pennsylvania, was a military camp, traversed by trains loaded with Gatling guns and bayonets, and was guarded by Governor Hartranft in person with five thousand soldiers. These strikes, penetrating twelve States and causing insurrections in ten of them, paralyzed the operation of twenty thousand miles of railroad, and directly and indirectly threw one million men temporarily out of employment. While they lasted they caused greater losses than any blockade which has been made by sea or land in the history of war. Non-sensational observers, like the Massachusetts Board of Railroad Commissioners, look to see the outburst repeated, possibly to secure a rise of wages. The movement of the railroad trains of this country is literally the circulation of its blood. Evidently, from the facts we have recited, the States cannot prevent its arrest by the struggle between these giant forces within society, outside the law.

Kerosene has become, by its cheapness, the people's light the world over. In the United States we used 220,000,000 gallons of petroleum last year. It has come into such demand abroad that our exports of it increased from 79,458,888 gallons in 1868, to 417,648,544 in 1879. It goes all over Europe, and to the far East. The Oriental demand for it is increasing faster than any other. We are assured by the eloquent petroleum editor of the New York Shipping List that "it blazes across the ruins of Babylon and waste Persepolis," and that "all over Polynesia, and Far Cathay, in Burmah, in Siam, in Java, the bronzed denizens toil and dream, smoke opium and swallow hasheesh, woo and win, love and hate, and sicken and die under the rays of this wonderful product of our fruitful caverns." However that may be, it is statistically true that China and the East Indies took over 10,000,000 gallons in 1877, and nearly 25,000,000 gallons in 1878. After articles of food, this country has but one export, cotton, more valuable than petroleum. It was worth $61,789,438 in our foreign trade in 1877; $46,574,974 in 1878; and $18,546,642 in the five months ending November 30, 1879. In the United States, in the cities as well as the country, petroleum is the general illuminator. We use more kerosene lamps than Bibles. The raw material of this world's light is produced in a territory beginning with Cattaraugus County in New York, and extending southwesterly through eight or nine counties of Pennsylvania, making a belt about one hundred and fifty miles long, and twelve or fifteen miles wide, and then, with an interval, running into West Virginia, Kentucky, and Tennessee, where the yield is unimportant. The bulk of the oil comes from two counties, Cattaraugus in New York, and McKean in Pennsylvania. There are a few places elsewhere that produce rock oil, such as the shales of England, Wales, and Scotland, but the oil is so poor that American kerosene, after being carried thousands of miles, can undersell it. Very few of the forty millions of people in the United States who burn kerosene know that its production, manufacture, and export, its price at home and abroad, have been controlled for years by a single corporation,—the Standard Oil Company. This company began in a partnership, in the early years of the civil war, between Samuel Andrews and John Rockefeller in Cleveland. Rockefeller had been a bookkeeper in some interior town in Ohio, and had afterwards made a few thousand dollars by keeping a flour store in Cleveland. Andrews had been a day laborer in refineries, and so poor that his wife took in sewing. He found a way of refining by which more kerosene could be got out of a barrel of petroleum than by any other method, and set up for himself a ten-barrel still in Cleveland, by which he cleared $500 in six months. Andrews' still and Rockefeller's savings have grown into the Standard Oil Company. It has a capital, nominally $3,500,000, but really much more, on which it divides among its stockholders every year millions of dollars of profits. It has refineries at Cleveland, Baltimore, and New York. Its own acid works, glue factories, hardware stores, and barrel shops supply it with all the accessories it needs in its business. It has bought land at Indianapolis on which to erect the largest barrel factory in the country. It has drawn its check for $1,000,000 to suppress a rival. It buys 30,000 to 40,000 barrels of crude oil a day, at a price fixed by itself, and makes special contracts with the railroads for the transportation of 13,000,000 to 14,000,000 barrels of oil a year. The four quarters of the globe are partitioned among the members of the Standard combinations.

One has the control of the China trade; another that of some country of Europe; another that of the United States. In New York, you cannot buy oil for East Indian export from the house that has been given the European trade; reciprocally, the East Indian house is not allowed to sell for export to Europe. The Standard produces only one fiftieth or sixtieth of our petroleum, but dictates the price of all, and refines nine tenths. Circulars are issued at intervals by which the price of oil is fixed for all the cities of the country, except New York, where a little competition survives. Such is the indifference of the Standard Oil Company to railroad charges that the price is made the same for points so far apart as Terre Haute, Chicago, and Keokuk. There is not to-day a merchant in Chicago, or in any other city in the New England, Western, or Southern States, dealing in kerosene, whose prices are not fixed for him by the Standard. In all cases these prices are graded so that a merchant in one city cannot export to another. Chicago, Cincinnati, or Cleveland is not allowed to supply the tributary towns. That is done by the Standard itself, which runs oil in its own tank cars to all the principal points of distribution. This corporation has driven into bankruptcy, or out of business, or into union with itself, all the petroleum refineries of the country except five in New York, and a few of little consequence in Western Pennsylvania. Nobody knows how many millions Rockefeller is worth. Current gossip among his business acquaintance in Cleveland puts his income last year at a figure second only, if second at all, to that of Vanderbilt. His partner, Samuel Andrews, the poor English day laborer, retired years ago with millions. Just who the Standard Oil Company are, exactly what their capital is, and what are their relations to the railroads, nobody knows except in part. Their officers refused to testify before the supreme court of Pennsylvania, the late New York Railroad Investigating Committee, and a committee of Congress. The New York committee found there was nothing to be learned from them, and was compelled to confess its inability to ascertain as much as it desired to know "of this mysterious organization, whose business and transactions are of such a character that its members declined giving a history or description, lest their testimony be used to convict them of crime."

Their great business capacity would have insured the managers of the Standard success, but the means by which they achieved monopoly was by conspiracy with the railroads. Mr. Simon Sterne, counsel for the merchants of New York in the New York investigation, declared that the relations of the railroads to the Standard exhibited "the most shameless perversion of the duties of a common carrier to private ends that has taken place in the history of the world." The Standard killed its rivals, in brief, by getting the great trunk lines to refuse to give them transportation. Commodore Vanderbilt is reported to have said that there was but one man—Rockefeller—who could dictate to him. Whether or not Vanderbilt said it, Rockefeller did it. The Standard has done everything with the Pennsylvania legislature, except refine it. In 1876 its organization was brought before Congress, and referred to a committee. A prominent member of the Standard, not a member of Congress, conducted the farce of inquiry from behind the seat of the chairman. Another member of the company, who was a member of Congress, came with the financial officer of the company before the committee, and sustained him in his refusal to testify about the organization, its members, or its relations with the railroads. The committee never reported. The facts they suppressed must be hunted out through newspaper articles, memorials from the oil producers and refiners, records of lawsuits, reports of chambers of commerce and of legislative investigating committees, and other miscellaneous sources of information.

The contract is in print by which the Pennsylvania Railroad agreed with the Standard, under the name of the South Improvement Company, to double the freights on oil to everybody, but to repay the Standard one dollar for every barrel of oil it shipped, and one dollar for every barrel any of its competitors shipped. This contract was produced in Congress, and was stigmatized by Representative Conger as "the most damnable and startling evidence yet produced of the possibility of railroad monopoly." Ostensibly this contract was given up, in deference to the whirlwind of indignation it excited. But Rockefeller, the manager of the Standard, was a man who could learn from defeat. He made no more tell-tale contracts that could be printed. He effected secret arrangements with the Pennsylvania, the New York Central, the Erie, and the Atlantic and Great Western.

What influences he used to make the railroad managers pliable may probably be guessed from the fact that one quarter of the stock of the Acme Oil Company, a partner in the Standard combination, on which heavy monthly dividends are paid, is owned by persons whose names Rockefeller would never reveal, which Mr. Archbold, the president of the company, said under oath he had not been told, and which the supreme court of Pennsylvania has not yet been able to find out. The Standard succeeded in getting from Mr. Vanderbilt free transportation for its crude oil from the wells in Pennsylvania, one hundred and fifty miles, to the refineries at Cleveland, and back. This stamped out competing refineries at Pittsburg, and created much of the raw material of the riots of July, 1877. Vanderbilt signed an agreement, March 25, 1872, that "all agreements for the transportation of oil after this date shall be upon a basis of perfect equality," and ever since has given the Standard special rates and privileges. He has paid it back in rebates millions of dollars, which have enabled it to crush out all competitors, although many of them, like the Octave Oil Company and the Titusville refiners, had done all their business over his road till they went into bankruptcy, broken by his contracts with the Standard. He united with the Erie in a war on the Pennsylvania Railroad, to force it to sell to the Standard all its refineries, and the great pipe lines by which the oil, like Croton water in the mains, was carried from the wells to the railroads. He then joined with the Erie and the Pennsylvania in a similar attack on the Baltimore and Ohio, which had to sell out to the Standard. So the Standard obtained the control of all the pipe lines and of the transportation, of everything, in fact, as a witness said before the New York Railroad Investigating Committee, except the bodies of the producers. Mr. Vanderbilt began, as did the Erie and Pennsylvania railroad kings, with paying back to the Standard, but to no other shipper, ten per cent. of its freight bills. He continued making one concession after another, till when he was doing the business for other shippers at $1.40 and $1.25 a barrel, he charged the Standard only eighty and eighty-one cents, and this was afterwards reduced to sixty cents a barrel. During the war against the Pennsylvania road to make it sell out to the Standard, the New York Central carried oil for less than nothing. Besides the other allowances, Mr. Vanderbilt paid the Standard through its alias, the American Transfer Company, a rebate of thirty-five cents a barrel on all the crude oil shipped by it or its competitors. When the oil producers, whom the Standard had cut off from all access to the world except through it, sought an exit through an out-of-the-way railroad and the Erie Canal, or down the Ohio River hundreds of miles to Huntingdon, thence by the Chesapeake and Ohio Railroad to Richmond, and so to the sea, Mr. Vanderbilt lowered his rates to the Standard so that it could undersell any one who used these devious routes. When the producers, June, 1879, completed their own tidewater pipe line, 104 miles long, to a junction with the Reading Railroad, obtaining in this way a direct connection with the seaboard, Mr. Vanderbilt reduced his rate to the public from $1.40 to $1.25 a barrel to thirty-five and twenty-five cents, and charged the Standard twenty, fifteen, finally but ten cents. For ten cents Mr. Vanderbilt hauled for the Standard a barrel weighing 390 pounds over 400 miles, and hauled back the empty cars, at the same time that he charged forty-five cents for hauling a can of milk weighing ninety pounds for sixty miles. So closely had the Standard octopus gripped itself about Mr. Vanderbilt that even at the outside rates its competitors could not get transportation from him. He allowed the Standard to become the owner of all the oil cars run over his road, and of all his terminal facilities for oil. As the Standard owned all but 200 of the oil cars run on the Erie, and leased all that road's terminal facilities, it could charge its rivals anything it pleased for the privileges of New York harbor. When Mr. Vanderbilt was questioned by Mr. Simon Sterne, of the New York committee, about these and other things, his answers were, "I don't know," "I forget," "I don't remember," to 116 questions out of 249 by actual count. At a time when the Standard Oil Company through its other self, the American Transfer Company, was receiving from the New York Central thirty-five cents a barrel on all oil shipped by itself or its competitors, and was getting other rebates which cost the New York Central over $2,000,000 from October 17, 1877, to March 31, 1879, Mr. Vanderbilt testified positively before the New York Investigating Committee that he knew nothing whatever about the American Transfer Company, its officers, or the payments to it. . . .

2

How to Capture the Growing Mass Markets

Patent Medicine Advertising

Soon after 1700 patent medicines from England were being imported into the United States, and a century later the nostrums were reaching out aggressively for new customers. One company cut down a forest so that passengers on passing trains could read its slogan painted on a hillside. The leading monthly magazines did not publish advertising before 1900, but patent medicines were hawked in daily papers, in the religious press, in the back pages of dime novels. This example is typical in its sensationalism; and the fact that it is signed by the "New England Medical Institute" reflects the low state of medical practice. Note (1) that the formula contains both cocaine and alcohol; (2) the appeal to individualism in the slogan "Be your own physician," and (3) the admission that it is a sham in the offer to mail out the finished product. See James Harvey Young's splendid *The Toadstool Millionaires: A Social History of Patent Medicines in America* (1961) and Frank Luther Mott's standard *A History of American Magazines, 1885-1905* (1957).

From the Waltham (Massachusetts) *Daily Tribune*, November 16, 1882, p. 4.

ERRORS OF YOUTH
Sufferers from
Nervous Debility,
Youthful Indiscretions,
Lost Manhood,
BE YOUR OWN PHYSICIAN

There are many sufferers from self-destroying maladies, who, having tried every advertised remedy in vain, have become discouraged and despair of a cure.

The knowledge of this fact led us to a long course of experiments, resulting in the discovery of new and concentrated remedies, by which thousands of our patients have been restored to perfect health, after other treatments had failed. For the benefit of numerous sufferers we herewith publish our prescription. Perfectly pure ingredients must be used.

℞ Cocain (from Erythroxlon coca) 1 drachm.
  Jerubebin 1-2 drachm.
  Hypophosphite quinia, 1-2 drachm.
  Geisemin, 8 grains
  Ext. igratiae amarae (alcoholic), 2 grains.
  Ext. Septandra, 2 scruples
  Glycerin, q. s.
    Mix

Make 60 pills. Take one pill at 3 p.m., and another on going to bed. In some cases it will be necessary for the patient to take two pills at bed time, making the number three a day. This remedy is adapted to every condition of nervous debility and weakness in either sex, and especially in those cases resulting from imprudence. The recuperative powers of this remedy are truly astonishing, and its use, continued for a short time, changes the languid, debilitated, nerveless condition to one of renewed life and vigor.

As we are constantly in receipt of letters of inquiry relative to this remedy, we would say to those who would prefer to obtain it from us, by remitting $3 in post office money order, or registered letter, a securely sealed package in its pure state will be sent by return mail from our private laboratory.

New England Medical Institute
24 Tremont Row
Boston, Mass.

3

A Harvard Man in Cattle Ranching

Richard Trimble's Letters to His Mother

Richard Trimble (1858-1924), Harvard 1880, was a classmate of Theodore Roosevelt, Frederic O. deBillier, and Hubert E. Teschemacher. When the latter two started a cattle company, Roosevelt and Trimble invested heavily in it and Trimble went to Wyoming to help manage it. His letters to his family in New York show some problems of managing a large-scale ranch. Trimble returned East after five years, and in 1901 became secretary-treasurer of the newly formed United States Steel Corporation, the first billion dollar company. In reading these selections note (1) ways of acquiring land, (2) the importance of prices to cattle ranching, (3) problems associated with fencing, water, feed, marketing, and the protection of property. See Gene M. Gressley, "Teschemacher and deBillier Cattle Company: A Study of Eastern Capital on the Frontier," *Business History Review*, XXXIII (1959), pp. 121-137; this can be supplemented by Lewis Atherton, *The Cattle Kings* (1961).

From Richard Trimble Papers, Western History and Archives Department, University of Wyoming.

Cotton Wood Ranch
December 13, 1882

Dᴇᴀʀ ᴍᴏᴍɪᴇ,

The surveyor who came out with Arthur starts back today so I send you a line in the hope that it will reach you by the 20th. On Sunday I put my bed & traps on the mail wagon at Hunton's & followed it as far as the Laramie bridge on one of the Co's horses. At Uva (the Laramie bridge) I found a team from the F ranch, the new one a few miles further up the Laramie river, so I got them to take my things & went with them to the ranch which we reached in time for dinner. Yesterday (Monday) the morning was spent in killing a beef & the afternoon in driving over here in the teeth of one of the winds for which this country is famous. The F ranch is right on the road & it is rather expensive to feed all the people who stop there, so the Co. is about to build a new ranch out of the way & abandon the present one. the outfit began today to cut logs for this new ranch & I have been out watching and taking a hand sometimes but a tender foot is of less use with an ax than in almost any other way. They are getting the logs out a mile or two from here & will have to haul them about twenty five miles. I shall be in Cheyenne about Xmas time to file a claim under this desert land act for 640 acres on this side of the Platte river. . . .

D Y Ranch
30 miles north of Ft. Fetterman
Feby. 22, 1883

Dear Momie,

From Uva Andrews & I started north and after three days ride, lovely weather all the way, came to his ranch where we are now. In a few days we are going to take a hunt & about the middle of March are going down to Laramie City, where Andrews has to appear as witness against a horse thief & where I expect to get two or three good cow ponies from Dan in order to make my summer as a tender foot pass with as little torture as possible. I am sorry thee has so little confidence in my ability to judge whether it is for my advantage to stay on the ranch or in Cheyenne. There are two sides to the cattle business, the theory & the practice, one of which is learned better in Cheyenne where cattle men congregate & the other on a ranch! . . .

Dear Creek Ranch
March 4th, 1883

Dear Family,

At the last minute our hunt was given up as I wrote you on Thursday. Williams, it seemed, didn't know that we wanted him to go & didn't want to leave his horses with nobody but the cook to look after them. He also said that he didn't think we would find any more game where we thought of going than we could find in a day's excursion from the ranch for the snow has all gone except an occasional drift. He thought the elk had probably gone back to the hills. In coming out from Fetterman he had seen a number of deer & there are hundreds of antelope within a few miles of us all the time. However, we have not been out for anything yet as there is still a whole deer hanging up in the cellar with the exception of a jack rabbit I shot behind the stable which went very well as a curry. The outfit has killed nothing for a long time. The other day I was walking up the creek in search of rabbits. I saw something in a small willow which at first I thought was a hawk's nest, but when I got nearer it turned out to be a good sized porcupine. He didn't seem at all afraid of me. I scratched his nose with a short twig. If I had known how to skin & stuff nicely I would have shot him for he had his winter coat on & his bristles, of about the *rich* color of Grind's beard, were eight or ten inches long & covered him thickly from the tip of his nose to the end of his tail. I am sorry that giving up the hunt will prevent my seeing a camp of Arapahoe Indians for Shavelord wanted to see some real, bold, bad, wild Indians in all their native nastiness & I hoped that some of their bead work and tanned skins might be worth getting. Andrews expects now to leave here on the 13th for Laramie City via Cheyenne. I expect to go with him at any rate as far as Uva where I will have a talk with Jim Shaw and seek what kind of a string of horses he can let me have for the summer. Of course I don't need *top* cow ponies for I can neither "rope" nor "cut out" the first year but if he can't let me have good, strong, gentle horses I shall go on down with A. & buy two or three ponies from Dan who told me when I was there that he was going to sell most of his horses on Laramie Plains. The fence question is progressing nicely. All fences on Govt land not enclosing claims lawfully taken up must come down & what struck me as the most serious question for the future of the cattle business is solved in the most satisfactory way possible. This will open up no end of water front for even where men have claims on the water if they can't fence large pastures back of it they must turn their own cattle loose & leave watering places every few miles for them . . . .

Cheyenne Club
Sept 14 [1883]

Dear Momie,

 . . . We had bad luck with our first shipment of cattle. They stampeded in a thunder storm three days drive from the railroad & we lost 290 out of 700, the remainder going in on a very poor market weighed 1089 & sold for $3.75 per hundred. This means that we must feed in order to get our money & I shall not let another creature go to Chicago directly. I am going out to the ranch tomorrow to meet a surveyor & have the lines of all our claims run over so we can know just where our fences must go. The fences on government land must be taken down at last & we are more than ready to comply with the law which is now in a shape to be enforced. I hope nothing will prevent Grind from coming out for it will be a very great pleasure to me to see him & have him with me, but with Tesch in Boston & our arrangements on feeding not yet completed my hands are pretty full & instead of winding up everything by the middle of November the prospect is that I shall have to be in Iowa and Nebraska the greater part of this winter. . . .

4

Pros and Cons of the Single Tax

Henry George and David Dudley Field, "Land and Taxation: A Conversation"

Henry George (1839-1897), like Henry Demarest Lloyd, was strongly influenced by his Christian upbringing. But whereas Lloyd leaned increasingly toward collectivism, George remained stanchly individualistic. As editor of California newspapers after 1869, George saw the effects of completion of the transcontinental railroads. Population growth caused land values and rents to soar, and landowners engrossed much of the community's wealth and income. But George did not repudiate private ownership of land. Instead, he urged that any increase in land values that was due merely to the growth of the community—the so-called "unearned increment"—should be taken by the government. All other taxes would be abolished; hence, the "single tax." George passionately stated his views in *Progress and Poverty* (1879), perhaps the most influential American book, in Australia and England as well as at home, of the century. In reading the following report of a conversation, note (1) George's tax proposals; (2) George's theoretical defense of his proposals; (3) two popular positions at the time regarding the proper functions of government; and (4) the relationship that George saw between taxation, progress, and civilization. See Charles Albro Barker, *Henry George* (1955) and George's writings.

From Henry George and David Dudley Field, "Land and Taxation: A Conversation," *North American Review*, vol. 141 (July 1885), pp. 1-14.

MR. DAVID DUDLEY FIELD. WILL YOU EXPLAIN TO ME how you expect to develop, in practice, your theory of the confiscation of land to the use of the state?

MR. HENRY GEORGE. By abolishing all other taxes, and concentrating taxation upon land-values.

F. Then suppose A to be the proprietor of a thousand acres of land on the Hudson, chiefly farming land, but at the same time having on it houses, barns, cattle, horses, carriages, furniture; how is he to be dealt with, under your theory?

G. He would be taxed upon the value of his land, and not upon the value of his improvements and stock.

F. Whether the value of his land has been increased by his cultivation or not?

G. The value of land is not really increased by cultivation. The value that cultivation adds is a value of improvement, which I would exempt. I would tax the land at its present value, excluding improvements; so that such a proprietor would have no more taxes to pay than the proprietor of one thousand acres of land, equal in capabilities, situation, etc., that remained in a state of nature.

F. But suppose the proprietor of such land to have let it lie waste for many years, while the farmer that I speak of has devoted his time and money to increasing the value of his thousand acres, would you tax them exactly alike?

G. Exactly.

F. Let us suppose B, an adjoining proprietor, has land that has never yielded a blade of grass, or any other product but weeds; and that A, a farmer, took his in the same condition when he purchased, and by his own thrift and expenditure has improved his land, so that now, without buildings, furniture, or stock, it is worth five times as much as B's thousand acres; B is taxed at the rate of a dime an acre; would you tax A at the rate of a dime an acre?

G. I would certainly tax him no more than B, for by the additional value that A has created he has added that much to the common stock of wealth, and he ought to profit by it. The effect of our present system, which taxes a man for values created by his labor and capital, is to put a fine upon industry, and repress improvement. The more houses, the more crops, the more buildings in the country, the better for us all, and we are doing ourselves an injury by imposing taxes upon the production of such things.

F. How are you to ascertain the value of land considered as waste land?

G. By its selling price. The value of land is more easily and certainly ascertained than any other value. Land lies out of doors, everybody can see it, and in every neighborhood a close idea of its value can be had.

F. Take the case of the owner of a thousand acres in the Adirondack wilderness that have been denuded of trees, and an adjoining thousand acres that have a fine growth of timber. How would you value them?

G. Natural timber is a part of land; when it has value, it adds to the value of the land.

F. The land denuded of timber would then be taxed less than land that has timber?

G. On general principles it would, where the value of the land was therefore lessened. But where, as in the Adirondacks, public policy forbids anything that would hasten the cutting of timber, natural timber might be considered an improvement, like planted timber, which should not add to taxable value.

F. Then suppose a man to have a thousand acres of wild timber land, and to have cut off the timber, and planted the land, and set up buildings, and generally improved it; would you tax him less than the man that has retained his land with the timber still on?

G. I would tax the value of his land irrespective of the improvements made by him, whether they consisted in clearing, in plowing, or in building. In other words, I would tax that value which is created by the growth of the community, not that created by individual effort. Land has no value on account of improvements made upon it, or on account of its natural capabilities. It is as population increases, and society develops, that land-values appear, and they rise in proportion to the growth of population and social development. For instance, the value of the land upon which this building stands is now enormously greater than it was years ago, not because of what its owner has done, but because of the growth of New York.

F. I am not speaking of New York City in particular; I am speaking of land generally.

G. The same principle is generally true. Where a settler takes up a quarter section on a Western prairie, and improves it, his land has no value so long as other land of the same quality can be had for nothing. The value he creates is merely the value of improvement. But when population comes, then arises a value that attaches to the land itself. That is the value I would tax.

F. Suppose the condition of the surrounding community in the West remained the same; two men go together and purchase two pieces of land of a thousand acres each; one leaves his with a valuable growth of timber, the other cuts off the timber, cultivates the land, and makes a well ordered farm. Would you tax the man that has left the timber upon his land more than you would tax the other man, provided that the surrounding country remained the same?

G. I would tax them both upon the value of the land at the time of taxation. At first, I take it, the clearing of the land would be a valuable improvement. On this, as on the value of his other improvements, I would not have the settler taxed. Thus taxation upon the two would be the same. In course of time, the growth of population might give value to the uncut timber, which, being included in the value of land, would make the taxation upon the man that had left his land in a state of nature heavier than upon the man that had converted his land into a farm.

F. A man that goes into the Western country and takes up land, paying the Government price, and does nothing to the land; how is he to be taxed?

G. As heavily as the man that has taken a like amount of land and improved it. Our present system is unjust and injurious in taxing the improver and letting the mere proprietor go. Settlers take up land, clear it, build houses, and cultivate crops, and for thus adding to the general wealth are immediately punished by taxation upon their improvements. This taxation is escaped by the man that lets his land lie idle, and, in addition to that, he is generally taxed less upon the value of his land than are those who have made their land valuable. All over the country, land in use is taxed more heavily than unused land. This is wrong. The man that holds land and neglects to improve it, keeps away somebody that would, and he ought to pay as much for the opportunity he wastes as the man that improves a like opportunity.

F. Then you would tax the farmer whose farm is worth $1,000, as heavily as you would tax the adjoining proprietor, who, with the same quantity of land, has added improvements worth $100,000; is that your idea?

G. It is. The improvements made by the capitalist would do no harm to the farmer, and would benefit the whole community, and I would do nothing to discourage them.

F. In whom would you have the title to land vested—in the state, or in individuals as now?

G. I would leave land-titles as at present.

F. Your theory does not touch the title to land, nor the mode of transferring the title, nor the enjoyment of it; but it is a theory confined altogether to the taxing of it?

G. In form. Its effect, however, if carried as far as I would like to carry it, would be to make the community the real owner of land, and the various nominal owners virtually tenants, paying ground rent in the shape of taxes.

F. Before we go to the method by which you would effect that result, let me ask you this question: A, a large landlord in New York, owns a hundred houses, worth each, say, $25,000 (scattered in different parts of the city); at what rate of valuation would you tax him?

G. On his houses, nothing. I would tax him on the value of the lots.

F. As vacant lots?

G. As if each particular lot were vacant, surrounding improvements remaining the same.

F. If you would have titles as now, then A, who owns a ten-thousand-dollar house and lot in the city, would still continue to be the owner, as he is at present?

G. He would still continue to be the owner, but as taxes were increased upon land-values he would, while still continuing to enjoy the full ownership of the house, derive less and less of the pecuniary benefits of the ownership of the lot, which would go in larger and larger proportions to the state, until, if the taxation of land-values were carried to the point of appropriating them entirely, the state would derive all those benefits, and, though nominally still the owner, he would become in reality a tenant with assured possession, so long as he continued to pay the tax, which might then become in form, as it would be in essence, a ground rent.

F. Now, suppose A to be the owner of a city lot and building, valued at $500,000; who would give a deed to it to B?

G. A would give the deed.

F. Then supposing A to own twenty lots, with twenty buildings on them, the lots being, as vacant lots, worth each $1,000, and the buildings being worth $49,000 each; and B to own twenty lots of the same value, as vacant lots, without any buildings; would you tax A and B alike?

G. I would.

F. Suppose that B, to buy the twenty lots, had borrowed the price, and mortgaged them for it; would you have the tax in that case apportioned?

G. I would hold the land for it. In cases in which it became necessary to consider the relations of mortgagee and mortgagor, I would treat them as joint owners.

F. If A, the owner of a city lot with a house upon it, should sell it to B, do you suppose that the price would be graduated by the value of the improvements alone?

G. When the tax upon the land had reached the point of taking the full annual value, it would.

F. To illustrate: Suppose A has a city lot, which, as a vacant lot, is worth annually $10,000, and there is a building upon it worth $100,000, and he sells them to B; you think the price would be graduated according to the value of the building, that is to say, $100,000, after the taxation had reached the annual value of $10,000?

G. Precisely.

F. To what purposes do you contemplate that the money raised by your scheme of taxation should be applied?

G. To the ordinary expenses of government, and such purposes as the supplying of water, of light, of power, the running of railways, the maintenance of public parks, libraries, colleges and kindred institutions, and such other beneficial objects as may from time to time suggest themselves; to the care of the sick and needy, the support of widows and orphans, and, I am inclined to think, to the payment of a fixed sum to every citizen when he came to a certain age.

F. Do you contemplate that money raised by taxation should be expended for the support of the citizen?

G. I see no reason why it should not be.

F. Would you have him fed and clothed at the public expense?

G. Not necessarily; but I think a payment might well be made to the citizen when he came to the age at which active powers decline, that would enable him to feed and clothe himself for the remainder of his life.

F. Let us come to practical results: The rate of taxation now in the city of New York, we will suppose, is 2.30 upon the assessed value. The assessed value is understood to be about sixty per cent. of the real value of property. Land assessed at $60,000 is really worth $100,000, and being assessed at 2.30 when valued at $60,000, should be assessed at about 1.40 on the real value; you would increase that amount indefinitely, if I understand you, up to the annual rental value of the land?

G. I would.

F. Which we will suppose to be five per cent.; is that it?

G. Let us suppose so.

F. Then your scheme contemplates the raising of 5 per cent. on the true value of all real estate as vacant land, to be used for the purposes you have mentioned. Have you thought of the increase in the army of office-holders that would be required for the collection and disbursement of this enormous sum of money?

G. I have.

F. What do you say to that?

G. That, as to collection, it would greatly reduce the present army of office-holders. A tax upon land-values can be levied and collected with a much smaller force than is now required for our multiplicity of taxes; and I am inclined to think, that, directly and indirectly, the plan I propose would permit the dismissal of three-fifths of the officials needed for the present purposes of government. This simplification of government would do very much to purify our politics; and I rely largely upon the improvement that the change I contemplate would make in social life, by lessening the intensity of the struggle for wealth, to permit the growth of such habits of thought and conduct as would enable us to get for the management of public affairs as much intelligence and as strict integrity as can now be obtained for the management of great private affairs.

F. Supposing it to be true that you would reduce the expense of collection, would you not, for the disbursement of these vast funds, require a much larger number of efficient men than are now required?

G. Not necessarily. But, whether this be so or not, the full scheme I propose can only be attained gradually. Until, at least, the total amount needed for what are now considered purely governmental purposes were obtained by taxation upon land-values, there would be a large reduction of office-holders, and no increase.

F. How do you propose to divide the taxation between the state and the municipalities?

G. As taxes are now divided. As to questions that might arise, there will be time enough to determine them when the principle has been accepted.

F. Your theory contemplates the raising of nearly four times as much revenue in the State of New York as is now raised; how many office-holders would it require to disburse this enormous sum of money among the various objects that you have mentioned?

G. My theory does not require that it should be disbursed among the objects I have mentioned, but simply that it should be used for public benefit.

F. Do you not think that the present rate of taxation is more than sufficient for all purposes of government?

G. Under the state of society that I believe would ensue, it would be much more than sufficient for present purposes of government. We should need far less for expenses of revenue collection, police, penitentiaries, courts, alms-houses, etc.

F. Then, to bring the matter down to a point, you propose for the present no change whatever in anything, except that the amount now raised by all methods of taxation should be imposed upon real estate considered as vacant?

G. For a beginning, yes.

F. Well, what do you contemplate as the ending of such a scheme?

G. The taking of the full annual value of land for the benefit of the whole people. I hold that land belongs equally to all, that land-values arise from the presence of all, and should be shared among all.

F. And this result you propose to bring about by a tax upon land-values, leaving the title, the privilege of sale, of rent, of testament, the same as at present?

G. Yes.

F. Your theory appears to me impracticable. I think that the raising of such an enormous sum of money, placing it in the coffers of the state, to be disbursed by the state in the manner you contemplate, would tend to the corruption of the government beyond all former precedent. The end you contemplate—of bettering the condition of all the people—is a worthy one. I believe that we—you and I—who are well to do in the world, and others in our condition, do neglect and have neglected our duty to those in a less fortunate condition, and that it is our highest duty to endeavor to relieve, so far as we can, the burdens of those who are now suffering from poverty and want. Therefore, far from deriding or scouting your theory, I examine it with respect and attention, desirous of getting from it whatever I can that may be good, while rejecting what I conceive to be erroneous. Taken altogether, as you have explained it, I do not see that it is a practicable scheme.

G. But your objections to it as impracticable only arise at the point, yet a long distance off, at which the revenues raised from land-values would be greater than those now raised. Is there anything impracticable in substituting, for the present corrupt, demoralizing, and repressive methods of taxation, a single tax upon land-values?

F. I think it possible to concentrate all taxation upon land, if that should be thought the best method. Many economists are of opinion that taxes should be raised from land alone, conceiving that rent is really paid by every consumer, but they include in land everything placed upon it out of which rent comes.

G. Then we could go together for a long while, and when the point was reached at which we would differ, we might be able to see that a purer government than any we have yet had might be possible. Certainly here is the gist of the whole problem. If men are too selfish, too corrupt, to co-operate for mutual benefit, there must always be poverty and suffering.

F. My theory of government is, that its chief function is to keep the peace between individuals, and allow each to develop his own nature for his own happiness. I would never raise a dollar from the people except for necessary purposes of government. I believe that the demoralization of our politics comes from the notion that public offices are spoils for partisans. A large class of men has grown up among us whose living is obtained from the state, that is to say, out of the people; we must get rid of these men, and, instead of creating offices, we must lessen their number.

G. I agree with you as to government in its repressive feature; and in no way could we so lessen the number of office-holders and take the temptation of private profit out of public affairs as by raising all public revenues by the tax upon land-values, which, easily assessed and collected, does not offer opportunities for evasion or add to prices. Though in form a tax, this would be in reality a rent; not a taking from the people, but a collecting of their legitimate revenues. The first and most important function of government is to secure the full and equal liberty of individuals; but the growing complexity of civilized life, and the growth of great corporations and combinations before which the individual is powerless, convince me that government must undertake more than to keep the peace between man and man, must carry on, when it cannot regulate, businesses that involve monopoly, and in larger and larger degree assume co-operative functions. If I could see any other means of doing away with the injustice involved in growing monopolies, of which the railroad is a type, than by extension of governmental functions, I should not favor that; for all my earlier thought was in the direction you have indicated—the position occupied by the Democratic party of the last generation. But I see none. However, if it were to appear that further extension of the functions of government would involve demoralization, then the surplus revenue might be divided per capita. But it seems to me that there must be in human nature the possibility of a reasonably pure government, when the ends of that government are felt by all to be the promotion of the general good.

F. I do not believe in spoliation, and I conceive that that would be spoliation which would take from one man his property and give it to another. The scheme of the Communists, as I understand it, appears to me to be not only unsound, but destructive of society. I do not mean to intimate that you are one of the Communists; on the contrary, I do not believe you are.

G. As to the sacredness of property, I thoroughly agree with you. As you say in your recent article on Industrial Co-operation in the NORTH AMERICAN REVIEW, "To take from one against his will that which he owns, and give it to another, would be a violation of that instinct of justice which God has implanted in the heart of every human being; a violation, in short, of the supreme law of the Most High;" and my objection to the present system is that it does this. I hold that that which a man produces is rightfully his, and his alone; that it should not be taken from him for any purpose, even for public uses, so long as there is any public property that might be employed for that purpose; and therefore I would exempt from taxation everything in the nature of capital, personal property or improvements, in short, that property which is the result of man's exertion. But I hold that land is not the rightful property of any individual. As you say again, "no one can have private property in privilege," and if the land belongs, as I hold it does belong, to all the people, the holding of any part of it is a privilege for which the individual holder should compensate the general owner according to the pecuniary value of the privilege. To exact this would not be to despoil any one of his rightful property, but to put an end to spoliation that now goes on. Your article in the REVIEW shows that you see the same difficulties I see, and would seek the same end—the amelioration of the condition of labor, and the formation of society upon a basis of justice. Does it not seem to you that something more is required than any such scheme of co-operation as that which you propose, which at best could be only very limited in its application, and which is necessarily artificial in its nature?

F. Undoubtedly. The hints that I have given in the article to which you refer, would affect a certain number of persons, not by any means the whole body politic. I conceive that a great deal more is necessary. There should be more sympathy, more mutual help. I think, as I have said, that we are greatly wanting in our duty to all the people around us, and I would do everything in my power to aid them and their children. I do not think that we have arrived at the true conception of our duty, of the duty of every American citizen to all other American citizens.

G. I think you are right in that; but does it not seem as though it were out of the power of mere sympathy, mere charity, to accomplish any real good? Is it not evident that there is at the bottom of all social evils an injustice, and until that injustice is replaced by justice, charity and sympathy will do their best in vain? The fact that there are among us strong, willing men unable to find work by which to get an honest living for their families, is a most portentous one. It speaks to us of an injustice that, if not remedied, must wreck society. It springs, I believe, from the fact that, while we secure to the citizen equal political rights, we do not secure to him that natural right more important still, the equal right to the land on which and from which he must live. To me it seems clear, as our Declaration of Independence asserts, that all men are endowed by their Creator with certain unalienable rights, and that the first of these rights—that which, in fact, involves all the rest, that without which none of the others can be exercised—is the equal right to land. Here are children coming into life to-day in New York; are they not endowed with the right to more than to struggle along as they best can in a country where they can neither eat, sleep, work, nor lie down without buying the privilege from some of certain human creatures like themselves, who claim to own, as their private property, this part of the physical universe, from the earth's center to the zenith?

F. I was not speaking of charity, but of sympathy leading to help—helping one to help himself—that is the help I mean, and not the charity that humbles him.

G. Then I cordially agree with you, and I look upon such sympathy as the most powerful agency for social improvement. But sympathy is little better than mockery until it is willing to do justice, and justice requires that all men shall be placed upon an equality so far as natural opportunities are concerned.

F. How would you secure that equality? Take the case of a child born to-day in a tenement-house, in one of those rooms that are said to be occupied by several families; and another child born at the same time in one of the most comfortable homes in our city. The parents of the first child are wasteful, intemperate, filthy; the parents of the second are thrifty, temperate, cleanly; how would you secure equality in opportunities of the first child with the second?

G. Equality in all opportunities could not be secured; virtuous parents are always an advantage, vicious parents a disadvantage; but equality of natural opportunities could be secured in the way I have proposed. And in a civilization where the equal rights of all to the bounty of their Creator were recognized, I do not believe there would be any tenement-houses, and very few, if any, parents such as those of which you speak. The vice and crime and degradation that so fester in our great cities are the effects, rather than the causes, of poverty.

F. The principle announced in the Declaration of Independence to which you have referred is one of the cardinal principles of American government—the inalienable right of all men to "life, liberty, and the pursuit of happiness." That, however, does not mean that all men are equal in opportunities or in positions. A child born to-day is entitled to the labors of his parents, or rather to the products of their labor, just as much as they are entitled to it, until he is able to take care of himself. One of the incentives to labor is to provide for the children of the laborer. The aim of our American civilization ought to be to furnish, so far as can be done rightfully, to every child born into the world, an equal opportunity with every other child, to work out his own good. This, however, is the theoretical proposition. It is impossible in practice to give to every child the same opportunity; what we should aim at is, to approximate to that state of things; this is the work of the philanthropist and Christian. In short, my belief is, that the truest statement of political ethics and political economy is to be found in the doctrines of the Christian religion.

G. In that I thoroughly agree with you. But Christianity that does not assert the natural rights of man, that has no protest when the earth which it declares was created by the Almighty as a dwelling-place for all his children is made the exclusive property of some of them, while others are denied their birthright,—seems to me a travesty. A Christian has something to do as a citizen and lawmaker. We must rest our social adjustments upon Christian principles if we would have a really Christian society. But to return to the Declaration of Independence, the equal right to life, liberty, and the pursuit of happiness; does it not necessarily involve the equal right to land, without which neither life, liberty, nor the freedom to pursue happiness is possible?

F. You do not propose to give to every child a piece of land; you only propose to secure its right, if I understand you, by taxing land as vacant land in the mode you propose?

G. That is all, but it is enough. In the complex civilization we have now attained it would be impossible to secure equality by giving to each a separate piece of land, or to maintain that equality, even if once secured; but by treating all land as the property of the whole people, we would make the whole people the landlords, and the individual users the tenants of all, thus securing to each his equal right.

F. In how long a time, if you were to have such legislation as you would wish, do you think we should arrive at the condition that you have mentioned?

G. I think immediately a substantial equality would be arrived at, such an equality as would do away with the spectacle of a man unable to find work, and would secure to all a good and easy living with a mere modicum of the hard labor and worriment now undergone by most of us. The great benefit would not be in the appropriation to public use of the unearned revenues now going to individuals, but in the opening of opportunities to labor, and the stimulus that would be given to improvement and production by the throwing open of unused land and the removal of taxation that now weights productive powers. And with the land made the property of the whole people, all social progress would be a progress toward equality. While other values tend to decline as civilization progresses, the value of land steadily advances. Such a great fact bespeaks some creative intent; and what that intent may be, it seems to me we can see when we reflect that if this value—a value created not by the individual, but by the whole community—were appropriated to the common benefit, the progress of society would constantly tend to make less important the difference between the strong and the weak, and thus, instead of those monstrous extremes toward which civilization is now hastening, would bring about conditions of greater and greater equality.

F. As a conclusion of the whole matter, if I understand this explanation of your scheme, it is this: that the state should tax the soil, and the soil only; that in doing so it should consider the soil as it came from the hands of the Creator, without anything that man has put upon it; that all other property—in short, everything that man has made—is to be acquired, enjoyed, and transmitted as at present; that the rate of annual taxation should equal the rate of annual rental; and that the proceeds of the tax should be applied not only to purposes of government, but to any other purposes that the legislature from time to time may think desirable, even to dividing them among the people at so much a head.

G. That is substantially correct.

F. I am glad to hear your explanation, though I do not agree with you, except as I have expressed myself.

5

The Knights of Labor and Collective Bargaining

Rules and Regulations Governing the Shoe Factories of Portsmouth, Ohio, March 1886

The Noble and Holy Order of the Knights of Labor was founded in 1869 as a secret fraternal and benefit society, with the ritual and flim-flam usual to such organizations. It grew rapidly, and turned increasingly toward economic and political reform. Although it accepted businessmen and farmers as well as wage earners (specifically barring only lawyers, bankers, liquor dealers, and gamblers), many of its branches came to act as trade unions. In 1885 it won a great victory over the Southwestern railroads controlled by Jay Gould, and the next year it reached its peak of perhaps 600,000 members. But in 1886 another strike against Gould was smashed, and the organization was shaken to pieces by factionalism and its own internal contradictions. A decade later it barely existed. The agreement that follows resembles a modern contract in its detailed outline of grievance and other procedures. Note (1) the machinery established for settling disputes, (2) the agreement concerning work hours, and (3) the provisions related to seniority and promotions. The longtime head of the Knights tells his story in Harry J. Carman and others, eds., *The Path I Trod: The Autobiography of Terence V. Powderly* (1940).

From Joseph A. Labadie Papers, Labadie Collection, University of Michigan.

Rᴜʟᴇs ᴀɴᴅ ʀᴇɢᴜʟᴀᴛɪᴏɴs ꜰᴏʀ ɢᴏᴠᴇʀɴɪɴɢ ᴛʜᴇ sʜᴏᴇ
factories of Portsmouth, Ohio, adopted by the
Joint Executive Board, March 11, 1886:

We, the Shoe Manufacturers and Employees of Portsmouth, O.,
believing it to be to our mutual benefit, do hereby agree to
arbitrate all differences; thus making strikes and lock-outs unnecessary. We as Manufacturers can not compel any one to join
the Knights of Labor, but would in the interest of harmony
prefer all to do so. Employees not now members of the Knights
of Labor from whatever cause must not be molested on that
account, and as a further precaution, do adopt the following
rules:

Rule No. 1]

The Shoe Factories shall be classed as "Union Shops," preference being given to Knights of Labor with the understanding
that this does not prohibit the employment of non-union men
and women.

Rule No. 2]

Should a grievance arise in any department of the Factories
the same must be referred to the Shop's Committee, whose duty
it shall be to endeavor to settle the same, failing in which they
shall notify the Executive Committee of the shop in which the
difficulty has arisen, the chairman of which must call a meeting
of the Committee within 24 hours after receiving notice; they
failing to settle the difficulty, there shall be a call for a joint
session of the Executive Board of both shops, together with the
Executive Board of the manufacturers; before whom the grievance shall be presented in writing, signed by the aggrieved party:
failing of settlement by this Board, the grievance shall immediately be referred to an Arbitration Committee, composed
of three disinterested parties, one of whom shall be selected by
the Manufacturers, and one by the Employees, and they two to

select the third whose decision in the matter shall be final and binding.

Rule No. 3]

The Executive Committee shall have power to settle all difficulties excepting where a question of wages is involved.

Rule No. 4]

The Employees shall remain at work pending a grievance.

Rule No. 5]

Whenever the Employers wish to reduce help the latest employed shall be first discharged, except when satisfactory reasons exist for doing otherwise.

Rule No. 6]

In dull seasons the work to be divided equally among the Employees as far as practicable.

Rule No. 7]

In filling vacancies preference shall be shown those longest in our employ, if eighteen years of age or over.

Rule No. 8]

Each factory shall regulate its own working hours; but in no case shall a day's work be more than 10 hours.

Rule No. 9]

No Employee shall be compelled to remain in the shop when there is no work for him or her, but shall not leave without obtaining permission from the proper authority in their department.

Should an Employee wilfully neglect his or her work they do so on their own responsibility.

Should an Employee be discharged for incompetency, the evidence shall be conclusive and the position must be filled by a skilled workman if available; if not then recourse shall be had to Rule 7.

These Rules to go into effect on and after March 15th, 1886, for one year.

Signed on the part of Manufacturers,

GEORGE PADAN,
HENRY PADAN,
IRVING DREW,
GEO. B. SELBY.

Signed on part of Knights of Labor,

DAN. SLATTERY,
OSCAR F. UPP,
JACOB IMM,
CHAS. W. ROW,
ELLA BENNETT,
DELIA LEE,
ANNA LLOYD,
JENNIE SEEL.

6

The Eight-Hour Day and the A. F. of L.

Statement of the National Eight-Hour Association, May 1886

Even as the Knight of Labor was collapsing, an association was emerging that was more explicitly trade unionist. In 1884 the Federation of Organized Trades and Labor Unions (which two years later became the American Federation of Labor) urged a campaign to reduce the working day to eight hours, beginning May 1, 1886. In the following handbill arguing for the eight-hour day, note (1) the stress on technological advance and its results: increased production, advances in output per man-hour, falling prices for farm products and manufactured goods; (2) the likelihood that an urban workman would be economically incapable of moving to a frontier farm; (3) the insufficiency of purchasing power due to the concentration of wealth and income; (4) the emphasis on economic interdependence; (5) internal inconsistencies and faulty reasoning. See Henry David, *The History of the Haymarket Affair* (1936); Philip Taft, *The A. F. of L. in the Time of Gompers* (1957); Ray Ginger, *Altgeld's America* (1958); and Lloyd Ulman, *The Rise of the National Trade Union* (1955).

Handbill in possession of Ray Ginger, Brandeis University.

Eight Hours for a Day's Labor
on and after May 1, 1886

THE NATIONAL EIGHT-HOUR ASSOCIATION PRESENTS the following reasons why the working classes will be benefited, and all the various kinds of business made more prosperous, through working less hours at daily labor:

If rightly distributed, there are enough of grain and manufactured products on the earth to-day to give every human being a reasonable amount of the comforts of life; but, through lack of knowledge of means of general distribution of labor, a large share of the food and manufactured products is allowed to remain in warehouse, store and factory; and wealth is accumulating in the hands of a few, while general business stagnates, and the poorer classes suffer from want of employment.

The present depressed conditions are rapidly aggravating the troubles of the poor. The idle classes, being compelled from necessity to sell their homes at a great sacrifice, thus become impoverished, while the rich, buying at the depreciated value, sell, when times are improved, at treble the prices which they pay; and hence the facilities of the rich man for rapidly becoming a millionaire.

There has been a time when relief from poverty in the cities could be had upon new lands, but machinery has caused such an abundance of farm produce, and such a fall in prices, as to leave but very little to the tiller of the soil for his labor—not sufficient, at any rate, to induce the poor to go to the new lands, even if they had the means to get there and could get them for nothing.

Patents are granted in the United States, latterly, on from 20,000 to 30,000 new machines and devices each year, the most of these being labor-saving. But while the purpose of these machines is to save labor, they pauperize the displaced laborers. Thirty years ago the workman toiled ten hours daily in the factory, and he does the same to-day, if he can get work. The only mission which the machine has served, latterly, is to cause depression in business through the discharge of laborers and mechanics into compulsory idleness, while it creates a vast product on farm, in store and factory, which the masses cannot buy. because of inability through lack of remunerative employment.

ᴛᴏ snow the misuse and the proper use of machinery, behold three men, all working prosperously together ten hours per day. A labor-saving machine is brought to them, which will do the work of one man. Two of the men misappropriate the same, and continue working with it ten hours, turning the third man into idleness, pauperism, and possibly crime. In the end the two are the losers by the misuse of the machine, they being compelled to support the third man in the poor-house or prison, while their trade is dull because they have destroyed the power of the third man to buy and consume that which they make. The proper use of the machine would have been to have allowed it to serve its purpose by lessening the working time for all three. The machine, then, would have been a blessing, and truly what it was designed to be—a labor-saver, bringing prosperity for all, with more rest and time for intellectual and moral improvement.

The time of daily toil, through labor-saving implements, has been lessened in the past century, from sixteen hours to ten, always, at every lessening, to the advantage of all classes. But, although a more rapid introduction of machinery has been made in the last twenty years than in a whole century before, there has been no shortening of daily working time for over thirty years. Consequently the productive power of the country, through machinery and long hours, is in excess of the ability to consume. Hence the discharge of workmen from factories, the increase of destitution and the general dullness of business.

The Eight-Hour Association asks for a reduction of all daily toil from ten hours to eight, for the reason that such reduction of time will give opportunity for two more men to work for every eight now employed. In other words, the work now performed by eight men will require ten men to achieve the same result. This will be twenty more men employed for every eighty, thus giving immediate, and for some years, constant labor to all who are willing and able to work.

That every one shall have steady employment at good wages, working eight hours daily, it is necessary that all agree and unite in this movement. In order for each workman to prosper it is essential that all other workmen prosper; because all people support each other by exchanging each others' production and services. Therefore everybody who has commodities or services for sale is interested in having everybody else have a sufficient income from his own earnings to make a mutual exchange. United action in this effort means not only strength but prosperity for all.

The advocates of eight hours for a day's labor advise all workers to take for this number of hours an eight-hour price, allowing the law of supply and demand to regulate wages in the future. We fully believe that while merchants, manufacturers and all employers will be benefited, the wages for laborers will soon be higher than ever heretofore, for the following reasons: A reduction of one-fifth of laboring-time for all that work will make a reduction of one-fifth of all kinds of products in the near future, which will make proportionate scarcity. With scarcity will come advance in prices for every commodity, giving merchants and manufacturers a fair profit, and wage-workers an advance in wages. Ere long, all being employed, the production will be as great as now, but, all earning wages, the consumption and demand will be greater than now, so that prices and wages will still continue better than at present.

Eight hours, instead of ten, means a gain of two hours each day—more than one day each week—*seventy-eight days a year!* —a time sufficient to enable every unlettered person to learn to read and write; time in which every foreigner can learn to speak the English language and familiarize himself with his political duty as an American citizen. The extra time thus gained in the year will afford every workingman not only a sufficient recreation, but opportunity to attend the State and county fairs, the National Exposition, and make a visit to the childhood home, with time to spare for a journey to Europe.

This appeal is in the interest of capital as well as labor. The plain facts are that the strikes, lock-outs, business failures, general business depression throughout the world, overflowing prisons and poor-houses, are the result of the producing power of the country being far in excess of the practical ability to consume. We make, raise and produce more than we can readily eat, wear, or dispose of. This results, first, in a falling of prices; then a lowering of wages, succeeded by strikes and resistance of wage-workers, and a final discharge of workmen into idleness. Then, as men are unable to buy, there is a great under-consumption, goods piling up on one side, while great want and destitution exist on the other. To remedy this, productive power, temporarily, must be lessened. To do this by destroying machinery is barbarous. It is wiser far to accomplish this result, and benefit all mankind, by lessening the hours in which machines and men labor in the work of production.

The benefit to the mercantile and manufacturing interests of the world by a shortening of production will be at once evident in the advance in prices and corresponding advance in profits; while every person having employment, earning wages, and better wages, will be able to buy at higher prices. Prosperity exists, and activity in business is manifest, when prices are tending upward. Stagnation, failure and distress prevail when prices are tending downward. Eight hours will send the life-currents of business pulsating throughout the entire commercial world, giving new life and energy to flagging industries that are now almost dead.

The advantage of eight hours to the laboring classes will be (1st) employment; (2d) steady employment; (3d) better wages; (4th) relief from anxiety that comes from idleness and poverty; (5th) an opportunity to lay aside the means for the purchase of a home; (6th) opportunity to see and get acquainted with the family by day-light; (7th) more time for intellectual improvement; (8th) a chance for outdoor recreation on the secular day, without being compelled to take Sunday for that purpose; (9th) the ability to obtain respectable dress and make a good appearance, whereby encouragement is given to attend church and social gatherings, resulting in intellectual, moral and spiritual improvement.

To establish this reform, and make its benefits universal throughout the United States, we earnestly urge all Unions, Labor organizations, societies, and persons interested in the peace of society, and in the pecuniary, intellectual and moral welfare of the nation, to *begin on May 1, 1886, and thereafter, to labor at all the mercantile, mechanical, manufacturing, and other regular employments, as far as may be, but eight hours each day.*

We do not urge eight hours in the interest of any one class. We ask it for the good of the prisoner who is suffering confinement and shame because want drove him there; we ask it for the pauper in the asylum, who sought that shelter rather than starve; we ask it for the toiling millions who find their daily earnings becoming less and less, with final discharge from work, idleness, poverty and crime the coming result; we ask it for merchants who are struggling to avoid bankruptcy through slow sales and the steady falling of prices of goods on their shelves; we ask it for manufacturers whose machinery is standing still, and we ask it for the transportation companies, the professional classes, capitalists—each and all.

To fully lay this matter before the people, through literature, discussion, lecture, sermon and study, *we recommend (Saturday, April 24, 1886, as a general holiday for the laboring classes, preparatory to inaugurating the Eight-Hour Movement seven days afterwards, on the first day of May.*

In this effort we fervently invoke the aid of the press, the clergy, legislators, teachers, employers, and all persons in authority. Give us employment for the idle masses who are struggling for bread; give us a chance to send pauper and criminal back to shop, and field, and factory, where they may get an honest living; give us back again health and bloom for the sunken-eyed, starving sewing-woman; give us homes for working-people, and a chance to earn them; give us an honest opportunity for every human being to possess the reasonable comforts of life—GIVE US EIGHT HOURS!

7

Monopoly as Seen by an Industrialist

Andrew Carnegie's "The Bugaboo of Trusts"

Andrew Carnegie (1835-1919) migrated from Scotland to the United States as a virtually penniless boy of twelve. Twenty years later his income exceeded $50,000 a year—at a time when the ordinary workman earned perhaps a dollar a day. In iron and steel manufacturing he pyramided his wealth until, in 1900, his personal share of the earnings of his company was $25,000,000. Selling out the next year to U. S. Steel as it was being formed, he spent much of his fortune on nonprofit projects, including the Carnegie Endowment for International Peace and some 2,800 buildings for public libraries. Although many of his publications were ghost-written, it remains true that Carnegie was one of the most verbal, and one of the most intelligent, business leaders of his day. In his article that follows, note (1) the extent of Carnegie's faith in the rule of law in economics; (2) his classic exposition of the origin of trusts in a situation of overproduction and unprofitable prices; and (3) his explanation of what would quickly undermine any effort at monopoly. See Victor S. Clark, *History of Manufactures in the United States, 1860-1914* (1928), and Edward C. Kirkland, *Industry Comes of Age: Business, Labor, and Public Policy, 1860-1897* (1961).

From Andrew Carnegie, "The Bugaboo of Trusts," *North American Review*, vol. 148 (February 1889), pp. 141-150.

The Bugaboo of Trusts

WE MUST ALL HAVE OUR TOYS; THE CHILD HIS
rattle, the adult his hobby, the man of pleasure
the fashion, the man of art his Master; and mankind in its various
divisions requires a change of toys at short intervals. The same
rule holds good in the business world. We have had our age
of "consolidations" and "watered stocks." Not long ago everything was a "syndicate"; the world is already becoming obsolete
and the fashion is for "Trusts," which will in turn no doubt
give place to some new panacea, that is in turn to be displaced
by another, and so on without end. The great laws of the economic world, like all laws affecting society, being the genuine
outgrowth of human nature, alone remain unchanged through
all these changes. Whenever consolidations, or watered stocks,
or syndicates, or Trusts endeavor to circumvent these, it always
has been found the result is that after the collision there is
nothing left of the panaceas, while the great laws continue to
grind out their irresistible consequences as before.

It is worth while to inquire into the appearance and growth
of Trusts and learn what environments produce them. Their
genesis is as follows: a demand exists for a certain article, beyond
the capacity of existing works to supply it. Prices are high, and
profits tempting. Every manufacturer of that article immediately
proceeds to enlarge his works and increase their producing power.
In addition to this the unusual profits attract the attention of
his principal managers or those who are interested to a greater
or less degree in the factory. These communicate the knowledge
of the prosperity of the works to others. New partnerships are
formed, and new works are erected, and before long the demand
for the article is fully satisfied, and prices do not advance. In a
short time the supply becomes greater than the demand, there
are a few tons or yards more in the market for sale required,
and prices begin to fall. They continue falling until the article is
sold at cost to the less favorably situated or less ably managed
factory; and even until the best managed and best equipped factory is not able to produce the article at the prices at which it

can be sold. Political economy says that here the trouble will end. Goods will not be produced at less than cost. This was true when Adam Smith wrote, but it is not quite true to-day. When an article was produced by a small manufacturer, employing, probably at his own home, two or three journeymen and an apprentice or two, it was an easy matter for him to limit or even to stop production. As manufacturing is carried on to-day, in enormous establishments with five or ten millions of dollars of capital invested, and with thousands of workers, it costs the manufacturer much less to run at a loss per ton or per yard than to check his production. Stoppage would be serious indeed. The condition of cheap manufacture is running full. Twenty sources of expense are *fixed charges*, many of which stoppage would only increase. Therefore the article is produced for months, and in some cases that I have known for years, not only without profit or without interest upon capital, but to the impairment of the capital invested. Manufacturers have balanced their books year after year only to find their capital reduced at each successive balance. While continuing to produce may be costly, the manufacturer knows too well that stoppage would be ruin. His brother manufacturers are of course in the same situation. They see the savings of many years, as well perhaps as the capital they have succeeded in borrowing, becoming less and less, with no hope of a change in the situation. It is in soil thus prepared that anything promising relief is gladly welcomed. The manufacturers are in the position of patients that have tried in vain every doctor of the regular school for years, and are now liable to become the victims of any quack that appears. Combinations—syndicates—trusts—they are willing to try anything. A meeting is called, and in the presence of immediate danger they decide to take united action and form a trust. Each factory is rated as worth a certain amount. Officers are chosen, and through these the entire product of the article in question is to be distributed to the public, at remunerative prices.

Such is the genesis of "Trusts" in manufactured articles. In transportation the situation, while practically the same, differs in some particulars. Many small railway lines are built under separate charters. A genius in affairs sees that the eight or ten separate organizations, with as many different ideas of management, equipment, etc., are as useless as were the two hundred and fifty petty kings in Germany, and, Bismarck-like, he sweeps them out of existence, creates a great through line, doubles the securities or stock, the interest upon which is paid out of the saving effected by consolidation, and all is highly satisfactory, as in the case of the New York Central. Or a line is built and managed with such sagacity as distinguishes the Pennsylvania Railroad, and it succeeds in developing the resources of the State so extensively that upon a line of three hundred and fifty miles between Pittsburgh and Philadelphia it nets about thirteen millions of dollars per annum. Twelve millions of dollars of this it shows upon its books. From one to two millions extra are expended in making one of the best lines in the world out of a road which was originally designed as a horse-railroad. We do not call our railroad combinations Trusts, but they are substantially such, since they aim at raising and maintaining transportation rates in certain districts. They are "combinations" or "systems" which aim at monopolies within these districts.

During the recent Presidential campaign it suited the purpose of one of the parties to connect Trusts with the doctrine of protection. But Trusts are confined to no country, and are not in any way dependent upon fiscal regulations. The greatest Trust of all just now is the Copper Trust, which is French, and has its headquarters in Paris. The Salt Trust is English, with its headquarters in London. The Wire-rod Trust is German. The only Steel-rail Trust that ever existed was an international one which embraced all the works in Europe. Trusts either in transportation or manufactures are the products of human weakness, and this weakness is co-extensive with the race.

There is one huge combination classed with Trusts which is so exceptional in its origin and history that it deserves a separate paragraph. I refer to the Standard Oil Company. So favorable an opportunity to control a product perhaps never arose as in the case of petroleum. At an early stage a few of the ablest business men that the world has ever seen realized the importance of the discovery, and invested largely in the purchase of property connected with it. The success of the petroleum business was phenomenal, and so was the success of these people. The profits they made, and, no doubt, as much capital as they could borrow, were fearlessly reinvested, and they soon became the principal owners, and finally, substantially the only owners of the territory which contained this great source of wealth. The Standard Oil Company would long ago have gone to pieces had it not been managed, upon the whole, in harmony with the laws which control business. It is generally admitted that the prices of oil to the consumer are as low to-day, and many think that they are even lower, than could have been attained had the business not been grouped and managed as one vast concern in the broad spirit for which the Standard Oil managers are famous. They are in the position somewhat of the Colemans, of Pennsylvania, who possess the chief source of the ore supply in the East. They own the Cornwall deposit of ore as the Standard Oil Company owns the source of the oil deposit. But as the company has continually to deal with the finding of oil in other localities, the price of its existence and success is the continuance of that exceptional ability in its councils and management displayed by its founders. Threatened opposition arises every now and then, and the chances are greatly in favor of the Standard Oil Company losing its practical monopoly, and going the way of all huge combinations. It is a hundred to one whether it will survive when the present men at the head retire; or perhaps I should say when the present man retires, for wonderful organizations imply a genius at the head, a commander-in-chief, with exceptionally able corps commanders no doubt, but still a Grant at the head. To those who quote the Standard Oil Company as an evidence that Trusts or combinations can be permanently successful, I say wait and see. I have spoken thus freely of that company because I am ignorant of its management, profits, and modes of action. I view it from the outside, as a student of political economy only, and as such have endeavored to apply to it the principles which I know *will* have their way, no matter how formidable the attempt made to defeat their operation.

We have given the genesis of trusts and combinations in their several forms. The question is, Do they menace the permanent interest of the nation? Are they a source of serious danger? Or are they to prove, as many other similar forms have proved, mere passing phases of unrest and transition? To answer this question let us follow the operation of the manufacturing trust which we have in imagination created, salt or sugar, nails, beams, or lead or copper; it is all the same. The sugar refiners, let us say, have formed a Trust after competing one with another through years of disastrous business, and all the sugar manufactured in the country in existing factories is sold through one channel at advanced prices. Profits begin to grow. Dividends are paid, and those who before saw their property vanishing before their eyes are now made happy. The dividends from that part of a man's capital invested in the sugar business yield him profit far above the capital he has invested in various other affairs. The prices of sugar are such that the capital invested in a new factory would yield enormously. He is perhaps bound not to enlarge his factory or to enter into a new factory, but his relatives and acquaintances soon discover the fresh opportunity for gain. He can advise them to push the completion of a small factory, which, of course, must be taken into the Trust. Or, even if he does not give his friends this intimation, capital is always upon the alert, especially when it is bruited about that a Trust has been formed, as in the case of sugar, and immediately new sugar manufactories spring up, as if by magic. The more successful the Trust, the surer these off-shoots are to sprout. Every victory is a defeat. Every factory that the Trust buys is the sure creator of another, and so on, *ad infinitum*, until the bubble bursts. The sugar refiners have tried to get more from capital in a special case than capital yields in general. They have endeavored to raise a part of the ocean of capital above the level of the surrounding waters, and over their bulwarks the floods have burst, and capital, like water, has again found its level. It is true that to regain this level a longer or a shorter period may be required, during which the article affected may be sold to the consumer in limited quantities at a higher rate than before existed. But for this the consumer is amply recompensed in the years that follow, during which the struggle between the discordant and competitive factories becomes severer than it ever was before, and lasts till the great law of the survival of the fittest vindicates itself. Those factories and managers that can produce to the best advantage eventually close the less competent. Capital wisely managed yields its legitimate profit. After a time, the growth of demand enables capital to receive an unusual profit. This in turn attracts fresh capital to the manufacture, and we have a renewal of the old struggle, the consumer reaping the benefit.

Such is the law, such has been the law, and such promises to be the law for the future; for, so far, no device has yet been devised that has permanently thwarted its operation. Given freedom of competition, and all combinations or trusts that attempt to exact from the consumer more than a legitimate return upon capital and services, write the charter of their own defeat. We have many proofs that this great law does not sleep and that it will not be suppressed. Some time ago, as I have stated, the steel rail manufacturers of Europe formed a trust and advanced the price of rails to such an extent that American manufacturers were able for the first and perhaps for the last time to export steel rails to Canada in competition with the European. But the misunderstandings and quarrels, inseparable from these attempted unions of competitors, soon broke the Trust. With vindictive feelings, added to what was before business rivalry, the struggle was renewed, and the steel rail industry of Europe has never recovered. It was found that the advance of prices had only galvanized into life concerns which never should have attempted to manufacture rails; and so that Trust died a natural death.

During the great depression which existed for several years in this country in the steel rail trade many anxious meetings were held under circumstances described in the genesis of Trusts, and it was resolved that the plan of restricting production should be tried. Fortunately reaction soon came. A demand for rails set in before the plan went into operation, and, as a matter of fact, no restriction of product was ever attempted, and the steel rail industry was thus saved from a great error.

We have recently seen the Lead Trust of this country shattered and its chief owners bankrupted. The newspapers a few weeks ago were filled with accounts of the convention of the growers of cattle in St. Louis, resolved to break down the combination of slaughterers and shippers in Chicago and Kansas City. No business was poorer in this country for many years than the manufacture of nails. It was overdone. To remedy this the manufacturers did not form a Trust so far as the sale of product was concerned, but they restricted production. A certain percentage of their machines was kept idle. This percentage was increased from time to time, and only the quantity made that the market would take at a certain price. But the result was that there were soon more machines in America for the manufacture of iron nails added to the works than the demand for nails will require for many years to come, and this combination of nail manufacturers went the way of all Trusts, and left the business in a worse plight than it was in before.

The Sugar Trust has already a noted competitor at its heels. The Copper Trust is in danger. All stand prepared to attack a "trust" or "combine" if it proves itself worth attacking; in other words, if it succeeds in raising its profits above the natural level of profits throughout the country it is subject to competition from every quarter, and must finally break down. It is unnecessary to devote much attention to the numerous Trusts in minor articles which one reads of, a new one appearing every few days and others passing out of existence, because they are all subject to the great law. The newspapers charge that Trusts exist or have existed in wall paper, shoe laces, lumber, coal, coke, brick, screw, rope, glass, school-books, insurance and hardware, and twenty more articles; but the fitting epitaph for these ephemeral creations is

> "If I was so soon to be done for,
> I wonder what I was begun for!"

We may exclaim with Macbeth, as he watched the shadowy descendants of Banquo filing past, "What, will the line stretch out to the crack of doom?" But as with Banquo's procession, so with Trusts, it is comforting to remember that as one approaches another disappears. They come like shadows, and so depart.

So much for Trusts in the manufacturing department. Let us now examine the railways, whose "pools" and "combinations" and "differentials" alarm some people. In all their various forms, these are the efforts of capital to protect itself from the play of economic forces, centered in free competition. In most cases the stocks of railways have been watered. Calculated upon the real capital invested the dividends of railway lines have been unusual, and much above the return which capital generally has yielded in other forms of investment. The entire capital stock of railways in the West as a rule has cost little or nothing, the proceeds of the bonds issued having been sufficient to build them. The efforts of railway managers to-day are therefore directed to obtain a return upon more capital than would be required to duplicate their respective properties. Their combinations and agreements of various kinds, which come to naught a few months after they are solemnly entered into, are evidences of this attempt. But, just as enormous profits on capital, received from the manufacture of any article, are sure to attract additional capital into the production of the article, so, in like manner, the unusual success of these railroads attracts new capital into their territory. New York Central paying dividends upon its eighty per cent. stock dividend culminates in the West Shore. The Pennsylvania Railroad, earning, as I have said, something like thirteen millions per annum upon its line in Pennsylvania, has its South Pennsylvania. One line between Chicago and Milwaukee being greatly profitable, fortunately brought into existence a parallel road. The two being unusually profitable, fortunately resulted in a third. There was one line between these points, and now there are six; and should the six combine to-morrow and exact from the public one per cent. more return upon capital than the average return, there would soon be seven, and very properly so.

This proves once more that there is no possibility of evading the great law, provided capital is free to embark in competing lines. In Great Britain and throughout Europe generally a different policy has been pursued in regard to railways from that of the free-to-all policy which we have followed. The railways and other transportation routes of Great Britain, in order to get permission to build, have cost nearly as much per mile as our cheapest Western lines have cost to build. Manchester, for instance, has recently decided to construct a canal, thirty miles long, to Liverpool, and the expense incurred in obtaining permission from Parliament to embark capital in this enterprise has cost nearly half a million of dollars up to this date. The Government, through a committee of Parliament, determines whether a proposed line is actually needed, and to settle this point everybody connected with existing transportation facilities in the neighborhood appears before the committee to prove that it is not needed, while the promoters of the scheme are at enormous expense to prove by hundreds of experts that it is. The empirical decision of the committee of the House of Commons on this question is not to be compared with the unerring decision of the capitalists interested. They know much better than any committee of the Legislature are likely to know whether the work in question will pay a fair dividend, and this is the best proof that it is required. The result of the American policy is seen in the fact that notwithstanding all the attempts upon the part of our railways to thwart the economic laws, nevertheless, the American people enjoy the cheapest transportation in the world. The railway rates upon freight in Europe, compared with those in America, show startling contrasts. The cost of freightage on English lines is upon the average more than double the American charge, and in many cases which I have examined it is three times as great. In not a few cases the British charge is far beyond three times the American.

A friend bought a cargo of grain at Leith, which had paid one dollar per ton freight from New York; it cost him ninety-six cents per ton to transport it thirty-five miles inland. Another purchased six hundred tons charcoal pig-iron upon Lake Superior, which cost four dollars per ton freight to Liverpool; he paid $2.87 per ton to carry it eighty miles inland by rail to his mills. For this amount our trunk lines carry rails five hundred and sixty miles, as against eighty miles in Britain. If Europe enjoyed our advantages of free competition in its transportation system, the development of its resources would be surprising, even at this late day in its history. There is in my opinion only cause for hearty congratulation as regards our railway policy. Its evils are trifling; its advantages over all other systems in the world enormous.

The people of America can smile at the efforts of all her railway magnates and of all her manufacturers to defeat the economic laws by Trusts or combinations, or pools, or "differentials," or anything of like character. Only let them hold firmly to the doctrine of free competition. Keep the field open. Freedom for all to engage in railroad building when and where capital desires subject to conditions open to all. Freedom for all to engage in any branch of manufacturing under like conditions.

There can then be no permanent extortion of profit beyond the average return from capital, nor any monopoly, either in transportation or manufacturing. Any attempt to maintain either must end in failure, and failure ultimately disastrous just in proportion to the temporary success of the foolish effort. It is simply ridiculous for a party of men to meet in a room and attempt by passing resolutions to change the great laws which govern human affairs in the business world, and this, whether they be railway presidents, bankers or manufacturers.

The fashion of Trusts has but a short season longer to run, and then some other equally vain device may be expected to appear when the next period of depression arrives; but there is not the slightest danger that serious injury can result to the sound principles of business from any or all of these movements. The only people who have reason to fear Trusts are those foolish enough to enter into them. The Consumer and the Transporter, not the Manufacturer and the Railway owner, are to reap the harvest.

Even since the foregoing was written, a new form has appeared upon the stage in the shape of "The Presidents' Agreement—an agreement among gentlemen," in which the parties engage to control, strangle and restrict the future development of our magnificent railway system under the laws of natural growth, at a time when the country requires this development as much as it ever did. These gentlemen are not going to engage in building lines which will give the public the benefit of healthy competition, or permit such to be built hereafter. It is safe to say that very soon this toy will be discarded, like its predecessors, for another, and that the very men apparently most pleased with this new rattle will then regard it with the greatest contempt, and go forward in the good work, as hitherto, developing the railway system wherever and whenever they think they see a fair chance for profit. Whenever existing railways exact from the public more than a fair return upon the actual capital invested, or upon the capital which would be required to duplicate existing lines, competing lines will be built—fortunately for the interests of the country—which is much more concerned in getting cheap transportation than it is in insuring dividends for capitalists; and whenever a percentage is to be obtained by the negotiation of railway securities, bankers will be found—also fortunately for the best interests of the country—who will gladly find a market for them without stopping to inquire whether monopolies are to be overthrown by the new lines.

It is not in the power of man to exact for more than a brief season, and a very brief season indeed, unusual profit upon actual capital invested either in Transportation or Manufacture, so long as all are free to compete, and this freedom, it may safely be asserted, the American people are not likely to restrict.

8

Factory Workers:
Who Got How Much and Why?

Payroll Ledger of 1889

Although immigration from Eastern and Southern Europe did not reach its peak until after 1900, long before that date so-called New Immigrants in large numbers were clustered in some towns in the United States, as shown by the following payroll for a cotton mill in Holyoke, Massachusetts, in 1889. Many of these persons had been peasants in their homelands, and the fact that much of the manpower available to manufacturing was unskilled had major consequences. First, it put a premium on the invention and use of machinery that could be operated with a minimum of skill. Second, it tended to preserve the huge discrepancy between the rates of skilled and unskilled labor. While the overseer (foreman) in this carding room was getting $24 a week, most of his subordinates were earning less than a fourth as much. See Rowland Tappan Berthoff, *British Immigrants in Industrial America, 1790-1950* (1953); John Higham, *Strangers in the Land: A Study of American Nativism, 1860-1925* (1955); and David Brody, *Steelworkers in America: The Non-union Era* (1960).

From Lyman Mills Papers, Baker Library, Harvard University.

From: Payroll Ledger, Carding Room, Lyman Mills No. 1, week ending 9 Nov. 1889

Names	Total Hours	Price	Amounts
Overseer			
J. W. Doran ...	60	40	24.00 ...
Sec. Hands			
P. Clifford ...	60	18	10.80 ...
P. Smith ...	60	18	10.80 ...
P. King ...	60	20	12.00 ...
Third Oilers and Roving H'ds			
R. Lathrop ...	60	12	7.20 ...
A. Blanchard ...	60	10	6.00 ...
A. Boulris ...	60	10	6.00 ...
J. Fox ...	15	8	1.20 ...
F. Rojcrak ...	60	7	4.20 ...
J. Tobake ...	19	8	1.52 ...
Scrubber			
J. Moriarity ...	60	5	3.00 ...
Picker Men			
M. Grincovitch ...	60	10	6.00 ...
M. Goetz ...	60	10	6.00 ...
J. Chazee ...	60	10	6.00 ...
A. Icyk ...	60	10	6.00 ...
J. Theolong ...	60	10	6.00 ...
J. Wodjikoski ...	60	9	5.40 ...
A. Theolong ...	60	9	5.40 ...
Strippers			
J. Tirmasky ...	60	9½	5.70 ...
F. Woijcek ...	60	9½	5.70 ...
J. Gay ...	60	9½	5.70 ...
M. Martinsky ...	60	9½	5.70 ...
J. Stafeka ...	60	9½	5.70 ...
M. Keroski ...	60	9½	5.70 ...
M. Conak ...	60	9½	5.70 ...
M. Matyska ...	60	9½	5.70 ...
J. Hospen ...	60	9½	5.70 ...
J. Yarmick ...	60	9½	5.70 ...
Lap Oiler & W'ste Mach Hds			
J. Peter ...	60	9½	5.70 ...
H. Roberts ...	60	9	5.40 ...
J. Chyc ...	60	8½	5.10 ...

Names	Total Hours		Price	Amounts
Grinders				
J. Danforth ...	60		15	9.00 ...
G. Meinay ...	60		15	9.00 ...
J. Manning ...	60		15	9.00 ...
F. Downie ...	60		15	9.00 ...
M. Morrison ...	60		15	9.00 ...
Geo Pray ...	60		15	9.00 ...
Railways and Drawing				
J. Laternak ...	60		7	4.20 ...
P. Yourka ...	60		8	4.80 ...
J. Lapoint ...	60		7	4.20 ...
A. Garcoa ...	60		7	4.20 ...
M. Wodjikoski ...	60		7	4.20 ...
N. Ash ...	60		7	4.20 ...
D. Chomerni ...	60		7	4.20 ...
C. Koslanki ...	60		7	4.20 ...
		Piece Work		
Slubbers				
M. Swaga ...	60	48	10	4.80 ...
D. Brooks ...	55	44	10	4.40 ...
A. Danian ...	60	52	10	5.20 ...
A. Lapoint ...	60	51	10	5.10 ...
M. Snay ...	60	48	10	4.80 ...
S. Duprey ...	50	45	10	4.50 ...
M. McNulty ...	50	42	10	4.20 ...
K. Connor ...	60	90	7	6.30 ...
M. Sullivan ...	60	88	7	6.16 ...
J. Sullivan ...	60	93	7	6.51 ...

9

A Deal in Wheat

Letter from a Chicago Brokerage Firm
to a Client in Boston

Farmers faced severe natural hazards: drought, blizzards, plagues
of locusts and boll weevils. Even more serious was the steadily
falling prices of their chief cash crops. Infuriated farmers raved
against "money lenders" and "speculators." Documents like the one
below would have enraged farmers even more, for the deal outlined
here involves no speculation at all if that term be taken to imply an
element of risk. Walker & Wrenn, a LaSalle Street firm of bankers
and brokers in Chicago, writes to a client in Boston. Note (1) the
extent to which buying and selling wheat was removed from the
farmers; (2) how the price difference in wheat futures between
Chicago and St. Louis could be exploited to make a sure profit; and
(3) evidence of how American life had been nationalized by the
new technologies of the nineteenth century. See Fred A. Shannon,
The Farmer's Last Frontier: Agriculture, 1860-1897 (1945) and
Frank Norris' exciting novel about deals in wheat on the Chicago
Board of Trade, *The Pit* (1903).

From J. M. Forbes & Co. Papers, Baker Library, Harvard University.

Chicago, July 27th, 1894

Mess. J. M. Forbes & Co.
Boston, Mass.

GENTLEMEN:

We beg to offer the following suggestions for your consideration in reference to your holdings of cash and September wheat here: This market is at present relatively several cents a bushel out of line with other markets, such as St. Louis, Toledo, New York, Baltimore etc. The cash wheat which you are holding here is mostly winter wheat of the old crop and if you take delivery of your September purchases the same kind of wheat, namely, old crop No. 2 Red Winter is most sure to be delivered to you. For this old wheat there has not been for several months, and there is not now, any demand whatever from any quarter within several cents per bushel of the market. The elevator men here have been using this seven million bushels of old Winter wheat in store as every delivery day comes around as a club to widen out the difference from one option to another and enable them to earn their carrying charges. Our suggestion is for you to dispose of a portion say, a half million bushels of your holdings here, and replace it with something for which there is more likely to be a demand than there is for this old Winter wheat here. We did think of advising you to let us pick up for you receipts of new No. 2 Red wheat coming in here which is a very choice quality and is sure to bring considerable premium over the old crop, but within the last few days, the Elevator men have been competing so strongly for it that it already commands a premium of one cent or more over the old wheat, and on this basis we would not advise you to go into it. We have, however, been negotiating, through friends of ours, with the elevator companies in St. Louis, and we think we can make arrangements with them to get delivery of choice new wheat on purchases of August and September wheat, and also to make a special reduction in the rate of storage provided a good sized lot of wheat is taken. We think that if an offer is made to them of 3/4 cent per month on, say, one half million bushels that they would accept it. The St. Louis market has been ranging from 4 to 4-3/4 under Chicago. The difference ought not to be more than three cents, which is the actual difference in freight rates from most Winter wheat points and before very long the difference will not exceed three cents a bushel. Our suggestion would be to sell half a million bushels of wheat here and buy it in St. Louis at four cents or more less money, and make the arrangement with the Elevator company for new wheat and special storage rate. There is instantaneous telegraphic connection between our board and St. Louis and the selling out here and the buying in St. Louis could be done at the same time. We would not advise making a change at a less difference than four cents a bushel, and it might take us perhaps a week to get 500,000 bushels changed over.

The quality of the St. Louis wheat is exceedingly choice. We have never seen anything so fine in our lives. We send you by mail several samples of the wheat which we have received during the past week or two. We think when European buyers find out how choice this new crop of Winter wheat is that there will be an active demand for it at a premium of at least two cents a bushel over the old wheat.

If, during the next week or two, it should be possible to get hold of new wheat here without having to pay too much premium for it, we would advise transferring the balance of what you have into No. 2 Red here, but at present it cannot be done on favorable terms. If there should be any change we will advise you.

Part II. Social and Intellectual History]

10

Why Americans Are Not Class-Conscious

A Socialist Analysis of Reform Movements

When Karl Marx and others founded the International Working-men's Association in 1864, it began to form sections in the United States. Their membership was very small, and was largely confined to German immigrants. Not until 1900, when Eugene V. Debs polled 96,000 votes for President on the Social Democratic ticket, did radical ideas affect significant numbers of English-speaking voters. The following letter analyzes the ideologies and the social conditions that impeded the spread of socialism in this country in the late nineteenth century. It was written August 20, 1871 to the Conference of Delegates of the I.W.A., at London, by the North American Central Committee. Note (1) what effect the authors thought the dream of success had upon the labor movement; (2) how reform parties were thought to affect the cause of labor; and (3) what the authors thought was wrong with the leadership of labor in the United States. See Ray Ginger, *Eugene V. Debs: A Biography* (1962 reprint) and Karl Marx and Frederick Engels, *Letters to Americans, 1845-1895* (1953)

From International Workingmen's Association, North American Central Committee Letterbook, 1871-1876, Wisconsin State Historical Society.

...WE ARE SORRY TO STATE THAT THE WORKING-
men in general,—even in spite of the industrial
development—are quite unconscious of their own position
towards capital and slow to show battle against their oppressors
for the following reasons:

I]

The great majority of workingmen in the Northern States
are Immigrants from Ireland, Germany, England etc. (in California Coolies imported under contract) having left their native
countrys for the purpose of seeking here that wealth they could
not obtain at home. This delusion transforms itself into a sort
of creed, and employers & capitalists, parvenus, having gained
their wealth in a former period, take great care in preserving this
self-deception among their employees, and so the German, the
Irish & every laborer works on in the belief of finally arriving
at the desired goal, until time & experience show its utter vanity,
the Capitalists themselves rendering its realization more & more
impossible. This visionary idea has been the cornerstone in founding the Trades-Unions—in this country at least—whilst now it
is the stumbling block over which they fall & perish. Nonetheless
a great number of working men can not part with this, their
favorite idea, because their mind is constantly confused & troubled by another medium:

II. The Reform Parties]

The so-called Reform Parties are growing up in the United
States over night and for every one disappearing there are two
others anxious & ready to step into its tracks. These parties assert,
that the emancipation of labor or rather the welfare of mankind
can be obtained peacefully & easily by universal suffrage, glit-
tering educational measures, benevolent & homestead societies,
universal language & other schemes & systems nicely put up in
their innumerable meetings & carried out by nobody. The leading
men of said parties, mostly men of science & philanthropists

perceive the rottenness of the governing classes as far as relating to their own ideas of morality, but they see only the surface of the question of labor & accordingly all their humanitarian advices do not touch but the exterior of it. Such a reform movement well advocated & intelligently presented to the workingmen is often gladly accepted, because the laborer wants to ameliorate his position and does not perceive the hollowness of that gilded nut shining before his eyes. The daily press does not fail to point out the ridiculous parts of these propositions, to shake them well up with the labor question and to present that so prepared staff & surrogate as a new gospel to their readers.

III]

The third obstacle is & has been the wrong guidance of the labor movement itself. A number of the so-called leaders have been activated by ambition or other selfish motives, whilst another number was honest & true but failed to take the right steps and began to reform, all reforms finally taking their abode in one of the political parties of the ruling class, the bourgeoisie. The best proof of this is given in the platform as passed by the first National Labor Congress at Baltimore 1866, compared with the platform passed in Cincinnati & St. Louis 1870 & 1871. . . . The first one (1866) endeavors to favor the workingman; in the latter (1870 & 1871) the main question is the money system of the United States, a question brought up by both parties of the ruling class, whenever an election is impending. . . .

11

"Only a Farmer's Daughter"

Handbill for a Sentimental Drama

The growth of cities greatly stimulated the demand for commercial entertainment. Americans swarmed to spectator sports; big-time boxing, baseball, football, and basketball all date from the last half of the nineteenth century. Nearly every village had a legitimate theater (often called "opera house" to avoid the connotation of sinfulness), and in 1880 fully 250 traveling companies were on the road. Although many of the actors and actresses were talented, the plays they acted in were likely to abound in melodramatic bombast or childish sentimentality. Typical is the plot of "Only a Farmer's Daughter": reading the synopsis might make one laugh and cry simultaneously. Note (1) the implications suggested in the name of the theater and the characterization of the play; (2) the kind of moral relationships implied in the society of the 1880s. See John R. Betts, "The Technological Revolution and the Rise of Sport," *Mississippi Valley Historical Review*, XL (1953-1954), pp. 231-256; Carl F. Wittke, *Tambo and Bones: A History of the American Minstrel Stage* (1930); and Arthur Hobson Quinn, *A History of the American Drama from the Civil War to the Present Day* (1936).

Playbill for People's Theatre, St. Louis, November 18, 1883, Harvard Theater Collection, Houghton Library.

PEOPLE'S THEATRE.

PROGRAMME.

TO-NIGHT.

The Great American Play

ONLY A

Farmer's Daughter,

CAST.

LIZZIE STARK, Mme LAURENT,	} The Adventurers	**Adelaide Cherie.**

JUSTINE, the Farmer's Daughter... CAMILLE KINZEY

Mother Stark, of Poverty Hollow .... Emma Frank

Mollie, Little Nellie's Attendant .... Etta Frank

Harold Lenox, the Wealthy Author ....Hugh T. Gibson

Jack Hartley,   the Adventuress'
Philip Bartram,   Accomplices.   Will F. Granger

Sammy Green, a Farmer Lad .... Fred Hunter

Higgins, the Butler .... H. J. Hirshberg

Keeper Taylor, of Sing Sing .... J. Dalton

Nelly, Mama's Treasure .... Little Mamie

SYNOPSIS:

ACT I.—Lizzie Stark, a poor sewing girl, helps her sweet-
heart to escape from Sing Sing.—Justine will not be de-
ceitful even to aid a woman in distress.—Lizzie becomes
embittered against the world and resolves to be a fool
no longer.—"Henceforth I live for Jack and myself."
(An interval of eight years between first and second
Acts.)

ACT II.—The Wealthy Author's Home.—Lizzie Stark, in
pursuance of her vow, appears as the adventuress.—
Her love for Jack undying and unyielding.—She
would sacrifice all for him. Jack, as Mr. Bartram, is
her accomplice.—They score a victory.

ACT III.—The Farmer's Daughter asserts her rights.—A
Mother's love.

ACT IV.—Poverty Hollow.—Poor little Nelly, Mother
Stark beats her, and makes her beg.—Her maniac
father.—Lizzie repents.—She would repair the wrong
she has done.—"Mother, your teaching has made me
what I am."—Spare me!—Mercy, Mercy! I came
to save you.—Thrilling tableaux.

ACT V.—Little Nelly's prayer.—Happy denouement.

12

Race Relations and an Economic Program

Henry W. Grady's "The South and Her Problems"

Henry Woodfin Grady (1850-1889), editor and publicist, was a Southerner born and bred. But while he urged the need for white supremacy and a Solid (Democratic) South, Grady also urged the desirability of moving forward from the old plantation system. With the Solid South he wished to merge a New South that would hold diversified farming and a large element of industry. In the following speech by Grady, delivered at the Dallas State Fair on October 26, 1887, note (1) the array of justifications for an anti-Negro viewpoint; (2) its relation to anti-Asian agitation, especially in the Far West; (3) the economic catastrophe worked in the South by the Civil War; (4) the growth of farm output and of manufacturing; (5) the hint of possible modification of the South's traditional low-tariff position; and, not least, (6) the florid rhetoric. See C. Vann Woodward, *Origins of the New South, 1877-1913* (1951), a great book; George B. Tindall, *South Carolina Negroes, 1877-1900* (1952); and John F. Stover, *Railroads of the South, 1865-1900* (1955.

From Henry Woodfin Grady, *The New South and Other Addresses,* edited by Edna Henry Lee (New York: Turpin, Maynard, Merrill & Co., 1904), pp. 47-70, 75-81.

Wʜᴀᴛ sʜᴀʟʟ ᴛʜᴇ sᴏᴜᴛʜ ᴅᴏ ᴛᴏ ʙᴇ sᴀᴠᴇᴅ? Through what paths shall she reach the end? Through what travail, or what splendors, shall she give to the Union this section, its wealth garnered, its resources utilized, and its rehabilitation complete—and restore to the world this problem solved in such justice as the finite mind can measure, or finite hands administer?

In dealing with this I shall dwell on two points.

First, the duty of the South in its relation to the race problem.

Second, the duty of the South in relation to its no less unique and important industrial problem.

I approach this discussion with a sense of consecration. I beg your patient and cordial sympathy. And I invoke the Almighty God, that having showered on this people His fullest riches, has put their hands to this task, that He will draw near unto us, as He drew near to troubled Israel, and lead us in the ways of honor and uprightness, even through a pillar of cloud by day, and a pillar of fire by night.

What of the negro? This of him. I want no better friend than the black boy who was raised by my side, and who is now trudging patiently with downcast eyes and shambling figure through his lowly way in life. I want no sweeter music than the crooning of my old "mammy," now dead and gone to rest, as I heard it when she held me in her loving arms, and bending her old black face above me stole the cares from my brain, and led me smiling into sleep. I want no truer soul than that which moved the trusty slave, who for four years while my father fought with the armies that barred his freedom, slept every night at my mother's chamber door, holding her and her children as safe as if her husband stood guard, and ready to lay down his humble life on her threshold.

History has no parallel to the faith kept by the negro in the South during the war. Often five hundred negroes to a single white man, and yet through these dusky throngs the women and children walked in safety, and the unprotected homes rested in peace. Unmarshaled the black battalions moved patiently to the fields in the morning to feed the armies their idleness would have starved, and at night gathered anxiously at the big house to "hear the news from marster," though conscious that his victory made their chains enduring. Everywhere humble and kindly; the bodyguard of the helpless; the rough companion of the little ones; the observant friend; the silent sentry in his lowly cabin; the shrewd counselor. And when the dead came home, a mourner at the open grave. A thousand torches would have disbanded every Southern army, but not one was lighted. When the master going to a war in which slavery was involved said to his slave, "I leave my home and loved ones in your charge," the tenderness between man and master stood disclosed. And when the slave held that charge sacred through storm and temptation, he gave new meaning to faith and loyalty. I rejoice that when freedom came to him after years of waiting, it was all the sweeter because the black hands from which the shackles fell were stainless of a single crime against the helpless ones confided to his care.

From this root, imbedded in a century of kind and constant companionship, has sprung some foliage. As no race had ever lived in such unresisting bondage, none was ever hurried with such swiftness through freedom into power. Into hands still trembling from the blow that broke the shackles, was thrust the ballot. In less than twelve months from the day he walked down the furrow a slave, a negro dictated in legislative halls from which Davis and Calhoun had gone forth, the policy of twelve commonwealths. When his late master protested against his misrule, the federal drum-beat rolled around his strongholds, and from a hedge of federal bayonets he grinned in good-natured insolence. From the proven incapacity of that day has he far advanced? Simple, credulous, impulsive—easily led and too often easily bought, is he a safer, more intelligent citizen now than then? Is this mass of votes, loosed from old restraints, inviting alliance or awaiting opportunity, less menacing than when its purpose was plain and its way direct?

My countrymen, right here the South must make a decision on which very much depends. Many wise men hold that the white vote of the South should divide, the color line be beaten down, and the Southern States ranged on economic or moral questions as interest or belief demands. I am compelled to dissent from this view. The worst thing, in my opinion, that could happen is that the white people of the South should stand in opposing factions, with the vast mass of ignorant or purchasable negro votes between. Consider such a status. If the negroes were skilfully led—and leaders would not be lacking—it would give them the balance of power—a thing not to be considered. If their vote was not compacted, it would invite the debauching bid of factions, and drift surely to that which was the most corrupt and cunning. With the shiftless habit and irresolution of slavery days still possessing him, the negro voter will not in this generation, adrift from war issues, become a steadfast partisan through conscience or conviction. In every community there are colored men who redeem their race from this reproach, and who vote under reason. Perhaps in time the bulk of this race may thus adjust itself. But, through what long and monstrous periods of political debauchery this status would be reached, no tongue can tell.

The clear and unmistakable domination of the white race, dominating not through violence, not through party alliance, but through the integrity of its own vote and the largeness of its sympathy and justice through which it shall compel the support of the better classes of the colored race—that is the hope and assurance of the South. Otherwise, the negro would be bandied from one faction to another. His credulity would be played upon, his cupidity tempted, his impulses misdirected, his passions inflamed. He would be forever in alliance with that faction which was most desperate and unscrupulous. Such a state would be worse than reconstruction, for then intelligence was banded, and its speedy triumph assured. But with intelligence and property divided—bidding and overbidding for place and patronage—irritation increasing with each conflict—the bitterness and desperation seizing every heart—political debauchery deepening, as each faction staked its all in the miserable game—there would be no end to this, until our suffrage was hopelessly sullied, our people forever divided, and our most sacred rights surrendered.

One thing further should be said in perfect frankness. Up to this point we have dealt with ignorance and corruption—but beyond this point a deeper issue confronts us. Ignorance may struggle to enlightenment, out of corruption may come the incorruptible. God speed the day when—every true man will work and pray for its coming—the negro must be led to know and through sympathy to confess that his interests and the interests of the people of the South are identical. The men who, from afar off, view this subject through the cold eye of speculation or see it distorted through partisan glasses insist that directly or indirectly the negro race shall be in control of the affairs of the South. We have no fears of this; already we are attracting to us the best elements of the race, and as we proceed our alliance will broaden; external pressure but irritates and impedes. Those who would put the negro race in supremacy would work against infallible decree, for the white race can never submit to its domination, because the white race is the superior race. But the supremacy of the white race of the South must be maintained forever, and the domination of the negro race resisted at all points and at all hazards—because the white race is the superior race. This is the declaration of no new truth. It has abided forever in the marrow of our bones, and shall run forever with the blood that feeds Anglo-Saxon hearts.

In political compliance the South has evaded the truth, and men have drifted from their convictions. But we can not escape this issue. It faces us wherever we turn. It is an issue that has been, and will be. The races and tribes of earth are of divine origin. Behind the laws of man and the decrees of war, stands the law of God. What God hath separated let no man join together. The Indian, the Malay, the Negro, the Caucasian, these types stand as markers of God's will. Let no man tinker with the work of the Almighty. Unity of civilization, no more than unity of faith, will never be witnessed on earth. No race has risen, or will rise, above its ordained place. Here is the pivotal fact of this great matter—two races are made equal in law, and in political rights, between whom the caste of race has set an impassable gulf. This gulf is bridged by a statute, and the races are urged to cross thereon. This cannot be. The fiat of the Almighty has gone forth, and in eighteen centuries of history it is written.

We would escape this issue if we could. From the depths of its soul the South invokes from heaven "peace on earth, and good will to man." She would not, if she could, cast this race back into the condition from which it was righteously raised. She would not deny its smallest or abridge its fullest privilege. Not to lift this burden forever from her people would she do the least of these things. She must walk through the valley of the shadow, for God has so ordained. But He has ordained that she shall walk in that integrity of race that was created in His wisdom and has been perpetuated in His strength. Standing in the presence of this multitude, sobered with the responsibility of the message I deliver to the young men of the South, I declare that the truth above all others to be worn unsullied and sacred in your hearts, to be surrendered to no force, sold for no price, compromised in no necessity, but cherished and defended as the covenant of your prosperity, and the pledge of peace to your children, is that the white race must dominate forever in the South, because it is the white race, and superior to that race by which its supremacy is threatened.

It is a race issue. Let us come to this point, and stand here. Here the air is pure and the light is clear, and here honor and peace abide. Juggling and evasion deceive not a man. Compromise and subservience have carried not a point. There is not a white man North or South who does not feel it stir in the gray matter of his brain and throb in his heart, not a negro who does not feel its power. It is not a sectional issue. It speaks in Ohio and in Georgia. It speaks wherever the Anglo-Saxon touches an alien race. It has just spoken in universally approved legislation in excluding the Chinaman from our gates, not for his ignorance, vice, or corruption, but because he sought to establish an inferior race in a republic fashioned in the wisdom and defended by the blood of a homogeneous people.

The Anglo-Saxon blood has dominated always and everywhere. It fed Alfred when he wrote the charter of English liberty; it gathered about Hampden as he stood beneath the oak; it thundered in Cromwell's veins as he fought his king; it humbled Napoleon at Waterloo; it has touched the desert and jungle with undying glory; it carried the drumbeat of England around the world and spread on every continent the gospel of liberty and of God; it established this republic, carved it from the wilderness, conquered it from the Indians, wrested it from England, and at last, stilling its own tumult, consecrated it forever as the home of the Anglo-Saxon, and the theater of his transcending achievement. Never one foot of it can be surrendered, while that blood lives in American veins and feeds American hearts, to the domination of an alien and inferior race.

And yet that is just what is proposed. Not in twenty years have we seen a day so pregnant with fate to this section as the sixth of next November. If President Cleveland is then defeated, which God forbid, I believe these States will be led through sorrows compared to which the woes of reconstruction will be as the fading dews of morning to the roaring flood. To dominate these States through the colored vote, with such aid as federal patronage may debauch or federal power determine, and thus through its chosen instruments perpetuate its rule, is in my opinion the settled purpose of the Republican party. I am appalled when I measure the passion in which this negro problem is judged by the leaders of the party.

Fifteen years ago Vice-President Wilson said—and I honor his memory as that of a courageous man: "We shall not have finished with the South until we force its people to change their thought, and think as we think." I repeat these words, for I heard them when a boy, and they fell on my ears as the knell of my people's rights—"to change their thought, and make them think as we think." Not enough to have conquered our armies—to have decimated our ranks, to have desolated our fields and reduced us to poverty, to have struck the ballot from our hands and enfranchised our slaves—to have held us prostrate under bayonets while the insolent mocked and thieves plundered—but their very souls must be rifled of their faiths, their sacred traditions cudgeled from memory, and their immortal minds beaten into subjection until thought had lost its integrity, and we were forced "to think as they think."

And just now General Sherman has said, and I honor him as a soldier: "The negro must be allowed to vote, and his vote must be counted; otherwise, so sure as there is a God in heaven, you will have another war, more cruel than the last, when the torch and dagger will take the place of the muskets of well-ordered battalions. Should the negro strike that blow, in seeming justice, there will be millions to assist them."

And this General took Johnston's sword in surrender! He

looked upon the thin and ragged battalions in gray, that for four years had held his teeming and heroic legions at bay. Facing them, he read their courage in their depleted ranks and gave them a soldier's parole. When he found it in his heart to taunt these heroes with this threat, why—careless as he was twenty years ago with fire, he is even more careless now with his words. If we could hope that this problem would be settled within our lives I would appeal from neither madness nor unmanliness. But when I know that, strive as I may, I must at last render this awful heritage into the untried hands of my son, already dearer to me than my life, and that he must in turn bequeath it unsolved to his children, I cry out against the inhumanity that deepens its difficulties with this incendiary threat and beclouds its real issue with inflaming passion.

This problem is not only enduring, but it is widening. The exclusion of the Chinese is the first step in the revolution that shall save liberty and law and religion to this land, and in peace and order, not enforced on the gallows or at the bayonet's end, but proceeding from the heart of an harmonious people, shall secure in the enjoyment of the rights and the control of this republic, the homogeneous people that established and has maintained it.

The next step will be taken when some brave statesman, looking Demagogy in the face, shall move to call to the stranger at our gates, "Who comes there?" admitting every man who seeks a home or honors our institutions and whose habit and blood will run with the native current; but excluding all who seek to plant anarchy or to establish alien men or measures on our soil; and will then demand that the standard of our citizenship be lifted and the right of acquiring our suffrage be abridged. When that day comes, and God speed its coming, the position of the South will be fully understood and everywhere approved. Until then, let us—giving the negro every right, civil and political, measured in that fullness the strong should always accord the weak—holding him in closer friendship and sympathy than he is held by those who would crucify us for his sake—realizing that on his prosperity ours depends—let us resolve that never by external pressure, or internal division, shall he establish domination, directly or indirectly, over that race that everywhere has maintained its supremacy. Let this resolution be cast on the lines of equity and justice. Let it be the pledge of honest, safe, and impartial administration, and we shall command the support of the colored race itself, more dependent than any other on the bounty and protection of government. Let us be wise and patient, and we shall secure through its acquiescence what otherwise we should win through conflict and hold in insecurity.

All this is no unkindness to the negro—but rather that he may be led in equal rights and in peace to his uttermost good. Not in sectionalism—for my heart beats true to the Union, to the glory of which your life and heart is pledged. Not in disregard of the world's opinion—for to render back this problem in the world's approval is the sum of my ambition and the height of human achievement. Not in reactionary spirit—but rather to make clear that new and grander way up which the South is marching to higher destiny, and on which I would not halt her for all the spoils that have been gathered unto parties since Catiline conspired and Caesar fought. Not in passion, my countrymen, but in reason—not in narrowness but in breadth—that we may solve this problem in calmness and in truth, and lifting its shadows let perpetual sunshine pour down on two races, walking together in peace and contentment. Then shall this problem have proved our blessing, and the race that threatened our ruin work our salvation as it fills our fields with the best peasantry the world has ever seen. Then the South—putting behind her all the achievements of her past—and in war and in peace they beggar eulogy—may stand upright among the nations and challenge the judgment of man and the approval of God, in having worked out in their sympathy, and in His guidance, this last and surpassing miracle of human government.

What of the South's industrial problem? When we remember that amazement followed the payment by thirty-seven million Frenchmen of a billion dollars indemnity to Germany, that the five million whites of the South rendered to the torch and sword three billions of property—that thirty million dollars a year, or six hundred million dollars in twenty years, has been given willingly of our poverty as pensions for Northern soldiers, the wonder is that we are here at all.

There is a figure with which history has dealt lightly, but

that, standing pathetic and heroic in the genesis of our new growth, has interested me greatly—our soldier farmer of '65. What chance had he for the future as he wandered amid his empty barns, his stock, labor, and implements gone—gathered up the fragments of his wreck—urging kindly his borrowed mule —paying sixty per cent. for all that he bought, and buying all on credit—his crop mortgaged before it was planted—his children in want, his neighborhood in chaos—working under new conditions and retrieving every error by a costly year—plodding all day down the furrow, hopeless and adrift, save when at night he went back to his broken home, where his wife, cheerful even then, renewed his courage, while she ministered to him in loving tenderness. Who would have thought as during those lonely and terrible days he walked behind the plow, locking the sunshine in the glory of his harvest and spreading the showers in the verdure of his field—no friend near save nature that smiled at his earnest touch, and God that sent him the message of good cheer through the passing breeze and the whispering leaves— that he would in twenty years, having carried these burdens uncomplaining, make a crop of $800,000,000. Yet this he has done, and from his bounty the South has rebuilded her cities, and recouped her losses. While we exult in his splendid achievement, let us take account of his standing.

Whence this enormous growth? For ten years the world has been at peace. The pioneer has now replaced the soldier. Commerce has whitened new seas, and the merchant has occupied new areas. Steam has made of the earth a chessboard, on which men play for markets. Our western wheat-grower competes in London with the Russian and the East Indian. The Ohio woolgrower watches the Australian shepherd, and the bleat of the now historic sheep of Vermont is answered from the steppes of Asia. The herds that emerge from the dust of your amazing prairies might hear in their pauses the hoofbeats of antipodean herds marching to meet them. Under Holland's dykes, the cheese and butter makers fight American dairies. The hen cackles around the world. California challenges vine-clad France. The dark continent is disclosed through meshes of light. There is competition everywhere. The husbandman, driven from his market, balances price against starvation and undercuts his rival. This conflict often runs to panic, and profit vanishes. The Iowa farmer burning his corn for fuel is not an unusual type.

Amid this universal conflict, where stands the South? While the producer of everything we eat or wear, in every land, is fighting through glutted markets for bare existence, what of the Southern farmer? In his industrial as in his political problem he is set apart—not in doubt, but in assured independence. Cotton makes him king. . . . To summarize: Our American fibre has increased its product nearly three-fold, while it has seen the product of its rival decrease one-third. It has enlarged its dominion in the old centers of population, supplanting flax and wool, and it peeps from the satchel of every business and religious evangelist that trots the globe. In three years the American crop has increased 1,400,000 bales, and yet there is less cotton in the world to-day than at any time for twenty years. The dominion of our king is established; this princely revenue assured, not for a year, but for all time. It is the heritage that God gave us when he arched our skies, established our mountains, girt us about with the ocean, tempered the sunshine, and measured the rain—ours and our children's forever. . . . In 1880 the South made 212,000 tons of iron. In 1887, 845,000 tons. She is now actually building, or has finished this year, furnaces that will produce more than her entire product of last year. Birmingham alone will produce more iron in 1889 than the entire South produced in 1887.

Our coal supply is exhaustless, Texas alone having 6,000 square miles. In marble and granite we have no rivals, as to quantity or quality. In lumber our riches are even vaster. More than fifty per cent. of our entire area is in forests, making the South the best timbered region in the world. We have enough merchantable yellow pine to bring in money, $2,500,000,000—a sum the vastness of which can only be understood when I say it nearly equals the assessed value of the entire South, including cities, forests, farms, mines, factories and personal property of every description whatsoever. Back of this are our forests of hard woods and measureless swamps of cypress and gum. Think of it. In cotton a monopoly. In iron and coal establishing a swift mastery. In granite and marble developing equal advantage and resource. In yellow pine and hard woods the world's treasury....

Texas produces a million and a half bales of cotton, which yield her $60,000,000. That cotton woven into common goods would add $75,000,000 to Texas's income from this crop, and employ 220,000 operatives, who would spend within her borders more than $30,000,000 in wages. Massachusetts manufactures 575,000 bales of cotton, for which she pays $31,000,000, and sells for $72,000,000, adding a value nearly equal to Texas's gross revenue from cotton, and yet Texas has a clean advantage for manufacturing this cotton of one per cent. a pound over Massachusetts.

The little village of Grand Rapids began manufacturing furniture simply because it was set in a timber district. It is now a great city and sells $10,000,000 worth of furniture every year, in making which 12,500 men are employed, and a population of 40,000 people supported. The best pine districts of the world are in eastern Texas. With less competition and wider markets than Grand Rapids has, will she ship her forests at prices that barely support the woodchopper and sawyer, to be returned in the making of which great cities are built or maintained? When her farmers and herdsmen draw from her cities $126,000,000 as the price of her annual produce, shall this enormous wealth be scattered through distant shops and factories, leaving in the hands of Texas no more than the sustenance, support, and the narrow brokerage between buyer and seller? As one-crop farming cannot support the country, neither can a resource of commercial exchange support a city. Texas wants immigrants—she needs them —for if every human being in Texas were placed at equi-distant points through the State no Texan could hear the sound of a human voice in your broad areas.

So how can you best attract immigration? By furnishing work for the artisan and mechanic if you meet the demand of your population for cheaper and essential manufactured articles. One half million workers would be needed for this, and with their families would double the population of your State. In these mechanics and their dependents, farmers would find a market for not only their staple crops but for the truck that they now despise to raise or sell, but is at last the cream of the farm.

Worcester county, Mass., takes $7,200,000 of our material and turns out $87,000,000 of products every year paying $20,000,000 in wages.

The most prosperous section of this world is that known as the Middle States of this republic. With agriculture and manufactures in the balance, and their shops and factories set amid rich and ample acres, the result is such deep and diffuse prosperity as no other section can show. Suppose those States had a monopoly of cotton and coal so disposed as to command the world's markets and the treasury of the world's timber, I suppose the mind is staggered in contemplating the majesty of the wealth and power they would attain. What have they that the South lacks?—and to her these things were added, and climate, ampler acres, and rich soil. It is a curious fact that three-fourths of the population and manufacturing wealth of this country is comprised in a narrow strip between Iowa and Massachusetts, comprising less than one-sixth of our territory, and that this strip is distant from the source of raw materials on which its growth is based, of hard climate and in a large part of sterile soil. Much of this forced and unnatural development is due to slavery, which for a century fenced enterprise and capital out of the South. Mr. Thomas, who, in the Lehigh Valley, owned a furnace in 1845 that set the pattern for iron-making in America, had at that time bought mines and forests where Birmingham now stands. Slavery forced him away. He settled in Pennsylvania. I have wondered what would have happened if that one man had opened his iron mines in Alabama and set his furnaces there at that time. I know what is going to happen since he has been forced to come to Birmingham and put up two furnaces nearly forty years after his survey.

Another cause that has prospered New England and the Middle States while the South languished, is the system of tariff taxes levied on the unmixed agriculture of these States for the protection of industries to our neighbors to the North, a system on which the Hon. Roger Q. Mills—that lion of the tribe of Judah—has at last laid his mighty paw and under the indignant touch of which it trembles to its center. That system is to be revised and its duties reduced, as we all agree it should be, though I should say in perfect frankness I do not agree with

Mr. Mills in it. Let us hope this will be done with care and industrious patience. Whether it stands or falls, the South has entered the industrial list to partake of its bounty if it stands, and if it falls, to rely on the favor with which nature has endowed her, and from this immutable advantage to fill her own markets and then have a talk with the world at large.

With amazing rapidity she has moved away from the one-crop idea that was once her curse. In 1880 she was esteemed prosperous. Since that time she added 393,000,000 bushels to her grain crops, and 182,000,000 head to her live stock. This has not lost one bale of her cotton crop, which, on the contrary, has increased nearly 200,000 bales. With equal swiftness has she moved away from the folly of shipping out her ore at $2 a ton and buying it back in implements at from $20 to $100 per ton; her cotton at 10 cents a pound, and buying it back in cloth at 20 to 80 cents a pound; her timber at 8 per thousand and buying it back in furniture at ten to twenty times as much. In the past eight years $250,000,000 have been invested in new shops and factories in her States; 225,000 artisans are now working that eight years ago were idle or worked elsewhere, and these added $227,000,000 to the value of her raw material—more than half the value of her cotton. Add to this the value of her increased grain crops and stock, and in the past eight years she has grown in her fields or created in her shops manufactures more than the value of her cotton crop. The incoming tide has begun to rise. Every train brings manufacturers from the East and West seeking to establish themselves or their sons near the raw material and in this growing market. Let the fullness of the tide roll in. . . .

13

Why America Is Not "Interesting"

Matthew Arnold's *Civilization in the United States*

Matthew Arnold (1822-1888), poet and critic, was the son of a prominent English educator. He served as a school inspector and as professor of poetry at Oxford University. In 1883 he visited the United States as a guest of Andrew Carnegie, and that winter he made a lecture tour here. He returned again in 1886. His appraisals of this country, from the stance of an urbane British academic, were published in periodicals and then collected in a book. In this essay, first published in *The Nineteenth Century* (London), note (1) Arnold's judgment of American political institutions; (2) what he thought of the life of the common man in America; (3) his views concerning equality in Europe and America; (4) what he meant by "interesting" and to what extent he thought American life interesting; and (5) what Arnold thought the United States needed in order to advance its civilization. See James Bryce, *The American Commonwealth* (1888) for the views of another qualified Englishman.

From Matthew Arnold, *Civilization in the United States: First and Last Impressions of America* (Boston: Cupples and Hurd, 1888), pp. 159-192.

PERHAPS IT IS NOT LIKELY THAT ANY ONE WILL now remember what I said three years ago here about the success of the Americans in solving the political and social problem. I will sum it up in the briefest possible manner. I said that the United States had constituted themselves in a modern age; that their institutions complied well with the form and pressure of those circumstances and conditions which a modern age presents. Quite apart from all question how much of the merit for this may be due to the wisdom and virtue of the American people, and how much to their good fortune, it is undeniable that their institutions do work well and happily. The play of their institutions suggests, I said, the image of a man in a suit of clothes which fits him to perfection, leaving all his movements unimpeded and easy; a suit of clothes loose where it ought to be loose, and sitting close where its sitting close is an advantage; a suit of clothes able, moreover, to adapt itself naturally to the wearer's growth, and to admit of all enlargements as they successively arise.

So much as to the solution, by the United States, of the political problem. As to the social problem, I observed that the people of the United States were a community singularly free from the distinction of classes, singularly homogeneous; that the division between rich and poor was consequently less profound there than in countries where the distinction of classes accentuates that division. I added that I believed there was exaggeration in the reports of their administrative and judicial corruption; and altogether, I concluded, the United States, politically and socially, are a country living prosperously in a natural modern condition, and conscious of living prosperously in such a condition. And being in this healthy case, and having this healthy consciousness, the community there uses its understanding with the soundness of health; it in general, as to its own political and social concerns, sees clear and thinks straight. Comparing the United States with ourselves, I said that while they are in this natural and healthy condition, we, on the contrary, are so little homogeneous, we are living with a system of classes so intense, with institutions and a society so little modern, so unnaturally complicated, that the whole action of our minds is hampered and falsened by it; we are in consequence wanting in lucidity, we do not see clear or think straight, and the Americans have here much the advantage of us.

Yet we find an acute and experienced Englishman * saying that there is no country, calling itself civilized, where one would not rather live than in the United States, except Russia! The civilization of the United States must somehow, if an able man

* Sir Lepel Griffin, a British official in India who had traveled in the United States [editor's note].

can think thus, have shortcomings, in spite of the country's success and prosperity. What is civilization? It is the humanization of man in society, the satisfaction for him, in society, of the true law of human nature. Man's study, says Plato, is to discover the right answer to the question *how to live?* our aim, he says, is very and true life. We are more or less civilized as we come more or less near to this aim, in that social state which the pursuit of our aim essentially demands. But several elements or powers, as I have often insisted, go to build up a complete human life. There is the power of conduct, the power of intellect and knowledge, the power of beauty, the power of social life and manners; we have instincts responding to them all, requiring them all. And we are perfectly civilized only when all these instincts in our nature, all these elements in our civilization, have been adequately recognized and satisfied. But of course this adequate recognition and satisfaction of all the elements in question is impossible; some of them are recognized more than others, some of them more in one community, some in another; and the satisfactions found are more or less worthy.

And, meanwhile, people use the term *civilization* in the loosest possible way, for the most part attaching to it, however, in their own mind some meaning connected with their own preferences and experiences. The most common meaning thus attached to it is perhaps that of a satisfaction, not of all the main demands of human nature, but of the demand for the comforts and conveniences of life, and of this demand as made by the sort of person who uses the term.

Now we should always attend to the common and prevalent use of an important term. Probably Sir Lepel Griffin had this notion of the comforts and conveniences of life much in his thoughts when he reproached American civilization with its shortcomings. For men of his kind, and for all that large number of men, so prominent in this country and who make their voice so much heard, men who have been at the public schools and universities, men of the professional and official class, men who do the most part of our literature and our journalism, America is not a comfortable place of abode. A man of this sort has in England everything in his favor; society appears organized expressly for his advantage. A Rothschild or a Vanderbilt can buy his way anywhere, and can have what comforts and luxuries he likes, whether in America or in England. But it is in England that an income of from three or four to fourteen or fifteen hundred a year does so much for its possessor, enables him to live with so many of the conveniences of far richer people. For his benefit, his benefit above all, clubs are organized and hansom cabs ply; service is abundant, porters stand waiting at the railway stations. In America all luxuries are dear except oysters and ice; service is in general scarce and bad; a club is a most expensive luxury: the cab-rates are prohibitive—more than half of the people who in England would use cabs must in America use the horse-cars, the tram. The charges of tailors and mercers are about a third higher than they are with us. I mention only a few striking points as to which there can be no dispute, and in which a man of Sir Lepel Griffin's class would feel the great difference between America and England in the conveniences at his command. There are a hundred other points one might mention, where he might feel the same thing. When a man is passing judgment on a country's civilization, points of this kind crowd to his memory, and determine his sentence.

On the other hand, for that immense class of people, the great bulk of the community, the class of people whose income is less than three or four hundred a year, things in America are favorable. It is easier for them there than in the Old World to rise and to make their fortune; but I am not now speaking of that. Even without making their fortune, even with their income below three or four hundred a year, things are favorable to them in America, society seems organized there for their benefit. To begin with, the humbler kind of work is better paid in America than with us; the higher kind, worse. The official, for instance, gets less, his office-keeper gets more. The public ways are abominably cut up by rails and blocked with horse-cars; but the inconvenience is for those who use private carriages and cabs, the convenience is for the bulk of the community who but for the horse-cars would have to walk. The ordinary railways cars are not delightful, but they are cheap, and they are better furnished and in winter are warmer than third-class carriages in England. Luxuries are, as I have said, very dear—above all, European luxuries; but a working-man's clothing is nearly as cheap as in

England, and plain food is on the whole cheaper. Even luxuries of a certain kind are within a laboring man's easy reach. I have mentioned ice; I will mention fruit also. The abundance and cheapness of fruit is a great boon to people of small incomes in America. Do not believe the Americans when they extol their peaches as equal to any in the world, or better than any in the world; they are not to be compared to peaches grown under glass. Do not believe that the American Newtown pippins appear in the New York and Boston fruit-shops as they appear in those of London and Liverpool; or that the Americans have any pear to give you like the Marie Louise. But what laborer, or artisan, or small clerk, ever gets hot-house peaches, or Newtown pippins, or Marie Louise pears? Not such good pears, apples, and peaches as those, but pears, apples, and peaches by no means to be despised, such people and their families do in America get in plenty.

Well, now, what would a philosopher or a philanthropist say in this case? which would he say was the more civilized condition —that of the country where the balance of advantage, as to the comforts and conveniences of life, is greatly in favor of the people with incomes below three hundred a year, or that of the country where it is greatly in favor of those with incomes above that sum?

Many people will be ready to give an answer to that question without the smallest hesitation. They will say that they are, and that all of us ought to be, for the greatest happiness of the greatest number. However, the question is not one which I feel bound now to discuss and answer. Of course, if happiness and civilization consists in being plentifully supplied with the comforts and conveniences of life, the question presents little difficulty. But I believe neither that happiness consists, merely or mainly, in being plentifully supplied with the comforts and conveniences of life, nor that civilization consists in being so supplied; therefore, I leave the question unanswered.

I prefer to seek for some other and better tests by which to try the civilization of the United States. I have often insisted on the need of more equality in our own country, and on the mischiefs caused by inequality over here. In the United States there is not our intense division of classes, our inequality; there is great equality. Let me mention two points in the system of social life and manners over there in which this equality seems to me to have done good. The first is a mere point of form, but it has its significance. Every one knows it is the established habit with us in England, if we write to people supposed to belong to the class of gentlemen, of addressing them by the title of *Esquire,* while we keep *Mr.* for people not supposed to belong to that class. If we think of it, could one easily find a habit more ridiculous, more offensive? The title of *Esquire,* like most of our titles, comes out of the great frippery shop of the Middle Age; it is alien to the sound taste and manner of antiquity, when men said *Pericles* and *Camillus.* But unlike other titles, it is applied or withheld quite arbitrarily. Surely, where a man has no specific title proper to him, the one plain title of *Master* or *Mr.* is enough, and we need not be encumbered with a second title of *Esquire,* now quite unmeaning, to draw an invidious and impossible line of distinction between those who are gentlemen and those who are not; as if we actually wished to provide a source of embarrassment for the sender of a letter, and of mortification for the receiver of it.

The French, those great authorities in social life and manners, find *Mr.* enough, and the Americans are more and more, I am glad to say, following the French example. I only hope they will persevere, and not be seduced by *Esquire* being "so English, you know." And I do hope, moreover, that we shall one day take the same course and drop our absurd *Esquire.*

The other point goes deeper. Much may be said against the voices and intonation of American women. But almost every one acknowledges that there is a charm in American women—a charm which you find in almost all of them, wherever you go. It is the charm of a natural manner, a manner not self-conscious, artificial, and constrained. It may not be a beautiful manner always, but it is almost always a natural manner, a free and happy manner; and this gives pleasure. Here we have, undoubtedly, a note of civilization, and an evidence, at the same time, of the good effect of equality upon social life and manners. I have often heard it observed that a perfectly natural manner is as rare among Englishwomen of the middle classes as it is general among American women of like condition with them. And so far as the observation is true, the reason of its truth no doubt is, that the Englishwoman is living in presence of an upper class, as it is called—in presence, that is, of a class of women recognized as being the right thing in style and manner, and whom she imagines criticising *her* style and manner, finding this or that to be amiss with it, this or that to be vulgar. Hence, self-consciousness and constraint in her. The American women lives in presence of no such class; there may be circles trying to pass themselves off as such a class, giving themselves airs as such, but they command no recognition, no authority. The American woman in general is perfectly unconcerned about their opinion, is herself, enjoys her existence, and has, consequently, a manner happy and natural. It is her great charm; and it is moreover, as I have said, a real note of civilization, and one which has to be reckoned to the credit of American life, and of its equality.

But we must get nearer still to the heart of the question raised as to the character and worth of American civilization. I have said how much the word civilization really means—the humanization of man in society; his making progress there towards his true and full humanity. Partial and material achievement is always being put forward as civilization. We hear a nation called highly civilized by reason of its industry, commerce, and wealth, or by reason of its liberty or equality, or by reason of its numerous churches, schools, libraries, and newspapers. But there is something in human nature, some instinct of growth, some law of perfection, which rebels against this narrow account of the matter. And perhaps what human nature demands in civilization, over and above all those obvious things which first occur to our thoughts,—what human nature, I say, demands in civilization, if it is to stand as a high and satisfying civilization, is best described by the word *interesting*. Here is the extraordinary charm of the old Greek civilization: that it is so *interesting*. Do not tell me only, says human nature, of the magnitude of your industry and commerce; of the beneficence of your institutions, your freedom, your equality; of the great and growing number of your churches and schools, libraries and newspapers; tell me also if your civilization—which is the grand name you give to all this development—tell me if your civilization is *interesting*.

An American friend of mine, Professor Norton, has lately pub-

lished the early letters of Carlyle. If any one wants a good antidote to the unpleasant effect left by Mr. Froude's "Life of Carlyle,"
let him read those letters. Not only of Carlyle will those letters
make him think kindly, but they will also fill him with admiring
esteem for the qualities, character, and family life, as there de-
lineated, of the Scottish peasant. Well, the Carlyle family were
numerous, poor, and struggling. Thomas Carlyle, the eldest son,
a young man in wretched health and worse spirits, was fighting
his way in Edinburgh. One of his younger brothers talked of
emigrating. "The very best thing he could do!" we should all say.
Carlyle dissuades him. "You shall never," he writes, "you shall
never seriously meditate crossing the great Salt Pool to plant
yourself in the Yankee-land. That is a miserable fate for any one,
at best; never dream of it. Could you banish yourself from all
that is interesting to your mind, forget the history, the glorious
institutions, the noble principles of old Scotland—that you might
eat a better dinner, perhaps?"

There is our word launched—the word *interesting*. I am not
saying that Carlyle's advice was good, or that young men should
not emigrate. I do but take note, in the word *interesting*, of a
requirement, a cry of aspiration, a cry not sounding in the imaginative Carlyle's own breast only, but sure of a response in his
brother's breast also, and in human nature.

Amiel, that contemplative Swiss whose journals the world has
been reading lately, tells us that "the human heart is, as it were,
haunted by confused reminiscences of an age of gold; or, rather,
by aspirations towards a harmony of things which every day
reality denies to us." He says that the splendor and refinement
of high life is an attempt by the rich and cultivated classes to
realize this ideal, and is "a form of poetry." And the interest which
this attempt awakens in the classes which are not rich or cultivated, their indestructible interest in the pageant and fairy tale,
as to them it appears, of the life in castles and palaces, the life
of the great, bears witness to a like imaginative strain in them
also, a strain tending after the elevated and the beautiful. In
short, what Goethe describes as "was uns alle bändigt, *das
Gemeine*—that which holds us all in bondage, the common and
ignoble," is, notwithstanding its admitted prevalence, contrary
to a deep-seated instinct of human nature, and repelled by it.

Of civilization, which is to humanize us in society, we demand, before we will consent to be satisfied with it—we demand, however much else it may give us, that it shall give us, too, the *interesting*.

Now, the great sources of the *interesting* are distinction and beauty: that which is elevated, and that which is beautiful. Let us take the beautiful first, and consider how far it is present in American civilization. Evidently, this is that civilization's weak side. There is little to nourish and delight the sense of beauty there. In the long-settled states east of the Alleghanies the landscape in general is not interesting, the climate harsh and in extremes. The Americans are restless, eager to better themselves and to make fortunes; the inhabitant does not strike his roots lovingly down into the soil, as in rural England. In the valley of the Connecticut you will find farm after farm which the Yankee settler has abandoned in order to go West, leaving the farm to some new Irish immigrant. The charm of beauty which comes from ancientness and permanence of rural life the country could not yet have in a high degree, but it has it in an even less degree than might be expected. Then the Americans come originally, for the most part, from that great class in English society amongst whom the sense for conduct and business is much more strongly developed than the sense for beauty. If we in England were without the cathedrals, parish churches, and castles of the catholic and feudal age, and without the houses of the Elizabethan age, but had only the towns and buildings which the rise of our middle class has created in the modern age, we should be in much the same case as the Americans. We should be living with much the same absence of training for the sense of beauty through the eye, from the aspect of outward things. The American cities have hardly anything to please a trained or a natural sense for beauty. They have buildings which cost a great deal of money and produce a certain effect—buildings, shall I say, such as our Midland Station at St. Pancras; but nothing such as Somerset House or Whitehall. One architect of genius they had—Richardson. I had the pleasure to know him: he is dead, alas! Much of his work was injured by the conditions under which he was obliged to execute it; I can recall but one building, and that of no great importance, where he seems to have had his own way, to be fully himself; but that is indeed excellent. In general, where the Americans succeed best in their architecture—in that art so indicative and educative of a people's sense for beauty—is in the fashion of their villa-cottages in wood. These are often original and at the same time very pleasing, but they are pretty and coquettish, not beautiful. Of the really beautiful in the other arts, and in literature, very little has been produced there as yet. I asked a German portrait-painter, whom I found painting and prospering in America, how he liked the country. "How *can* an artist like it?" was his answer. The American artists live chiefly in Europe; all Americans of cultivation and wealth visit Europe more and more constantly. The mere nomenclature of the country acts upon a cultivated person like the incessant pricking of pins. What people in whom the sense for beauty and fitness was quick could have invented, or could tolerate, the hideous names ending in *ville*, the Briggsvilles, Higginsvilles, Jacksonvilles, rife from Maine to Florida; the jumble of unnatural and inappropriate names everywhere? On the line from Albany to Buffalo you have, in one part, half the names in the classical dictionary to designate the stations; it is said that the folly is due to a surveyor who, when the country was laid out, happened to possess a classical dictionary; but a people with any artist-sense would have put down that surveyor. The Americans meekly retain his names; and, indeed, his strange Marcellus or Syracuse is perhaps not much worse than their congenital Briggsville.

So much as to beauty, and as to the provision, in the United States, for the sense of beauty. As to distinction, and the interest which human nature seeks from enjoying the effect made upon it by what is elevated, the case is much the same. There is very little to create such an effect, very much to thwart it. Goethe says somewhere that "the thrill of awe is the best thing humanity has":—

Das Schaudern ist der Menschheit bestes Theil.

But, if there be a discipline in which the Americans are wanting, it is the discipline of awe and respect. An austere and intense religion imposed on their Puritan founders the discipline of respect, and so provided for them the thrill of awe; but this religion is dying out. The Americans have produced plenty of men strong, shrewd, upright, able, effective; very few who are highly distinguished. Alexander Hamilton is indeed a man of rare distinction; Washington, though he has not the high mental distinction of Pericles or Caesar, has true distinction of style and character. But these men belong to the pre-American age. Lincoln's recent American biographers declare that Washington is but an Englishman, an English officer; the typical American, they say, is Abraham Lincoln. Now Lincoln is shrewd, sagacious, humorous, honest, courageous, firm; he is a man with qualities deserving the most sincere esteem and praise, but he has not distinction.

In truth, everything is against distinction in America, and against the sense of elevation to be gained through admiring and respecting it. The glorification of "the average man," who is quite a religion with statesmen and publicists there, is against it. The addiction to "the funny man," who is a national misfortune there, is against it. Above all, the newspapers are against it.

It is often said that every nation has the government it deserves. What is much more certain is that every nation has the newspapers it deserves. The newspaper is the direct product of the want felt; the supply answers closely and inevitably to the demand. I suppose no one knows what the American newspapers are, who has not been obliged, for some length of time, to read either those newspapers or none at all. Powerful and valuable contributions occur scattered about in them. But on the whole, and taking the total impression and effect made by them, I should say that if one were searching for the best means to efface and kill in a whole nation the discipline of respect, the feeling for what is elevated, one could not do better than take the American newspapers. The absence of truth and soberness in them, the poverty in serious interest, the personality and sensation-mongering, are beyond belief. There are a few newspapers which are in whole, or in part, exceptions. The *New York Nation,* a weekly paper, may be paralleled with the *Saturday Review* as it was in its old and good days; but the *New York Nation* is conducted by a foreigner, and has an extremely small sale. In general, the daily papers are such that when one returns home one is moved to admiration and thankfulness not only at the great

London papers, like the *Times* or the *Standard,* but quite as much at the great provincial newspapers, too,—papers like the *Leeds Mercury* and the *Yorkshire Post* in the north of England, like the *Scotsman* and the *Glasgow Herald* in Scotland.

The Americans used to say to me that what they valued was news, and that this their newspapers gave them. I at last made the reply: "Yes, news for the servants' hall!" I remember that a New York newspaper, one of the first I saw after landing in the country, had a long account, with the prominence we should give to the illness of the German Emperor or the arrest of the Lord Mayor of Dublin, of a young woman who had married a man who was a bag of bones, as we say, and who used to exhibit himself as a skeleton; of her growing horror in living with this man, and finally of her death. All this in the most minute detail, and described with all the writer's powers of rhetoric. This has always remained by me as a specimen of what the Americans call news.

You must have lived amongst their newspapers to know what they are. If I relate some of my own experiences, it is because these will give a clear enough notion of what the newspapers over there are, and one remembers more definitely what has happened to oneself. Soon after arriving in Boston, I opened a Boston newspaper and came upon a column headed: "Tickings." By *tickings* we are to understand news conveyed through the tickings of the telegraph. The first "ticking" was: "Matthew Arnold is sixty-two years old"—an age, I must just say in passing, which I had not then reached. The second "ticking" was: "Wales says, Mary is a darling"; the meaning being that the Prince of Wales expressed great admiration for Miss Mary Anderson. This was at Boston, the American Athens. I proceeded to Chicago. An evening paper was given me soon after I arrived; I opened it, and found under a large-type heading, "*We have seen him arrive,*" the following picture of myself: "He has harsh features, supercilious manners, parts his hair down the middle, wears a single eyeglass and ill-fitting clothes." Notwithstanding this rather unfavorable introduction, I was most kindly and hospitably received at Chicago. It happened that I had a letter for Mr. Medill, an elderly gentleman of Scotch descent, the editor of the chief newspaper in those parts, the *Chicago Tribune.* I called on him, and we conversed amicably together. Some time afterwards, when I had gone back to England, a New York paper published a criticism of Chicago and its people, purporting to have been contributed by me to the *Pall Mall Gazette* over here. It was a poor hoax, but many people were taken in and were excusably angry. Mr. Medill of the *Chicago Tribune* amongst the number. A friend telegraphed to me to know if I had written the criticism. I, of course, instantly telegraphed back that I had not written a syllable of it. Then a Chicago paper is sent to me; and what I have the pleasure of reading, as the result of my contradiction is this: "Arnold denies; Mr. Medill [my old friend] refuses to accept Arnold's disclaimer; says Arnold is a cur."

I once declared that in England the born lover of ideas and of light could not but feel that the sky over his head is of brass and iron. And so I say that, in America, he who craves for the *interesting* in civilization, he who requires from what surrounds him satisfaction for his sense of beauty, his sense for elevation, will feel the sky over his head to be of brass and iron. The human problem, then, is as yet solved in the United States most imperfectly; a great void exists in the civilization over there; a want of what is elevated and beautiful, of what is interesting.

The want is grave; it was probably, though he does not exactly bring it out, influencing Sir Lepel Griffin's feelings when he said that America is one of the last countries in which one would like to live. The want is such as to make any educated man feel that many countries, much less free and prosperous than the United States, are yet more truly civilized; have more which is interesting, have more to say to the soul; are countries, therefore, in which one would rather live.

The want is graver because it is so little recognized by the mass of Americans; nay, so loudly denied by them. If the community over there perceived the want and regretted it, sought for the right ways of remedying it, and resolved that remedied it should be; if they said, or even if a number of leading spirits amongst them said: "Yes, we see what is wanting to our civilization, we see that the average man is a danger, we see that our newspapers are a scandal, that bondage to the common and ignoble is our snare; but under the circumstances our civilization could not well have been expected to begin differently. What

you see are *beginnings,* they are crude, they are too predomin-
antly material, they omit much, leave much to be desired—but
they could not have been otherwise, they have been inevitable,
and we will rise above them"; if the Americans frankly said this,
one would not have a word to bring against it. One would *then*
insist on no shortcoming, one would accept their admission that
the human problem is at present quite insufficiently solved by
them, and would press the matter no further. One would con-
gratulate them on having solved the political problem and the
social problem so successfully, and only remark, as I have said
already, that in seeing clear and thinking straight on *our* political
and social questions, we have great need to follow the example
they set us on theirs.

But now the Americans seem, in certain matters, to have
agreed, as a people, to deceive themselves, to persuade themselves that they have what they have not, to cover the defects
in their civilization by boasting, to fancy that they well and
truly solve, not only the political and social problem, but the
human problem too. One would say that they do really hope to
find in tall talk and inflated sentiment a substitute for that real
sense of elevation which human nature, as I have said, instinctively craves—and a substitute which may do as well as the
genuine article. The thrill of awe, which Goethe pronounces to
be the best thing humanity has, they would fain create by proclaiming themselves at the top of their voices to be "the greatest
nation upon earth," by assuring one another, in the language of
their national historian, that "American democracy proceeds in
its ascent as uniformly and majestically as the laws of being, and
is as certain as the decrees of eternity."

Or, again, far from admitting that their newspapers are a
scandal, they assure one another that their newspaper press is
one of their most signal distinctions. Far from admitting that in
literature they have as yet produced little that is important, they
play at treating American literature as if it were a great independent power; they reform the spelling of the English language
by the insight of their average man. For every English writer
they have an American writer to match; and him good Americans
read. The Western States are at this moment being nourished
and formed, we hear, on the novels of a native author called

Roe, instead of those of Scott and Dickens. Far from admitting that their average man is a danger, and that his predominance has brought about a plentiful lack of refinement, distinction, and beauty, they declare in the words of my friend Colonel Higginson, a prominent critic at Boston, that "Nature said, some years since: 'Thus far the English is my best race, but we have had Englishmen enough; put in one drop more of nervous fluid and make the American.'" And with that drop a new range of promise opened on the human race, and a lighter, finer, more highly organized type of mankind was born. Far from admitting that the American accent, as the pressure of their climate and of their average man has made it, is a thing to be striven against, they assure one another that it is the right accent, the standard English speech of the future. It reminds me of a thing in Smollett's dinner-party of authors. Seated by "the philosopher who is writing a most orthodox refutation of Bolingbroke, but in the meantime has just been presented to the Grand Jury as a public nuisance for having blasphemed in an alehouse on the Lord's day"—seated by this philosopher is "the Scotchman who is giving lectures on the pronunciation of the English language."

The worst of it is, that all this tall talk and self-glorification meets with hardly any rebuke from sane criticism over there. I will mention, in regard to this, a thing which struck me a good deal. A Scotchman who has made a great fortune at Pittsburg, a kind friend of mine, one of the most hospitable and generous of men, Mr. Andrew Carnegie, published a year or two ago a book called "Triumphant Democracy," a most splendid picture of American progress. The book is full of valuable information, but religious people thought that it insisted too much on mere material progress, and it did not enough set forth America's deficiencies and dangers. And a friendly clergyman in Massachusetts, telling me how he regretted this, and how apt the Americans are to shut their eyes to their own dangers, put into my hands a volume written by a leading minister among the Congregationalists, a very prominent man, which he said supplied a good antidote to my friend Mr. Carnegie's book. The volume is entitled "Our Country." I read it through. The author finds in evangelical Protestantism, as the orthodox Protestant sects present it, the grand remedy for the deficiencies and dangers of America.

On this I offer no criticism; what struck me, and that on which I wish to lay stress, is, the writer's entire failure to perceive that such self-glorification and self-deception as I have been mentioning is one of America's dangers, or even that it *is* self-deception at all. He himself shares in all the self-deception of the average man among his countrymen; he flatters it. In the very points where a serious critic would find the Americans most wanting he finds them superior; only they require to have a good dose of evangelical Protestantism still added. "Ours is the elect nation," preaches this reformer of American faults—"ours is the elect nation for the age to come. We are the chosen people." Already, says he, we are taller and heavier than other men, longer lived than other men, richer and more energetic than other men, above all, "of finer nervous organization" than other men. Yes, this people, who endure to have the American newspaper for their daily reading, and to have their habitation in Briggsville, Jacksonville, and Marcellus—this people is of finer, more delicate nervous organization than other nations! It is Colonel Higginson's "drop more of nervous fluid," over again. This "drop" plays a stupendous part in the American rhapsody of self-praise. Undoubtedly the Americans are highly nervous, both the men and the women. A great Paris physician says that he notes a distinct new form of nervous disease, produced in American women by worry about servants. But this nervousness developed in the race out there by worry, overwork, want of exercise, injudicious diet, and a most trying climate—this morbid nervousness, our friends ticket as the fine susceptibility of genius, and cite it as a proof of their distinction, of their superior capacity for civilization! "The roots of civilization are the nerves," says our Congregationalist instructor, again; "and, other things being equal, the finest nervous organization will produce the highest civilization. Now, the finest nervous organization is ours."

The new West promises to beat in the game of brag even the stout champions I have been quoting. Those belong to the old Eastern States; and the other day there was sent to me a Californian newspaper which calls all the Easterners "the unhappy denizens of a forbidding clime," and adds: "The time will surely come when all roads will lead to California. Here will be the home of art, science, literature, and profound knowledge."

Common-sense criticism, I repeat, of all this hollow stuff there is in America next to none. There are plenty of cultivated, judicious, delightful individuals there. They are our hope and America's hope; it is through their means that improvement must come. They know perfectly well how false and hollow the boastful stuff talked is; but they let the storm of self-laudation rage, and say nothing. For political opponents and their doings there are in America hard words to be heard in abundance; for the real faults in American civilization, and for the foolish boasting which prolongs them, there is hardly a word of regret or blame, at least in public. Even in private, many of the most cultivated Americans shrink from the subject, are irritable and thin-skinned when it is canvassed. Public treatment of it, in a cool and sane spirit of criticism, there is none. In vain I might plead that I had set a good example of frankness, in confessing over here, that, so far from solving our problems successfully, we in England find ourselves with an upper class materialized, a middle class vulgarized, and a lower class brutalized. But it seems that nothing will embolden an American critic to say firmly and aloud to his countrymen and to his newspapers, that in America they do not solve the human problem successfully, and that with their present methods they never can. Consequently, the masses of the American people do really come to believe all they hear about their finer nervous organization, and the rightness of the American accent, and the importance of American literature; that is to say, they see things not as they are, but as they would like them to be; they deceive themselves totally. And by such self-deception they shut against themselves the door to improvement, and do their best to make the reign of *das Gemeine* eternal. In what concerns the solving of the political and social problem they see clear and think straight; in what concerns the higher civilization they live in a fools' paradise. This it is which makes a famous French critic speak of "the hard unintelligence of the people of the United States"— *la dure inintelligence des Américans du Nord*—of the very people who in general pass for being specially intelligent; and so, within certain limits, they are. But they have been so plied with nonsense and boasting that outside those limits, and where it is a question of things in which their civilization is weak, they seem, very many of them, as if in such things they had no power of perception whatever, no idea of a proper scale, no sense of the difference between good and bad. And at this rate they can never, after solving the political and social problem with success, go on to solve happily the human problem too, and thus at last to make their civilization full and interesting.

To sum up, then. What really dissatisfies in American civilization is the want of the *interesting*, a want due chiefly to the want of those two great elements of the interesting, which are elevation and beauty. And the want of these elements is increased and prolonged by the Americans being assured that they have them when they have them not. And it seems to me that what the Americans now most urgently require, is not so much a vast additional development of orthodox Protestantism, but rather a steady exhibition of cool and sane criticism by their men of light and leading over there. And perhaps the very first step of such men should be to insist on having for America, and to create if need be, better newspapers.

To us, too, the future of the United States is of incalculable importance. Already we feel their influence much, and we shall feel it more. We have a good deal to learn from them; we shall find in them, also, many things to beware of, many points in which it is to be hoped our democracy may not be like theirs. As our country becomes more democratic, the malady here may no longer be that we have an upper class materialized, a middle class vulgarized, and a lower class brutalized. But the predominance of the common and ignoble, born of the predominance of the average man, is a malady too. That the common and ignoble is human nature's enemy, that, of true human nature, distinction and beauty are needs, that a civilization is insufficient where these needs are not satisfied, faulty where they are thwarted, is an instruction of which we, as well as the Americans, may greatly require to take fast hold, and not to let go. We may greatly require to keep, as if it were our life, the doctrine that we are failures after all, if we cannot eschew vain boasting and vain imaginations,—eschew what flatters in us the common and ignoble, and approve things that are truly excellent.

I have mentioned evangelical Protestantism. There is a text

which evangelical Protestantism—and, for that matter, Catholicism too—translates wrong and takes in a sense too narrow. The text is that well-known one, "except a man be born again, he cannot see the kingdom of God." Instead of *again*, we ought to translate *from above;* and instead of taking the kingdom of God in the sense of a life in Heaven above, we ought to take it, as its speaker meant it, in the sense of the reign of saints, a renovated and perfected human society on earth,—the ideal society of the future. In the life of such a society, in the life *from above,* the life born of inspiration or *the spirit*—in that life elevation and beauty are not everything; but they are much, and they are indispensable. Humanity cannot reach its ideal while it lacks them, "Except a man be born *from above,* he cannot have part in the society of the future."

14

Farming in the Corn Belt

Diary of H. C. Downer

During the very years that wheat and cotton farmers were being goaded into political revolt by economic disaster, men could do quite well at diversified farming in the prairie states such as Illinois and Iowa. To explain why these states went Republican in 1896, the following extracts from the diary of H. C. Downer might be useful. Downer, near Lee in DeKalb County in northern Illinois, could afford more than once to make the 60-mile trip into Chicago to visit the Columbian Exposition. Note also the frequency of visiting back and forth and the preoccupation with weather conditions. And please observe that even the new hog-house has cupolas. See Fred A. Shannon, *The Farmer's Last Frontier: Agriculture, 1860-1897* (1945); Chester McA. Destler, *American Radicalism, 1865-1901* (1946); Lewis Atherton, *Main Street on the Middle Border* (1954); and Roy V. Scott, *The Agrarian Movement in Illinois, 1880-1896* (1962).

From H. C. Downer Diary, Illinois State Historical Society.

October 1893]

F RI. 6. FRED AND MARY CAME HOME FROM CHICAGO. Cold and rainy.

Mon. 9. "Chicago Day" at the World's Fair. Father and I went in on the early train this morning. Fifty-one tickets sold at Lee. 713,646 paid admissions at the Fair. Grounds literally covered with people. Music and special exercises through the day and fire-works and procession of floats in the evening. Anniversary of Chicago fire.

Tues. 10. I came home from Chicago at noon. Father came

this evening. Uncle David and family came with him. Weather warm and pleasant.

Fri. 13. Uncle David started for home this morning. Wea. foggy and rainy.

Sat. 14. County Superintendent of Schools, Gross, was here to dinner.

Thur. 19. Uncle Eb and cousin Rozie came here from Aurora. They have been to the World's Fair.

Sun. 22. Uncle Eb, Mary and I at meeting this forenoon. Rev. Pierce is the new minister. Fred took Uncle Eb and Rozie to Shabbona this evening. They visit there and at DeKalb before they go home.

Mon. 23. Wea. warm and pleasant for a week.

Tues. 24. Cold wave last night.

Tues. 31. Father came home from Au. Uncle Alfred is there & he went down to see him. Was at W. F. yesterday.

November 1893]

Sat. 11. Wea. warm past week; wet and foggy several mornings but clear rest of day; mer. at 60°; nights not cold.

Wed. 15. Cold and cloudy; ground frozen all day.

Sun. 12. Cold rain.

Sun. 19. Mary and I at meeting.

Tues. 21. Four inches of wet snow. 8 or 10 acres of corn yet to husk.

Wed. 22. Cold, cloudy & windy.

Fri. 24. Clear and cold; mer. at zero this morning. Gus Martens and man com. building a hog-house—40 × 24, 8 ft. high.

Mon. 27. Wet snow all day. About seven loads of corn to husk. About 10 inches of snow on the ground.

Wed. 29. Rain last night and this morning.

Thur. 30. Snowing nearly all day.

December 1893]

Fri. 1. Clear and cold; mer. 11° below zero this morning.

Sat. 2. Snowing all day.

Mon. 4. Mer. 8° below zero.

Tues. 5. Pleasant; snow melted in the sun.

Wed. 6. Mer. 2° below zero; light snow this p.m.

Fri. 8. Warm and pleasant.

Mon. 11. Snow last night.

Tues. 12. Hogs let into new hog-house; building finished excepting cupolas.

Wed. 13. Jessie Hall came for a week's visit. Mer. 10° below 0 this morn.

Fri. 15. Rain last night and this forenoon. Sleighing nearly spoiled.

Sat. 23. Warm and foggy. Frost out of ground.

Sun. 24. At meeting this a.m.

Mon. 25. Cloudy, windy and misty. Warm this morning but grew colder all day. Is freezing to-night. Ground bare.

Fri. 29. Cousin Mamie Downer came for a visit.

January 1894]

Mon. 1. Warm and clear; strong south wind; ground bare.

Tues. 2. At Aurora yesterday and today. At a "Suprise" at Mr. and Mrs. P. Cofield's this evening in honor of their 20th wedding anniversary. About 60 present.

Sat. 6. One inch of snow last night.

Sun. 7. Mamie, Mary and I at meeting this forenoon. Mer. 3° below 0 this morning.

Thur. 4. I'm husking corn.

Fri. 12. Father went to Aurora.

Sat. 13. Warm and pleasant the past week.

Sun. 14. At meeting morning and evening. . . .

15

Race Relations and an Economic Program

Booker T. Washington and the Atlanta Compromise

Booker T. Washington (1856-1915) was born a slave in Virginia and reared in West Virginia after emancipation. He worked his way through Hampton Institute for three years and got further education elsewhere. In 1881 he was called to take charge of the new Tuskegee Institute in Alabama, which he fashioned chiefly into a vocational college for Negroes. Frederick Douglass, long the foremost Negro in the country, died in 1895, and a few months later Washington on the wings of this speech flew into his place. Speaking to a largely white audience in Atlanta, Washington asked for economic opportunity for his people; they in return would not insist, temporarily at least, on social equality or even on political rights. "Cast down your bucket where you are" has become famous, and the remark, "In all things that are purely social we can be as separate as the fingers, yet one as the hand in all things essential to mutual progress," calls to mind the Supreme Court decision in *Plessy* v. *Ferguson* upholding the separate-but-equal doctrine. In reading this document note (1) what Washington meant by the phrase "Cast down your bucket where you are"; (2) wherein Washington thought the progress of the Negro lay; and (3) Washington's basic justification for Negro education. Washington tells his own story in *Up From Slavery* (1901; 1959 reprint). The emergence of opposition to Washington's views can be seen in W. E. Burghardt DuBois' eloquent *The Souls of Black Folk* (1903; 1961 reprint).

From *Address of Booker T. Washington . . . Delivered at the Opening of the Atlanta Cotton States and International Exposition, September 18, 1895* (pamphlet in Boston Public Library).

MR. PRESIDENT AND GENTLEMEN OF THE BOARD OF
Directors and Citizens:

One-third of the population of the South is of the Negro race.
No enterprise seeking the material, civil or moral welfare of
this section, can disregard this element of our population and
reach the highest success. I but convey to you, Mr. President and
Directors, the sentiment of the masses of my race, when I say
that in no way have the value and manhood of the American
Negro been more fittingly and generously recognized, than by
the managers of this magnificent Exposition at every stage of its
progress. It is a recognition that will do more to cement the
friendship of the two races than any occurrence since the dawn
of our freedom.

Not only this, but the opportunity here afforded will awaken
among us a new era of industrial progress. Ignorant and inex-
perienced, it is not strange that in the first years of our new
life we began at the top instead of at the bottom, that a seat in
Congress or the State Legislature was more sought than real
estate or industrial skill, that the political convention or stump
speaking had more attractions than starting a dairy farm or
truck garden.

A ship lost at sea for many days suddenly sighted a friendly
vessel. From the mast of the unfortunate vessel was seen the
signal: "Water, water, we die of thirst!" The answer from the
friendly vessel at once came back: "Cast down your bucket where
you are." A second time the signal, "Water, water; send us
water!" ran up from the distressed vessel, and was answered,
"Cast down your bucket where you are." And a third and fourth
signal for water was answered: "Cast down your bucket where
you are." The captain of the distressed vessel, at last heeding
the injunction, cast down his bucket, and it came up full of
fresh, sparkling water from the mouth of the Amazon river. To
those of my race who depend on bettering their condition in a
foreign land, or who under-estimate the importance of cultivating
friendly relations with the Southern white man, who is their next
door neighbor, I would say, "Cast down your bucket where you

are"—cast it down in making friends in every manly way of the
people of all races by whom we are surrounded.

Cast it down in agriculture, mechanics, in commerce, in domestic service and in the professions. And in this connection,
it is well to bear in mind, that whatever other sins the South may
be called to bear, that when it comes to business, pure and simple,
it is in the South that the Negro is given a man's chance in the
commercial world, and in nothing is this Exposition more eloquent than in emphasizing this chance. Our greatest danger is,
that in the great leap from slavery to freedom, we may overlook
the fact that the masses of us are to live by the productions of
our hands, and fail to keep in mind that we shall prosper in
proportion as we learn to dignify and glorify common labor and
put brains and skill into the common occupations of life, shall
prosper in proportion as we learn to draw the line between the
superficial and the substantial, the ornamental gewgaws of life
and the useful. No race can prosper till it learns that there is as
much dignity in tilling a field as in writing a poem. It is at the
bottom of life we must begin, and not at the top. Nor should we
permit our grievances to overshadow our opportunities.

To those of the white race who look to the incoming of those of
foreign birth and strange tongue and habits, for the prosperity of
the South, were I permitted, I would repeat what I say to my
own race—"Cast down your bucket where you are." Cast it down
among the 8,000,000 Negroes whose habits you know, whose
fidelity and love you have tested in days when to have proved
treacherous meant the ruin of your firesides. Cast down your
bucket among these people who have, without strikes and labor
wars, tilled your fields, cleared your forests, builded your railroads and cities, and brought forth treasures from the bowels of
the earth and helped make possible this magnificent representation of the progress of the South. Casting down your bucket
among my people, helping and encouraging them as you are
doing on these grounds, and to education of head, hand and
heart, you will find that they will buy your surplus land, make
blossom the waste places in your fields and run your factories.
While doing this, you can be sure in the future, as in the past,
that you and your families will be surrounded by the most
patient, faithful, law-abiding and unresentful people that the
world has seen. As we have proved our loyalty to you in the past,

in nursing your children, watching by the sick bed of your mothers and fathers and often following them with tear-dimmed eyes to their graves, so in the future in our humble way, we shall stand by you with a devotion that no foreigner can approach, ready to lay down our lives, if need be, in defence of yours, interlacing our industrial, commercial, civil and religious life with yours in a way that shall make the interests of both races one. In all things that are purely social we can be as separate as the fingers, yet one as the hand in all things essential to mutual progress.

There is no defence or security for any of us except in the highest intelligence and development of all. If anywhere there are efforts tending to curtail the fullest growth of the Negro, let these efforts be turned into stimulating, encouraging and making him the most useful and intelligent citizen. Effort or means so invested, will pay a thousand per cent. interest. These efforts will be twice blessed—"blessing him that gives and him that takes."

There is no escape through law of man or God, from the inevitable:

> "The laws of changeless justice bind,
>   Oppressor with oppressed;
> And close as sin and suffering joined,
>   We march to fate abreast."

Nearly sixteen millions of hands will aid you in pulling the load upwards, or they will pull against you the load downwards. We shall constitute one-third and more of the ignorance and crime of the South, or one third its intelligence and progress; we shall contribute one-third to the business and industrial prosperity of the South, or we shall prove a veritable body of death, stagnating, depressing, retarding every effort to advance the body politic.

Gentlemen of the Exposition, as we present to you our humble effort at an exhibition of our progress, you must not expect over much. Starting thirty years ago with ownership here and there in a few quilts, and pumpkins and chickens (gathered from miscellaneous sources), remember the path that has led from these to the inventions and production of agricultural implements, buggies, steam engines, newspapers, books, statuary, carving, paintings, the management of drug stores and banks, has not been trodden without contact with thorns and thistles. While we take pride in what we exhibit as a result of our independent efforts, we do not for a moment forget that our part in this exhibition would fall far short of your expectations but for the constant help that has come to our educational life, not only from the Southern States, but especially from Northern philanthropists, who have made their gifts a constant stream of blessing and encouragement.

The wisest among my race understand that the agitation of questions of social equality is the extremest folly, and that progress in the enjoyment of all the privileges that will come to us must be the result of severe and constant struggle, rather than of artificial forcing. No race that has anything to contribute to the markets of the world is long in any degree ostracized. It is important and right that all privileges of the law be ours, but it is vastly more important that we be prepared for the exercises of these privileges. The opportunity to earn a dollar in a factory just now is worth infinitely more than the opportunity to spend a dollar in an opera house.

In conclusion, may I repeat that nothing in thirty years has given us more hope and encouragement, and drawn us so near to you of the white race, as this opportunity offered by the Exposition; and, here bending, as it were, over the altar that represents the results of the struggles of your race and mine, both starting practically empty-handed three decades ago, I pledge that in your effort to work out the great and intricate problem which God has laid at the doors of the South, you shall have at all times the patient, sympathetic help of my race; only let this be constantly in mind, that while from representations in these buildings of the product of field, of forest, of mine, of factory, letters and art, much good will come, yet far above and beyond material benefits, will be that higher good, that let us pray God will come, in a blotting out of sectional differences and racial animosities and suspicions, in a determination to administer absolute justice, in a willing obedience among all classes to the mandates of the law. This, coupled with our material prosperity, will bring into our beloved South a new Heaven and a new earth.

16

Ethical Dilemmas of Practicing Law

Clarence Darrow Talks About Right and Wrong

Clarence Darrow (1857-1938) is best remembered for his late trials in criminal law, but in fact his legal career was amazingly varied. After serving as corporation counsel of Chicago, he was general attorney of the Chicago and Northwestern Railroad until 1894. Then for nearly two decades his most famous cases involved trade unions and their officials, but he continued to do corporate work. He was also a noted reformer, and for most of his life he stood close to socialism. In a memorial address in 1902 to his late law partner, ex-Governor John Peter Altgeld, Darrow pointed to the moral scars carried by men of his time: "In the commercial revolution of this generation, many wise, humane and righteous men have found themselves with the reactionary forces that are strangling liberty and destroying popular government throughout the world." He analyzes the seeming contradictions in his own behavior in this letter, probably written in 1895 to Ellen Gates Starr. In reading this letter note (1) the author's view of the principles upon which society was based; (2) upon what ethical grounds he defended his own actions; and (3) his references to a higher law and what he meant by that phrase. My own analysis is in "Clarence Seward Darrow, 1857-1938," *Antioch Review*, XIII (1953), pp. 52-66; the tone of a big corporate practice is superbly caught by Robert T. Swaine, *The Cravath Firm and Its Predecessors, 1819-1947* (1946).

Carbon copy in Clarence Darrow Papers, Library of Congress.

M<small>Y</small> DEAR MISS S.:

If I did not care for you and your friendship, as well as that of the other members of the "settlement," Hull House, Chicago, I would do as you requested, not answer your letter. I hope you know that I would understand the spirit in which you wrote. I know *you* know and appreciate the feeling of friendship which prompted you to write as you did.

Although you may not think it, I am very sensative to public opinion, even the opinion of those who are glad to criticise what I do. But when it comes to the opinion of those whom I know to be my sincere friends, and well wishers, like yourself, I feel it much more deeply. I should be very sorry to have you change your opinion of me, as I am sorry to have so many other of my good friends feel hurt (almost personally) in reference to the matter of which you wrote. I have always acted legally on my own judgment. I know I have many times made mistakes. I have sometimes admitted them, but I believe I never sought to evade the consequences of anything I have done, or to make any defense or excuse for my acts.

I wish to put this matter before you from my own stand point, and in so doing will endeavor, not to place myself in the position so frequently occupied by those who wish to excuse something they know to be wrong. An ordinance was passed by the city council granting certain valuable rights to an Electric Co., or to some people purporting to be an electric co. I never heard of this ordinance until after it was passed. The Mayor refused to sign it in the shape in which it passed. I was employed in getting as favorable amendments to the ordinance as I could, and to otherwise act as their attorney.

I did not know how this ordinance was passed, I do not know now. I however know enough about municipal affairs to believe it was passed for boodle like every other ordinance granting valuable privileges in this city.

I undertook to serve this company or these people, believing they had an ordinance, procured by the aid of boodle. Judged by the ordinary commercial and legal standard of ethics I did right. Every law and every instructor constantly teaches that all clients have the right to have their cases represented and to receive the benefit and protection of the law. I know that in your mind this is no justification, it is no justification in mine. I do not care a cent for all the ordinary rules of ethics or conduct. They are mostly wrong. I am satisfied that judged by the higher law, in which we both believe I could not be justified, and that I am practically a thief. I am taking money that I did not earn, which comes to me from men who did not earn it, but who get it, because they have a chance to get it. I take it without performing any useful service to the world, and I take a thousand times as much as my services are worth even assuming they were useful and honest.

This is my position, judged by the high rules of conduct and ethics in which I believe and which I have in my way, and to the best of my ability tried to urge the world to adopt. I came to Chicago about eight years ago, before I came I lived in a small country town.

Those modern thoughts about the rights of labor, and the wrongs of the world, had just taken possession of me. My attention was called to these by a friend named Swift, whom I believe you have met once in Boston. We discussed these questions not only abstractly, but as applied to our own life and our own conduct. He took one view and I another, both agreed the ideal life was well nigh unlivable, both had in view doing some good. His father owned a drug store, he died and Swift was appointed administrator of his father's estate. He took all the patent medicines out in the back yard and broke the bottles; he then left his town without money, refused to compromise with the world, lived as best he could, was nearly a tramp. He raised a Coxey army, marched to Washington, is now I believe shunned by most earnest people who cannot follow him. He is no doubt loved by those who know him, but has lived his life as he thought right and best, has perhaps done some good in his way by refusing to compromise with evil, and be a party or participate in wrong. I believed then and I believe now, that society is organized injustice, that business is legal fraud, that a land owner is a pirate, who takes money from the poor for standing on the ground which should be free to all, that society consists of two classes, the despoiler and despoiled, that all who directly or indirectly live off the proceeds of labor are enjoying the fruits of robbery, and the poor are their victims.

I determined then to give my energies and ability to help change the system under which all of us are compelled to live. I did not take the course that was adopted by my friend, like him I chose deliberately, and have followed consistently. I came to Chicago. I determined to take my chance with the rest, to get what I could out of the system and use it to destroy the system. I came without friends or money. Society provides no fund out of which such people can live while preaching heresy. It compels us to get our living out of society as it is or die. I do not choose yet to die although perhaps it would be the best. Long ago I laid out my course in life. I have followed it without much variation ever since. I care nothing whatever for money except to use it in this work and to bring me such comforts as I want and to help my friends.

After being here a short time I took a position in the law department of the city, where I learned something of municipal affairs. I then served a railroad company for three years. I have since sold my professional services to every corporation or individual who cared to buy, the only exception I have made is that I have never given them to oppress the weak, or convict the innocent. Aside from this I have used them to the best of my ability to serve my clients almost every one of whom are criminals judged by the higher law in which I firmly believe. I have taken their ill gotten gains and have tried to use it to prevent suffering, sometimes I have succeeded, often I have failed. My preaching and my practicing have ever been the same. I have always tried to show a state and a way to reach it where men and women can be honest and tender. I have never advised any one not to get a living out of this society, for I want the best of society to live. I believe that there is absolutely no difference in my conduct whether I serve a corporation conceived in oppression and fraud as all of them are, or whether I take rent from a tenant or sell goods to the poor, all of it is bad, none of it could live in a world that is beautiful and just. My conduct in this matter, if the facts generally believed are true, is nearer right than anything I have ever done for money in a business way. I have harmed no one who cannot afford to lose, and who has the least moral right to their possessions. Now, as when I went to serve the railroad company the only question that is pertinent from my standpoint is: what are his motives? and what attitude will he assume toward those things he condemns? If I let my professional business change my views of life, or allow it to influence me as a citizen to the support of measures in which I do not believe, I am wrong. Otherwise as I see the light I am doing my duty. It may be that people cannot look at this in the way I view it, I believe the wisest do. I may be condemned and lose influence, this I expected at the time and it hurt me, hurt me grievously, I would have been glad not to have taken the employment, and thus escape the censure which I have received and will receive, and which I knew would come. But had I refused it, I would have done so, not because I thought it wrong, but because I thought it would not pay. I will not allow myself to be influenced by that consideration. I have defended the poor and weak, have done it without pay, will do it again. I cannot defend them without bread, I cannot get this except from those who have it, and by giving some measure of conformity to what is.

While I am very sensative to public opinion I have never in my life considered it in determining my course, I hope I never will. I have even dared to do right in the face of public opinion, and this is always dangerous. I believe that after a while most of the people, nearly all the laborers, will believe I was right and that I am true to their cause. I hope they will, but I must abide it if they do not. The qualities which you say I possess, and the usefulness which you say might come to me, are due only to taking the same course in other matters that I have taken here. I do not believe that on the whole I would have been as useful in any other way, and yet no one can know. I could have taken the course pursued by my friend Swift, I chose the other. In my mind there is no middle ground, we must take one path or the other. I do not say that he did wrong, but I cannot say that I was wrong, only infinite wisdom can determine this, and I am inclined to think, that if such a judgment is ever pronounced it will be determined that neither one did wrong. I dont want you to think that I did this or anything for the money because I like money, for I do not, I did it as I mean to do all things because I thought it best, because I believe that the only way any person or deed can be judged is by the purpose and the full results.

17

The Function of the Novelist

Stephen Crane Interviews William Dean Howells

William Dean Howells (1837-1920) for four decades wrote a novel a year, of which a half-dozen rank with the permanent treasury of fiction in English. He was also an outstanding magazine editor, serving as editor-in-chief of the *Atlantic Monthly* for ten years and conducting the "Easy Chair" column in *Harper's Monthly* from 1900 to 1920. In these posts he fought to gain an audience for realist writers: Europeans like Tolstoi, Turgenev, and Zola; Americans like Garland, Dreiser, and Stephen Crane. Crane (1871-1900) interviewed Howells in 1894 about his conception of the writer's task, and published this story in the *New York Times*. The young reporter had finished *The Red Badge of Courage* in the summer of 1893, but it was not published until 1895. His great short stories were also written after this interview. Note (1) Howells' view of the novelist's role; (2) what Howells meant by realism; (3) what he meant by proportion and perspective; and (4) what Howells thought about an author's obligation to the reading public. On Howells see Edwin H. Cady, *The Road to Realism* (1956) and *The Realist at War* (1958) as well as the two volumes superbly edited by Henry Nash Smith and William M. Gibson, *Mark Twain-Howells Letters* (1960). Thomas Beer, *Stephen Crane* (1923), remains lively.

From *The New York Times*, October 28, 1894, p. 20, col. 7.

Wᴵᴸᴸᴵᴬᴹ ᴅᴇᴀɴ ʜᴏᴡᴇʟʟs ʟᴇᴀɴᴇᴅ ʜɪs ᴄʜᴇᴇᴋ ᴜᴘᴏɴ the two outstretched fingers of his right hand and gazed thoughtfully at the window—the panes black from the night without, although studded once or twice with little electric stars far up on the west side of the Park. He was looking at something which his memory had just brought to him.

"I have a little scheme," he said at last, slowly. "I saw a young girl out in a little Ohio town once—she was the daughter of the carpetwoman there—that is to say, her mother made rag carpets and rugs for the villagers. And this girl had the most wonderful instinct in manners and dress. Her people were of the lowest of the low in a way and yet this girl was a lady. She used to completely amaze me—to think how this girl could grow there in that squalor. She was as chic as chic could be, and yet the money spent and the education was nothing—nothing at all. Where she procured her fine taste you could not imagine. It was deeply interesting to me—it overturned so many of my rooted social dogmas. It was the impossible, appearing suddenly. And then there was another in Cambridge—a wonderful type. I have come upon them occasionally here and there. I intend to write something of the kind if I can. I have thought of a good title, too, I think—a name of a flower—'The Ragged Lady.'"

"I suppose this is a long way off," said the other man reflectively. "I am anxious to hear what you say in 'The Story of a Play.' Do you raise your voice toward reforming the abuses that are popularly supposed to hide in the manager's office for use upon the struggling artistic playwright and others? Do you recite the manager's divine misapprehension of art?"

"No, I do not," said Mr. Howells.

"Why?" said the other man.

"Well, in the first place, the manager is a man of business. He preserves himself. I suppose he judges not against art, but between art and art. He looks at art through the crowds."

"I don't like reformatory novels anyhow," said the other man.

"And in the second place," continued Mr. Howells, "it does no good to go at things hammer and tongs in this obvious way.

I believe that every novel should have an intention. A man should mean something when he writes. Ah, this writing merely to amuse people—why, it seems to me altogether vulgar. A man may as well blacken his face and go out and dance on the street for pennies. The author is a sort of trained bear, if you accept certain standards. If literary men are to be the public fools, let us at any rate have it clearly understood, so that those of us who feel differently can take measures. But, on the other hand, a novel should never preach and berate and storm. It does no good. As a matter of fact, a book of that kind is ineffably tiresome. People don't like to have their lives half cudgeled out in that manner, especially in these days, when a man, likely enough, only reaches for a book when he wishes to be fanned, so to speak, after the heat of the daily struggle. When a writer desires to preach in an obvious manner he should announce his intention—let him cry out then that he is in the pulpit. But it is the business of the novel—"

"Ah!" said the other man.

"It is the business of the novel to picture the daily life in the most exact terms possible, with an absolute and clear sense of proportion. That is the important matter—the proportion. As a usual thing, I think, people have absolutely no sense of proportion. Their noses are tight against life, you see. They perceive mountains where there are no mountains, but frequently a great peak appears no larger than a rat trap. An artist sees a dog down the street—well, his eye instantly relates the dog to its surroundings. The dog is proportioned to the buildings and the trees. Whereas, many people can conceive of that dog's tail resting upon a hill top."

"You have often said that the novel is a perspective," observed the other man.

"A perspective, certainly. It is a perspective made for the benefit of people who have no true use of their eyes. The novel, in its real meaning, adjusts the proportion. It preserves the balances. It is in this way that lessons are to be taught and reforms to be won. When people are introduced to each other they will see the resemblances, and won't want to fight so badly."

"I suppose that when a man tries to write 'what the people want'—when he tries to reflect the popular desire, it is a bad quarter of an hour for the laws of proportion."

"Do you recall any of the hosts of stories that began in love and ended a little further on? Those stories used to represent life to the people, and I believe they do now to a large class. Life began when the hero saw a certain girl, and it ended abruptly when he married her. Love and courtship was not an incident, a part of life—it was the whole of it. All else was of no value. Men of that religion must have felt very stupid when they were engaged at anything but courtship. Do you see the false proportion? Do you see the dog with his tail upon the hill top? Somebody touched the universal heart with the fascinating theme—the relation of man to maid—and, for many years, it was as if no other relation could be recognized in fiction. Here and there an author raised his voice, but not loudly. I like to see the novelists treating some of the other important things of life—the relation of mother and son, of husband and wife, in fact all those things that we live in constantly. The other can be but fragmentary."

"I suppose there must be two or three new literary people just back of the horizon somewhere," said the other man. "Books upon these lines that you speak of are what might be called unpopular. Do you think them a profitable investment?"

"From my point of view it is the right—it is sure to be a profitable investment. After that it is a question of perseverance, courage. A writer of skill cannot be defeated because he remains true to his conscience. It is a long, serious conflict sometimes, but he must win, if he does not falter. Lowell said to me one time: 'After all, the barriers are very thin. They are paper. If a man has his conscience and one or two friends who can help him, it becomes very simple at last.'"

"Mr. Howells," said the other man, suddenly, "have you observed a change in the literary pulse of the country within the last four months? Last winter, for instance, it seemed that realism was about to capture things, but then recently I have thought I saw coming a sort of counter wave, a flood of the other —a reaction, in fact. Trivial, temporary, perhaps, but a reaction, certainly."

Mr. Howells dropped his hand in a gesture of emphatic assent. "What you say is true. I have seen it coming. * * * I suppose we shall have to wait."

Stephen Crane

18

The Rebirth of American Poetry

Edwin Arlington Robinson Writes
a Sonnet to Zola

Edwin Arlington Robinson (1869-1935) wrote in his early sonnet to Walt Whitman:

> The master-songs are ended, and the man
> That sang them is a name . . .

It seemed true. For more than two decades after Whitman suffered paralysis in 1873, poetry in the United States was academic; it was ornamental; it was shallow. Robinson marks the change. In spite of his wide acquaintance with traditional forms of verse, he was an original. He studied at Harvard from 1891 to 1893, then he went home to Maine and wrote. His first book was published by himself in a small edition in 1896, and the following sonnet can be found there. Note (1) how the sonnet turns away from "poetic" pretenses toward a language and diction that often seem colloquial; and (2) the poem's insistence that a price is paid for innocence: that the tree in the Garden of Eden was the Tree of the Knowledge of Good and Evil. See Roy Harvey Pearce, *The Continuity of American Poetry* (1961).

From Edwin Arlington Robinson, "Zola," in *The Torrent and the Night Before* (The Author, Gardiner, Maine, 1896), p. 10.

Zola

Because he puts the compromising chart
Of hell before your eyes, you are afraid;
Because he counts the price that you have paid
For innocence, and counts it from the start,
You loathe him. But he sees the human heart
Of God meanwhile, and in God's hand has weighed
Your squeamish and emasculate crusade
Against the grim dominion of his art.

Never until we conquer the uncouth
Connivings of our shamed indifference
(We call it Christian faith!) are we to scan
The racked and shrieking hideousness of Truth
To find, in hate's polluted self-defence
Throbbing, the pulse, the divine heart of man.

19

Music and Culture in Boston and on the Frontier

Willa Cather Contrasts Two Worlds

Willa Cather (1873-1947) was one of the trio of tough-minded women writers—the others were Edith Wharton and Ellen Glasgow —who grew to maturity in the last quarter of the nineteenth century. Born in Virginia, she was reared in Nebraska among Bohemians, Norwegians, and other immigrants, and this setting figures in much of her best work. Her experiences caused her to realize that over a period of thirty years the musical comprehension of even a trained pianist might be "dissolved in soapsuds, or worked into bread, or milked into the bottom of a pail." The following short story is achingly poignant in its contrast of the cultural riches of Boston with the cultural poverty of the frontier; while the United States was becoming more integrated and homogeneous, it was still far from completely so. Victories over the plains, with their monotony and grinding toil and silences, could be "dearer bought than those of war." See E. Brown and Leon Edel, *Willa Cather* (1953).

From Willa Sibert Cather, "A Wagner Matinee," *The Troll Garden* (McClure, Phillips & Co., New York, 1903), pp. 195-210.

I RECEIVED ONE MORNING A LETTER, WRITTEN IN pale ink on glassy, blue-lined note-paper, and bearing the postmark of a little Nebraska village. This communication, worn and rubbed, looking as though it had been carried for some days in a coat pocket that was none too clean, was from my uncle Howard and informed me that his wife had been left a small legacy by a bachelor relative who had recently died, and that it would be necessary for her to go to Boston to attend to the settling of the estate. He requested me to meet her at the station and render her whatever services might be necessary. On examining the date indicated as that of her arrival, I found it no later than to-morrow. He had characteristically delayed writing until, had I been away from home for a day, I must have missed the good woman altogether.

The name of my Aunt Georgiana called up not alone her own figure, at once pathetic and grotesque, but opened before my feet a gulf of recollection so wide and deep, that, as the letter dropped from my hand, I felt suddenly a stranger to all the present conditions of my existence, wholly ill at ease and out of place amid the familiar surroundings of my study. I became, in short, the gangling farmer-boy my aunt had known, scourged with chilblains and bashfulness, my hands cracked and sore from the corn husking. I felt the knuckles of my thumb tentatively, as though they were raw again. I sat again before her parlour organ, fumbling the scales with my stiff, red hands, while she, beside me, made canvas mittens for the huskers.

The next morning, after preparing my landlady somewhat, I set out for the station. When the train arrived I had some difficulty in finding my aunt. She was the last of the passengers to alight, and it was not until I got her into the carriage that she seemed really to recognize me. She had come all the way in a day coach; her linen duster had become black with soot and her black bonnet grey with dust during the journey. When we arrived at my boarding-house the landlady put her to bed at once and I did not see her again until the next morning.

Whatever shock Mrs. Springer experienced at my aunt's appearance, she considerately concealed. As for myself, I saw my aunt's misshapen figure with that feeling of awe and respect with which we behold explorers who have left their ears and fingers north of Franz-Joseph-Land, or their health somewhere along the Upper Congo. My Aunt Georgiana had been a music teacher at the Boston Conservatory, somewhere back in the latter sixties. One summer, while visiting in the little village among the Green Mountains where her ancestors had dwelt for generations, she had kindled the callow fancy of the most idle and shiftless of all the village lads, and had conceived for this How-

ard Carpenter one of those extravagant passions which a handsome country boy of twenty-one sometimes inspires in an angu-
lar, spectacled woman of thirty. When she returned to her duties
in Boston, Howard followed her, and the upshot of this inexplic-
able infatuation was that she eloped with him, eluding the
reproaches of her family and the criticisms of her friends by
going with him to the Nebraska frontier. Carpenter, who, of
course, had no money, had taken a homestead in Red Willow
County, fifty miles from the railroad. There they had measured
off their quarter section themselves by driving across the prairie
in a wagon, to the wheel of which they had tied a red cotton
handkerchief, and counting off its revolutions. They built a dug-
out in the red hillside, one of those cave dwellings whose in-
mates so often reverted to primitive conditions. Their water they
got from the lagoons where the buffalo drank, and their slender
stock of provisions was always at the mercy of bands of roving
Indians. For thirty years my aunt had not been further than
fifty miles from the homestead.

But Mrs. Springer knew nothing of all this, and must have
been considerably shocked at what was left of my kinswoman.
Beneath the soiled linen duster which, on her arrival, was the
most conspicuous feature of her costume, she wore a black stuff
dress, whose ornamentation showed that she had surrendered
herself unquestioningly into the hands of a country dressmaker.
My poor aunt's figure, however, would have presented astonishing difficulties to any dressmaker. Originally stooped, her shoul-
ders were now almost bent together over her sunken chest. She
wore no stays, and her gown, which trailed unevenly behind,
rose in a sort of peak over her abdomen. She wore ill-fitting false
teeth, and her skin was as yellow as a Mongolian's from constant
exposure to a pitiless wind and to the alkaline water which
hardens the most transparent cuticle into a sort of flexible leather.

I owed to this woman most of the good that ever came my
way in my boyhood, and had a reverential affection for her.
During the years when I was riding herd for my uncle, my aunt,
after cooking the three meals—the first of which was ready at
six o'clock in the morning—and putting the six children to bed,
would often stand until midnight at her ironing-board, with
me at the kitchen table beside her, hearing me recite Latin de-

clensions and conjugations, gently shaking me when my drowsy head sank down over a page of irregular verbs. It was to her, at her ironing or mending, that I read my first Shakspere, and her old text-book on mythology was the first that ever came into my empty hands. She taught me my scales and exercises, too—on the little parlour organ, which her husband had bought her after fifteen years, during which she had not so much as seen any instrument, but an accordion that belonged to one of the Norwegian farmhands. She would sit beside me by the hour, darning and counting while I struggled with the "Joyous Farmer," but she seldom talked to me about music, and I understood why. She was a pious woman; she had the consolations of religion and, to her at least, her martyrdom was not wholly sordid. Once when I had been doggedly beating out some easy passages from an old score of *Euryanthe* I had found among her music books, she came up to me and, putting her hands over my eyes, gently drew my head back upon her shoulder, saying tremulously, "Don't love it so well, Clark, or it may be taken from you. Oh! dear boy, pray that whatever your sacrifice may be, it be not that."

When my aunt appeared on the morning after her arrival, she was still in a semi-somnambulant state. She seemed not realize that she was in the city where she had spent her youth, the place longed for hungrily half a lifetime. She had been so wretchedly train-sick throughout the journey that she had no recollection of anything but her discomfort, and, to all intents and purposes, there were but a few hours of nightmare between the farm in Red Willow County and my study on Newbury Street. I had planned a little pleasure for her that afternoon, to repay her for some of the glorious moments she had given me when we used to milk together in the straw-thatched cowshed and she, because I was more than usually tried, or because her husband had spoken sharply to me, would tell me of the splendid performance of the *Huguenots* she had seen in Paris, in her youth. At two o'clock the Symphony Orchestra was to give a Wagner programme, and I intended to take my aunt; though, as I conversed with her I grew doubtful about her enjoyment of it. Indeed, for her own sake, I could only wish her taste for such things quite dead, and the long struggle mercifully ended at last. I suggested our visiting the Conservatory and the Common before lunch, but she seemed altogether too timid to wish to venture out. She questioned me absently about various changes in the city, but she was chiefly concerned that she had forgotten to leave instructions about feeding half-skimmed milk to a certain weakling calf, "old Maggie's calf, you know, Clark," she explained, evidently having forgotten how long I had been away. She was further troubled because she had neglected to tell her daughter about the freshly-opened kit of mackerel in the cellar, which would spoil if it were not used directly.

I asked her whether she had ever heard any of the Wagnerian operas, and found that she had not, though she was perfectly familiar with their respective situations, and had once possessed the piano score of *The Flying Dutchman*. I began to think it would have been best to get her back to Red Willow County without waking her, and regretted having suggested the concert.

From the time we entered the concert hall, however, she was a trifle less passive and inert, and for the first time seemed to perceive her surroundings. I had felt some trepidation lest she might become aware of the absurdities of her attire, or might experience some painful embarrassment at stepping suddenly into the world to which she had been dead for a quarter of a century. But, again, I found how superficially I had judged her. She sat looking about her with eyes as impersonal, almost as stony, as those with which the granite Rameses in a museum watches the froth and fret that ebbs and flows about his pedestal —separated from it by the lonely stretch of centuries. I have seen this same aloofness in old miners who drift into the Brown hotel at Denver, their pockets full of bullion, their linen soiled, their haggard faces unshaven; standing in the thronged corridors as solitary as though they were still in a frozen camp on the Yukon, conscious that certain experiences have isolated them from their fellows by a gulf no haberdasher could bridge.

We sat at the extreme left of the first balcony, facing the arc of our own and the balcony above us, veritable hanging gardens, brilliant as tulip beds. The matinée audience was made up chiefly of women. One lost the contour of faces and figures, indeed any effect of line whatever, and there was only the colour of bodices past counting the shimmer of fabrics soft and firm, silky and sheer; red, mauve, pink, blue, lilac, purple, ecru, rose, yellow, cream, and white, all the colours that an impressionist finds in a sunlit landscape, with here and there the dead shadow of a frock coat. My Aunt Georgiana regarded them as though they had been so many daubs of tube-paint on a palette.

When the musicians came out and took their places, she gave a little stir of anticipation, and looked with quickening interest down over the rail at that invariable grouping, perhaps the first wholly familiar thing that had greeted her eye since she had left old Maggie and her weakling calf. I could feel how all those details sank into her soul, for I had not forgotten how they had sunk into mine when I came fresh from ploughing forever and forever between green aisles of corn, where, as in a treadmill, one might walk from daybreak to dusk without perceiving a shadow of change. The clean profiles of the musicians, the gloss of their linen, the dull black of their coats, the beloved shapes of the instruments, the patches of yellow light thrown by the green shaded lamps on the smooth, varnished bellies of the 'cellos and the bass viols in the rear, the restless, wind-tossed forest of fiddle necks and bows—I recalled how, in the first orchestra I had ever heard, those long bow strokes seemed to draw the heart out of me, as a conjurer's stick reels out yards of paper ribbon from a hat.

The first number was the *Tannhauser* overture. When the horns drew out the first strain of the Pilgrim's chorus, my Aunt Georgiana clutched my coat sleeve. Then it was I first realized that for her this broke a silence of thirty years; the inconceivable silence of the plains. With the battle between the two motives, with the frenzy of the Venusberg theme and its ripping of strings, there came to me an overwhelming sense of the waste and wear we are so powerless to combat; and I saw again the tall, naked house on the prairie, black and grim as a wooden fortress; the black pond where I had learned to swim, its margin pitted with sun-dried cattle tracks; the rain gullied clay banks about the naked house, the four dwarf ash seedlings where the dish-cloths were always hung to dry before the kitchen door. The world there was the flat world of the ancients; to the east, a cornfield that stretched to daybreak; to the west, a corral that reached to sunset; between, the conquests of peace, dearer bought than those of war.

The overture closed, my aunt released my coat sleeve, but she said nothing. She sat staring at the orchestra through a dullness of thirty years, through the films made little by little by each of the three hundred and sixty-five days in every one of them. What, I wondered, did she get from it? She had been a good pianist in her day, I knew, and her musical education had been broader than that of most music teachers of a quarter of a century ago. She had often told me of Mozart's operas and Meyerbeer's, and I could remember hearing her sing, years ago, certain melodies of Verdi's. When I had fallen ill with a fever in her house she used to sit by my cot in the evening—when the cool, night wind blew in through the faded mosquito netting tacked over the window and I lay watching a certain bright star that burned red above the cornfield—and sing "Home to our mountains, O, let us return!" in a way fit to break the heart of a Vermont boy near dead of homesickness already.

I watched her closely through the prelude to *Tristan and Isolde*, trying vainly to conjecture what that seething turmoil of strings and winds might mean to her, but she sat mutely staring at the violin bows that drove obliquely downward, like the pelting streaks of rain in a summer shower. Had this music any message for her? Had she enough left to at all comprehend this power which had kindled the world since she had left it? I was in a fever of curiosity, but Aunt Georgiana sat silent upon her peak in Darien. She preserved this utter immobility throughout the number from the *Flying Dutchman*, though her fingers worked mechanically upon her black dress, as though, of themselves, they were recalling the piano score they had once played. Poor old hands! They had been stretched and twisted into mere tentacles to hold and lift and knead with; the palm, unduly swollen, the fingers bent and knotted—on one of them a thin, worn band that had once been a wedding ring. As I pressed and gently quieted one of those groping hands, I remembered with quivering eyelids their services for me in other days.

Soon after the tenor began the "Prize Song," I heard a quick drawn breath and turned to my aunt. Her eyes were closed, but the tears were glistening on her cheeks, and I think, in a moment more, they were in my eyes as well. It never really died, then—the soul that can suffer so excruciatingly and so interminably; it withers to the outward eye only; like that strange moss which can lie on a dusty shelf half a century and yet, if placed in water, grows green again. She wept so throughout the development and elaboration of the melody.

During the intermission before the second half of the concert, I questioned my aunt and found that the "Prize Song" was not new to her. Some years before there had drifted to the farm in Red Willow County a young German, a tramp cow puncher, who had sung the chorus at Beyruth, when he was a boy, along with the other peasant boys and girls. Of a Sunday morning he used to sit on his gingham-sheeted bed in the hands' bedroom which opened off the kitchen, cleaning the leather of his boots and saddle, singing the "Prize Song," while my aunt went about her work in the kitchen. She had hovered about him until she had prevailed upon him to join the country church, though his sole fitness for this step, in so far as I could gather, lay in his boyish face and his possession of this divine melody. Shortly afterward he had gone to town on the Fourth of July, been drunk for several days, lost his money at a faro table, ridden a saddled Texan steer on a bet, and disappeared with a fractured collar-bone. All this my aunt told me huskily, wanderingly, as though she were talking in the weak lapses of illness.

"Well, we have come to better things than the old *Trovatore* at any rate, Auntie Georgie?" I queried, with a well meant effort at jocularity.

Her lip quivered and she hastily put her handkerchief up to her mouth. From behind it she murmured, "And you have been hearing this ever since you left me, Clark?" Her question was the gentlest and saddest of reproaches.

The second half of the programme consisted of four numbers from the *Ring*, and closed with Siegfried's funeral march. My aunt wept quietly, but almost continuously, as a shallow vessel overflows in a rain-storm. From time to time her dim eyes looked up at the lights which studded the ceiling, burning softly under their dull glass globes; doubtless they were stars in truth to her. I was still perplexed as to what measure of musical comprehension was left to her, she who had heard nothing but the singing of Gospel Hymns at Methodist services in the square frame schoolhouse on Section Thirteen for so many years. I was wholly unable to gauge how much of it had been dissolved in soapsuds, or worked into bread, or milked into the bottom of a pail.

The deluge of sound poured on and on; I never knew what she found in the shining current of it; I never knew how far it bore her, or past what happy islands. From the trembling of her face I could well believe that before the last numbers she had been carried out where the myriad graves are, into the grey, nameless burying grounds of the sea; or into some world of death vaster yet, where, from the beginning of the world, hope has lain down with hope and dream with dream and, renouncing, slept.

The concert was over; the people filed out of the hall chattering and laughing, glad to relax and find the living level again, but my kinswoman made no effort to rise. The harpist slipped its green felt cover over his instrument; the flute-players shook the water from their mouthpieces; the men of the orchestra went out one by one, leaving the stage to the chairs and music stands, empty as a winter cornfield.

I speak to my aunt. She burst into tears and sobbed pleadingly. "I don't want to go, Clark, I don't want to go!"

I understood. For her, just outside the door of the concert hall, lay the black pond with the cattle-tracked bluffs; the tall, unpainted house, with weather-curled boards; naked as a tower, the crook-backed ash seedlings where the dish-cloths hung to dry; the gaunt, moulting turkeys picking up refuse about the kitchen door.

Part III. Political and Constitutional History]

20

Reform of the Federal Civil Service

President Arthur's Proclamation of May 7, 1883

Although a Federal Civil Service Commission existed from 1871, it was financially starved by Congress and was ineffective. But agitation for reform was kept up by a small group of editors and other professionals, most of them men who were morally affronted by abuses of government patronage. In 1881 they founded the National Civil Service Reform League. The November elections the following year saw the Republicans suffer sweeping losses in the crucial Northeast, and there was little doubt that alleged support of the spoils system had been a telling charge against them (No. 22). Republican Congressmen felt compelled to make civil service reform a party measure, even though it meant curtailing their own power; the resultant Pendleton Act became law on January 16, 1883. In these ensuing regulations promulgated by President Arthur, note (1) the ban on compulsory political activity and contributions; (2) the restricted scope, which left most Federal jobholders unprotected; (3) the modest nature of the examinations required; and (4) the fact that the appointing official was not required to appoint the applicant who had done best on the competitive examination. See Ari Hoogenboom, *Outlawing the Spoils: A History of the Civil Service Reform Movement, 1865-1883* (1961); Paul P. Van Riper, *History of the United States Civil Service* (1958); and Leonard D. White, *The Republican Era, 1869-1901* (1958).

From Chester A. Arthur, Proclamation of May 7, 1883, in James D. Richardson (ed.), *Messages and Papers of the Presidents,* vol. 8 (n.p.: 1900), pp. 161-166.

IN THE EXERCISE OF THE POWER VESTED IN THE
President by the Constitution, and by virtue of the
seventeen hundred and fifty-third section of the Revised Statutes
and of the civil-service act approved January 16, 1883, the following rules for the regulation and improvement of the executive
civil service are hereby promulgated:

Rule I.]

No person in said service shall use his official authority or
influence either to coerce the political action of any person or
body or to interfere with any election.

Rule II.]

No person in the public service shall for that reason be under
any obligations to contribute to any political fund or to render
any political service, and he will not be removed or otherwise
prejudiced for refusing to do so. . . .

Rule V.]

There shall be three branches of the service classified under
the civil-service act (not including laborers or workmen or officers required to be confirmed by the Senate), as follows:

1. Those classified in the Departments at Washington shall be
designated "The classified departmental service."

2. Those classified under any collector, naval officer, surveyor,
or appraiser in any customs district shall be designated "The
classified customs service."

2. Those classified under any postmaster at any post-office,
including that at Washington, shall be designated "The classified
postal service."

4. The classified customs service shall embrace the several customs districts where the officials are as many as fifty, now the
following: New York City, N. Y.; Boston, Mass.; Philadelphia,
Pa.; San Francisco, Cal.; Baltimore, Md.; New Orleans, La.;

Chicago, Ill.; Burlington, Vt.; Portland, Me.; Detroit, Mich.; Port Huron, Mich.

5. The classified postal service shall embrace the several post-offices where the officials are as many as fifty, now the following: Albany, N. Y.; Baltimore, Md.; Boston, Mass.; Brooklyn, N. Y.; Buffalo, N. Y.; Chicago, Ill.; Cincinnati, Ohio; Cleveland, Ohio; Detroit, Mich.; Indianapolis, Ind.; Kansas City, Mo.; Louisville, Ky.; Milwaukee, Wis.; Newark, N. J.; New Orleans, La.; New York City, N. Y.; Philadelphia, Pa.; Pittsburg, Pa.; Providence, R. I.; Rochester, N. Y.; St. Louis, Mo.; San Francisco, Cal.; Washington, D. C.

Rule VI.]

1. There shall be open competitive examinations for testing the fitness of applicants for admission to the service. Such examinations shall be practical in their character and, so far as may be, shall relate to those matters which will fairly test the relative capacity and fitness of the persons examined to discharge the duties of the branch of the service which they seek to enter.

2. There shall also be competitive examinations of a suitable character to test the fitness of persons for promotion in the service.

Rule VII.]

1. The general examinations under the first clause of Rule VI for admission to the service shall be limited to the following subjects: (1) Orthography, penmanship, and copying; (2) arithmetic—fundamental rules, fractions, and percentage; (3) interest, discount, and elements of bookkeeping and of accounts; (4) elements of the English language, letter writing, and the proper construction of sentences; (5) elements of the geography, history, and government of the United States.

2. Proficiency in each of these subjects shall be credited in grading the standing of the persons examined in proportion to the value of a knowledge of such subjects in the branch or part of the service which the applicant seeks to enter.

3. No one shall be entitled to be certified for appointment whose standing upon a just grading in the general examination

shall be less than 65 per cent of complete proficiency in the first three subjects mentioned in this rule, and that measure of proficiency shall be deemed adequate.

4. But for places in which a lower degree of education will suffice the Commission may limit the examinations to, first, penmanship, copying, and orthography; second, the fundamental rules of arithmetic; but no person shall be certified under this examination of a less grading than 65 per cent on each subject.

5. The Commission may also order examinations of a higher grade or upon additional or special subjects, to test the capacity and fitness which may be needed in any special place or branch of the service.

Rule VIII.]

No question in any examination or proceeding by or under the Commission or examiners shall call for the expression or disclosure of any political or religious opinion or affiliation, nor shall any discrimination be made by reason thereof if known; and the Commission and its examiners shall discountenance all disclosure before either of them of such opinion by or concerning any applicants for examination or by or concerning anyone whose name is on any register awaiting appointment. . . .

Rule XVI.]

1. Whenever any officer having the power of appointment or employment shall so request, there shall be certified to him by the Commission or the proper examining board four names for the vacancy specified, to be taken from those graded highest on the proper register of those in his branch of the service and remaining eligible, regard being had to the apportionment of appointments to States and Territories; and from the said four a selection shall be made for the vacancy.

2. These certifications for the service at Washington shall be made in such order as to apportion, as nearly as may be practicable, the original appointments thereto among the States and Territories and the District of Columbia upon the basis of population as ascertained at the last preceding census. . . .

There are excepted from examination the following: (1) The confidential clerk or secretary of any head of a Department or office; (2) cashiers of collectors; (3) cashiers of postmasters; (4) superintendents of money-order divisions in post-offices; (5) the direct custodians of money for whose fidelity another officer is under official bond, but these exceptions shall not extend to any official below the grade of assistant cashier or teller; (6) persons employed exclusively in the secret service of the Government, or as translators or interpreters or stenographers; (7) persons whose employment is exclusively professional; (8) chief clerks, superintendents, and chiefs of divisions or bureaus. But no person so excepted shall be either transferred, appointed, or promoted, unless to some excepted place, without an examination under the Commission. Promotions may be made without examinations in offices where examinations for promotion are not now held until rules on the subject shall be promulgated. . . .

21

Negroes and the Constitution

Justice Harlan Dissents in the Civil Rights Case

The *Civil Rights Cases* (1883) arose under the Civil Rights Act of 1875 (18 *U. S. Statutes at Large* 335), which forbade inns, public conveyances, and places of public amusement from discriminating against Negroes. The Supreme Court decision written by Justice Joseph P. Bradley and ruled that the thirteenth Amendment dealt only with involuntary servitude and added: "Mere discriminations on account of race or color were not regarded as badges of slavery." The Fourteenth Amendment was intended to ban "state action of a particular character. . . . Individual invasion of individual rights is not the subject-matter of the amendment." Neither amendment gave Congress the powers it had sought to exercise, and the pertinent sections of the law were invalid. A Kentuckian, Justice John Marshall Harlan, was the sole dissenter. In his opinion, note (1) the reference to "those fundamental rights which are the essence of civil freedom" (What are they?) and the contention that the Thirteenth Amendment Joseph P. Bradley and ruled that the Thirteenth Amendment dealt by freeing the slaves had bestowed those rights and had bestowed upon Congress power to enforce them; (2) the quasi-public nature of the facilities regulated; (3) the call for judicial self-restraint; (4) the express authorization to Congress to enforce all provisions of the Fourteenth Amendment. See Rayford W. Logan, *The Negro in American Life and Thought: The Nadir, 1877-1901* (1954), and *Plessy* v. *Ferguson*, 163 U. S. 537 (1896).

From Justice Harlan, dissenting, in *Civil Rights Cases*, 109 U.S. 3 (1883).

Mr. JUSTICE HARLAN DISSENTING:

The opinion in these cases proceeds, it seems to me, upon grounds entirely too narrow and artificial. I cannot resist the conclusion that the substance and spirit of the recent Admendments of the Constitution have been sacrificed by a subtle and ingenious verbal criticism. "It is not the words of the law but the internal sense of it that makes the law; the letter of the law is the body; the sense and reason of the law is the soul." Constitutional provisions, adopted in the interest of liberty, and for the purpose of securing, through national legislation, if need be, rights inhering in a state of freedom, and belonging to American citizenship, have been so construed as to defeat the ends the people desired to accomplish, which they attempted to accomplish, and which they supposed they had accomplished by changes in their fundamental law. By this I do not mean that the determination of these cases should have been materially controlled by considerations of mere expediency or policy. I mean only, in this form, to express an earnest conviction that the court has departed from the familiar rule requiring, in the interpretation of constitutional provisions, that full effect be given to the intent with which they were adopted. . . .

Whether the legislative department of the government has transcended the limits of its constitutional powers, "Is at all times," said this court in *Fletcher* v. *Peck*, 6 Cranch, 128, "a question of much delicacy, which ought seldom, if ever, to be decided in the affirmative, in a doubtful case. * * * The opposition between the Constitution and the law should be such that the judge feels a clear and strong conviction of their incompatibility with each other." More recently in *Sinking Fund Cases*, 99 U. S., 718, we said: "It is our duty, when required in the regular course of judicial proceedings, to declare an Act of Congress void if not within the legislative power of the United States, but this declaration should never be made except in a clear case. Every possible presumption is in favor of the validity of a statute, and this continues until the contrary is shown beyond a rational doubt. One branch of the government cannot encroach on the domain of another without danger. The safety of our institutions depends in no small degree on a strict observance of this salutary rule." . . .

The 1st section of the 13th Amendment provides that "Neither slavery nor involuntary servitude, except as a punishment for crime, whereof the party shall have been duly convicted, shall exist within the United States, or any place subject to their jurisdiction." Its 2d section declares that "Congress shall have power to enforce this article by appropriate legislation." This Amendment was followed by the Civil Rights Act of April 9, 1866, which, among other things, provided that "All persons born in the United States, and not subject to any foreign power, excluding Indians not taxed, are hereby declared to be citizens of the United States." 14 Stat. at L., 27. The power of Congress, in this mode, to elevate the enfranchised race to national citizenship, was maintained by the supporters of the Act of 1866 to be as full and complete as its power, by general statute, to make the children, being of full age, of persons naturalized in this country, citizens of the United States without going through the process of naturalization. The Act of 1866, in this respect, was also likened to that of 1843, in which Congress declared "That the Stockbridge Tribe of Indians, and each and every one of them, shall be deemed to be and are hereby declared to be citizens of the United States to all intents and purposes, and shall be entitled to all the rights, privileges and immunities of such citizens, and shall in all respects be subject to the laws of the United States." If the Act of 1866 was valid in conferring national citizenship upon all embraced by its terms, then the colored race, enfranchised by the 13th Amendment, became citizens of the United States prior to the adoption of the 14th Amendment. But, in the view which I take of the present case, it is not necessary to examine this question.

The terms of the Thirteenth Amendment are absolute and universal. They embrace every race which then was, or might thereafter be, within the United States. No race, as such, can be excluded from the benefits or rights thereby conferred. Yet, it is historically true that that Amendment was suggested by the condition, in this country, of that race which had been declared, by this court, to have had—according to the opinion entertained by the most civilized portion of the white race, at the time of the adoption of the Constitution—"no rights which the white man was bound to respect," none of the privileges or immunities secured by that instrument to citizens of the United States. It had reference, in a peculiar sense, to a people which (although the larger part of them were in slavery) had been invited by an Act of Congress to aid in saving from overthrow a government which, theretofore, by all of its departments, had treated them as an inferior race, with no legal rights or privileges except such as the white race might choose to grant them.

These are the circumstances under which the Thirteenth Amendment was proposed for adoption. They are now recalled only that we may better understand what was in the minds of the people when that Amendment was considered, and what were the mischiefs to be remedied and the grievances to be redressed by its adoption.

We have seen that the power of Congress, by legislation, to enforce the master's right to have his slave delivered up on claim was *implied* from the recognition of that right in the National Constitution. But the power conferred by the Thirteenth Amendment does not rest upon implication or inference. Those who framed it were not ignorant of the discussion, covering many years of our country's history, as to the constitutional power of Congress to enact the Fugitive Slave Laws of 1793 and 1850. When, therefore, it was determined, by a change in the fundamental law, to uproot the institution of slavery wherever it existed in the land, and to establish universal freedom, there was a fixed purpose to place the authority of Congress in the premises beyond the possibility of a doubt. Therefore, *ex industria,* power to enforce the Thirteenth Amendment, by appropriate legislation, was expressly granted. Legislation for that purpose, my brethren concede, may be direct and primary. But to what specific ends may it be directed? This court has uniformly held that the National Government has the power, whether expressly given or not, to secure and protect rights conferred or guarantied by the Constitution. *U. S.* v. *Reese,* 92 U. S., 214 [XXIII, 563]; *Strauder* v. *W. Va.,* 100 U. S., 303 [XXV, 664]. That doctrine ought not now to be abandoned when the inquiry is not as to an implied power to protect the master's rights, but what may Congress, under powers expressly granted, do for the protection of freedom and the rights necessarily inhering in a state of freedom.

The 13th Amendment, it is conceded, did something more than to prohibit slavery as an *institution*, resting upon distinctions of race, and upheld by positive law. My brethren admit that it established and decreed universal *civil freedom* throughout the United States. But did the freedom thus established involve nothing more than exemption from actual slavery? Was nothing more intended than to forbid one man from owning another as property? Was it the purpose of the Nation simply to destroy the institution, and then remit the race, theretofore held in bondage, to the several States for such protection, in their civil rights, necessarily growing out of freedom, as those States, in their discretion, might choose to provide? Were the States against whose protest the institution was destroyed, to be left free, so far as national interference was concerned, to make or allow discriminations against that race, as such, in the enjoyment of those fundamental rights which by universal concession, inhere in a state of freedom? Had the 13th Amendment stopped with the sweeping declaration, in its 1st section, against the existence of slavery and involuntary servitude, except for crime, Congress would have had the power, by implication, according to the doctrines of *Prigg* v. *Commonwealth of Pennsylvania*, repeated in *Strauder* v. *West Virginia*, to protect the freedom established and, consequently, to secure the enjoyment of such civil rights as were fundamental in freedom. That it can exert its authority to that extent is made clear, and was intended to be made clear, by the express grant of power contained in the 2d section of the Amendment.

That there are burdens and disabilities which constitute badges of slavery and servitude, and that the power to enforce by appropriate legislation the 13th Amendment may be exerted by legislation of a direct and primary character, for the eradication, not simply of the institution, but of its badges and incidents, are propositions which ought to be deemed indisputable. They lie at the foundation of the Civil Rights Act of 1866. Whether that Act was authorized by the 13th Amendment alone, without the support which it subsequently received from the 14th Amendment, after the adoption of which it was re-enacted with some additions, my brethren do not consider it necessary to inquire. But I submit, with all respect to them, that its constitutionality is conclusively shown by their opinion. They admit, as I have said, that the 13th Amendment established freedom; that there are burdens and disabilities, the necessary incidents of slavery, which constitute its substance and visible form; that Congress, by the Act of 1866, passed in view of the 13th Amendment, before the 14th was adopted, undertook to remove certain burdens and disabilities, the necessary incidents of slavery, and to secure to all citizens of every race and color, and without regard to previous servitude, those fundamental rights which are the essence of civil freedom, namely, the same right to make and enforce contracts, to sue, be parties, give evidence, and to inherit, purchase, lease, sell and convey property as is enjoyed by white citizens; that under the 13th Amendment, Congress has to do with slavery and its incidents; and that legislation, so far as necessary or proper to eradicate all forms and incidents of slavery and involuntary servitude, may be direct and primary, operating upon the acts of individuals, whether sanctioned by state legislation or not. These propositions being conceded, it is impossible, as it seems to me, to question the constitutional validity of the Civil Rights Act of 1866. I do not contend that the 13th Amendment invests Congress with authority, by legislation, to define and regulate the entire body of the civil rights which citizens enjoy, or may enjoy, in the several States. But I hold, that since slavery, as the court has repeatedly declared, *Slaughter-House Cases*, 16 Wall., 36 [73 U. S., XVIII., 394]; *Strauder* v. *W. Va.*, 100 U. S., 303 [XXV., 664], was the moving or principal cause of the adoption of that Amendment, and since that institution rested wholly upon the inferiority, as a race, of those held in bondage, their freedom necessarily involved immunity from, and protection against, all discrimination against them, because of their race, in respect of such civil rights as belong to freemen of other races. Congress, therefore, under its express power to enforce that Amendment, by appropriate legislation, may enact laws to protect that people against the deprivation, *because of their race*, of any civil rights granted to other freemen in the same State; and such legislation may be of a direct and primary character, operating upon States, their offices and agents and, also, upon, at least, such individuals and corporations as exercise public functions and wield power and authority under the State. . . .

It remains now to inquire: what are the legal rights of colored persons in respect of the accommodations, privileges and facilities of public conveyances, inns and places of public amusement? . . .

In many courts it has been held that, because of the public interest in such a corporation, the land of a railroad company cannot be levied on and sold under execution by a creditor. The sum of the adjudged cases is that a railroad corporation is a governmental agency, created primarily for public purposes, and subject to be controlled for the public benefit. Upon this ground the State, when unfettered by contract, may regulate, in its discretion, the rates of fares of passengers and freight. And upon this ground, too, the State may regulate the entire management of railroads in all matters affecting the convenience and safety of the public; as, for example, by regulating speed, compelling stops of prescribed length at stations, and prohibiting discriminations and favoritism. If the corporation neglect or refuse to discharge its duties to the public, it may be coerced to do so by appropriate proceedings in the name or in behalf of the State.

Such being the relations these corporations hold to the public, it would seem that the right of a colored person to use an improved public highway, upon the terms accorded to freemen of other races, is as fundamental, in the state of freedom established in this country, as are any of the rights which my brethren concede to be so far fundamental as to be deemed the essence of civil freedom. "Personal liberty consists," says Blackstone, "in the power of locomotion, of changing situation or removing one's person to whatever places one's own inclination may direct, without restraint, unless by due course of law." But of what value is this right of locomotion, if it may be clogged by such burdens as Congress intended by the Act of 1875 to remove? They are burdens which lie at the very foundation of the institution of slavery as it once existed. They are not to be sustained, except upon the assumption that there is, in this land of universal liberty, a class which may still be discriminated against, even in respect of rights of a character so necessary and supreme, that, deprived of their enjoyment in common with others, a freeman is not only branded as one inferior and infected, but, in the competitions of life, is robbed of some of the most essential means of existence; and all this solely because they belong to a particular race which the nation has liberated. The 13th Amendment alone obliterated the race line, so far as all rights fundamental in a state of freedom are concerned.

Second, as to inns. The same general observations which have been made as to railroads are applicable to inns. The word "inn" has a technical legal signification. It means, in the Act of 1875, just what it meant at common law. A mere private boarding-house is not an inn, nor is its keeper subject to the responsibilities, or entitled to the privileges of a common innkeeper. "To constitute one an innkeeper, within the legal force of that term, he must keep a house of entertainment or lodging for all travelers or wayfarers who might choose to accept the same, being of good character or conduct." Redfield, Carriers, etc., section 575. Says *Judge* Story:

"An innkeeper may be defined to be the keeper of a common inn for the lodging and entertainment of travelers and passengers, their horses and attendants. An innkeeper is bound to take in all travelers and wayfaring persons, and to entertain them, if he can accommodate them, for a reasonable compensation; and he must guard their goods with proper diligence. * * * If an innkeeper improperly refuses to receive or provide for a guest, he is liable to be indicted therefor. * * * They (carriers of passengers) are no more at liberty to refuse a passenger, if they have sufficient room and accommodations, than an innkeeper is to refuse suitable room and accommodations to a guest." Story, Bailments, sections 475-6.

In *Rex* v. *Ivens,* 7 Carrington & Payne, 213, 32 E. C. L., 495, the court speaking by *Mr. Justice* Coleridge, said:

"An indictment lies against an innkeeper who refuses to receive a guest, he having at the time room in his house; and either the price of the guest's entertainment being tendered to him, or such circumstances occurring as will dispense with that tender. This law is founded in good sense. The innkeeper is not to select his guests. He has no right to say to one, you shall come to my inn; and to another, you shall not; as everyone coming and conducting himself in a proper manner has a right to be received; and for this purpose innkeepers are a sort of public servants, they having in return a kind of privilege of entertaining travelers and supplying them with what they want."

These authorities are sufficient to show that a keeper of an inn is in the exercise of a *quasi* public employment. The law gives him special privileges and he is charged with certain duties and responsibilities to the public. The public nature of his employment forbids him from discriminating against any person asking admission as a guest on account of the race or color of that person.

Third. As to places of public amusement. It may be argued that the managers of such places have no duties to perform with which the public are, in any legal sense, concerned, or with which the public have any right to interfere; and that the exclusion of a black man from a place of public amusement, on account of his race; or the denial to him, on that ground, of equal accommodations at such places, violates no legal right for the vindication of which he may invoke the aid of the courts. My answer is, that places of public amusement, within the meaning of the Act of 1875, are such as are established and maintained under direct license of the law. The authority to establish and maintain them comes from the public. The colored race is a part of that public. The local government granting the license represents them as well as all other races within its jurisdiction. A license from the public, to establish a place of public amusement, imports, in law, equality of right, at such places, among all the members of that public. This must be so, unless it be— which I deny—that the common municipal government of all the people may, in the exertion of its powers, conferred for the benefit of all, discriminate or authorize discrimination against a particular race, solely because of its former condition of servitude.

I also submit, whether it can be said—in view of the doctrines of this court as announced in *Munn* v. *Illinois*, 94 U. S., 113 [XXIII., 77], and re-affirmed in *Peik* v. *C. & N. W. R. Co.*, 94 U. S., 164 [XXIII., 97]—that the management of places of public amusement is a purely private matter, with which government has no rightful concern? In the *Munn Case* the question was whether the State of Illinois could fix, by law, the maximum of charges for the storage of grain in certain warehouses in that State, *the private property of individual citizens.* After quoting a remark attributed to *Lord Chief Justice* Hale, to the effect that when private property is "affected with a public interest it ceases to be *juris privati* only," the court says:

"Property does become clothed with a public interest when used in a manner to make it of public consequence and affect the community at large. When, therefore, one devotes his property to a use in which the public has an interest, he, in effect, grants to the public an interest in that use and must submit to be controlled by the public for the common good to the extent of the interest he has thus created. He may withdraw his grant by discontinuing the use, but, so long as he maintains the use, he must submit to the control."

The doctrines of *Munn* v. *Illinois* have never been modified by this court, and I am justified, upon the authority of that case, in saying that places of public amusement, conducted under the authority of the law, are clothed with a public interest, because used in a manner to make them of public consequence and to affect the community at large. The law may, therefore, regulate, to some extent, the mode in which they shall be conducted and, consequently, the public have rights in respect of such places, which may be vindicated by the law. It is, consequently, not a matter purely of private concern.

Congress has not, in these matters, entered the domain of state control and supervision. It does not, as I have said, assume to prescribe the general conditions and limitations under which inns, public conveyances and places of public amusement, shall be conducted or managed. It simply declares, in effect, that since the Nation has established universal freedom in this country, for all time, there shall be no discrimination, based merely upon race or color, in respect of the accommodations and advantages of public conveyances, inns and places of public amusement.

I am of the opinion that such discrimination practiced by corporations and individuals in the exercise of their public or *quasi* public functions is a badge of servitude, the imposition of which Congress may prevent under its power, by appropriate legislation, to enforce the 13th Amendment; and, consequently, without reference to its enlarged power under the 14th Amendment, the Act of March 1, 1875, is not, in my judgment, repugnant to the Constitution.

It remains now to consider these cases with reference to the power Congress has possessed since the adoption of the 14th Amendment. Much that has been said as to the power of Congress under the 13th Amendment is applicable to this branch of the discussion, and will not be repeated.

Before the adoption of the recent Amendments, it had become, as we have seen, the established doctrine of this court that negroes, whose ancestors had been imported and sold as slaves, could not become citizens of a State, or even of the United States, with the rights and privileges guarantied to citizens by the National Constitution; further, that one might have all the rights and privileges of a citizen of a State without being a citizen in the sense in which that word was used in the National Constitution, and without being entitled to the privileges and immunities of citizens of the several States. Still further; between the adoption of the 13th Amendment and the proposal by Congress of the 14th Amendment, on June 16, 1866, the statute-books of several of the States, as we have seen, had become loaded down with enactments which, under the guise of Apprentice, Vagrant and Contract Regulations, sought to keep the colored race in a condition, practically, of servitude. It was openly announced that whatever might be the rights which persons of that race had, as freemen, under the guaranties of the National Constitution, they could not become citizens of a State, with the privileges belonging to citizens, except by the consent of such State; consequently, that their civil rights, as citizens of the State, depended entirely upon state legislation. To meet this new peril to the black race, that the purposes of the Nation might not be doubted or defeated, and by way of further enlargement of the power of Congress, the 14th Amendment was proposed for adoption.

Remembering that this court, in the *Slaughter-House Cases*, declared that the one pervading purpose found in all the recent Amendments, lying at the foundation of each, and without which none of them would have been suggested, was "The freedom of the slave race, the security and firm establishment of that freedom, and the protection of the newly-made freeman and citizen from the oppression of those who had formerly exercised unlimited dominion over him"—that each Amendment was addressed primarily to the grievances of that race—let us proceed to consider the language of the 14th Amendment.

Its 1st and 5th sections are in these words:

"Sec. 1. All persons born or naturalized in the United States, and subject to the jurisdiction thereof, are citizens of the United States and of the State wherein they reside. No State shall make or enforce any law which shall abridge the privileges or immunities of citizens of the United States; nor shall any State deprive any person of life, liberty or property, without due process of law; nor deny to any person within its jurisdiction the equal protection of the laws.

*   *   *   *   *   *

Sec. 5. That Congress shall have power to enforce, by appropriate legislation, the provisions of this article."

It was adjudged in *Strauder* v. *West Virginia,* 100 U. S., 303 [XXV., 664] and *Ex parte Virginia,* 100 U. S., 339 [676], and my brethren concede, that positive rights and privileges were intended to be secured, and are in fact secured, by the 14th Amendment.

But when, under what circumstances and to what extent, may Congress, by means of legislation, exert its power to enforce the provisions of this Amendment? The theory of the opinion of the majority of the court—the foundation upon which their reasoning seems to rest—is, that the General Government cannot, in advance of hostile state laws or hostile state proceedings, actively interfere for the protection of any of the rights, privileges and immunities secured by the 14th Amendment. It is said that such rights, privileges and immunities are secured by way of *prohibition* against state laws and state proceedings affecting such rights and privileges, and by power given to Congress to legislate for the purpose of carrying *such prohibition* into effect; also, that congressional legislation must necessarily be predicated upon such supposed state laws or state proceedings, and be directed to the correction of their operation and effect.

In illustration of its position, the court refers to the clause of the Constitution forbidding the passage by a State of any law impairing the obligation of contracts. That clause does not, I submit, furnish a proper illustration of the scope and effect of the 5th section of the 14th Amendment. No express power is given Congress to enforce, by primary direct legislation, the prohibition upon state laws impairing the obligation of contracts. Authority is, indeed, conferred to enact all necessary and proper laws for carrying into execution the enumerated powers of Congress and all other powers vested by the Constitution in the Government of the United States or in any department or officer thereof. And, as heretofore shown, there is also, by necessary implication, power in Congress, by legislation, to protect a right derived from the National Constitution. But a prohibition upon a State is not a *power* in *Congress* or *in the National Government*. It is simply a *denial* of power to the *State*. And the only mode in which the inhibition upon state laws impairing the obligation of contracts can be enforced, is, indirectly, through the courts, in suits where the parties raise some question as to the constitutional validity of such laws. The judicial power of the United States extends to such suits for the reason that they are suits arising under the Constitution. The 14th Amendment presents the first instance in our history of the investiture of Congress with affirmative power, by *legislation,* to *enforce* an express prohibition upon the States. It is not said that the *judicial* power of the Nation may be exerted for the enforcement of that Amendment. No enlargement of the judicial power was required, for it is clear that had the 5th section of the 14th Amendment been entirely omitted, the judiciary could have stricken down all state laws and nullified all state proceedings in hostility to rights and privileges secured or recognized by that Amendment. The power given, is in terms, by congressional *legislation,* to enforce the provisions of the Amendment.

The assumption that this Amendment consists wholly of prohibitions upon state laws and state proceedings in hostility to its provisions, is unauthorized by its language. The first clause of the 1st section—"All persons born or naturalized in the United States, and subject to the jurisdiction thereof, are citizens of the United States, and of the State wherein they reside"—is of a distinctly affirmative character. In its application to the colored race, previously liberated, it created and granted, as well citizenship of the United States, as citizenship of the State in which they respectively resided. It introduced all of that race, whose ancestors had been imported and sold as slaves, at once, into the political community known as the "People of the United States." They became, instantly, citizens of the United States, *and* of their respective States. Further, they were brought, by this supreme act of the Nation, within the direct operation of that provision of the Constitution which declares that "The citizens of each State shall be entitled to all privileges and immunities of citizens in the several States." Art. 4, sec. 2.

The citizenship thus acquired, by that race, in virtue of an affirmative grant from the Nation, may be protected, not alone by the judicial branch of the government, but by congressional legislation of a primary direct character; this, because the power of Congress is not restricted to the enforcement of prohibitions upon state laws or state action. It is, in terms distinct and positive, to enforce "the *provisions* of *this article*" of Amendment; not simply those of a prohibitive character, but the provisions— *all* of the provisions—affirmative and prohibitive, of the Amendment. It is, therefore, a grave misconception to suppose that the 5th section of the Amendment has reference exclusively to express prohibitions upon state laws or state action. If any right was created by that Amendment, the grant of power, through appropriate legislation, to enforce its provisions, authorizes Congress, by means of legislation, operating throughout the entire Union, to guard, secure and protect that right.

It is, therefore, an essential inquiry what, if any, right, privilege or immunity was given, by the Nation, to colored persons, when they were made citizens of the State in which they reside? Did the constitutional grant of state citizenship to that race, of its own force, invest them with any rights, privileges and immunities whatever? That they became entitled, upon the adoption of the 14th Amendment, "to all privileges and immunities of citizens in the several States," within the meaning of section 2 of article 4 of the Constitution, no one, I suppose, will for a moment question. What are the privileges and immunities to which, by that clause of the Constitution they became entitled? To this it may be answered, generally, upon the authority of the adjudged cases, that they are those which are fundamental in citizenship in a free republican government, such as are "common to the citizens in the latter States under their constitutions and laws by virtue of their being citizens." Of that provision it has been said, with the approval of this court, that no other one in the Constitution has tended so strongly to constitute the citizens of the United States one people. *Ward* v. *Maryland*, 12 Wall., 418; *Corfield* v. *Coryell*, 4 Wash. C. C., 371; *Paul* v. *Va.*, 8 Wall., 168; *Slaughter-House Cases*, 16 Id., 36.

Although this court has wisely forborne any attempt, by a comprehensive definition, to indicate all of the privileges and immunities to which the citizen of a State is entitled, of right, when within the jurisdiction of other States, I hazard nothing, in view of former adjudications, in saying that no State can sustain her denial to colored citizens of other States, while within her limits, of privileges or immunities, fundamental in republican citizenship, upon the ground that she accords such privileges and immunities only to her white citizens and withholds them from her colored citizens. . . .

The language of this court with reference to the 15th Amendment, adds to the force of this view. In *United States* v. *Cruikshank*, it was said: "In *United States* v. *Reese*, 92 U. S., 214, we held that the 15th Amendment has invested the citizens of the United States with a new constitutional right, which is exemption from discrimination in the exercise of the elective franchise, on account of race, color or previous condition of servitude. From this it appears that the right of suffrage is not a necessary attribute of national citizenship, but that exemption from discrimination in the exercise of that right on account of race, etc., is. The right to vote in the States comes from the States; but the right of exemption from the prohibited discrimination comes from the United States. The first has not been granted or secured by the Constitution of the United States, but the last has been."

Here, in language at once clear and forcible, is stated the principle for which I contend. It can scarcely be claimed that exemption from race discrimination, in respect of civil rights, against those to whom state citizenship was granted by the Nation, is any less, for the colored race, a new constitutional right, derived from and secured by the National Constitution, than is exemption from such discrimination in the exercise of the elective franchise. It cannot be that the latter is an attribute of national citizenship, while the other is not essential in national citizenship, or fundamental in state citizenship.

If, then, exemption from discrimination, in respect of civil rights, is a new constitutional right, secured by the grant of state citizenship to colored citizens of the United States—and I do not see how this can now be questioned—why may not the Nation, by means of its own legislation of a primary direct character, guard, protect and enforce that right? It is a right and privilege which the nation conferred. It did not come from the States in which those colored citizens reside. It has been the established doctrine of this court during all its history, accepted as essential to the national supremacy, that Congress, in the absence of a positive delegation of power to the State Legislatures, may, by its own legislation, enforce and protect any right derived from or created by the National Constitution. It was so declared in *Prigg* v. *Commonwealth of Pennsylvania*. It was reiterated in *United States* v. *Reese*, 92 U. S., 214, where the court said that "Rights and immunities created by and dependent upon the Constitution of the United States can be protected by Congress. The form and manner of the protection may be such as Congress, in the legitimate exercise of its discretion, shall provide. These may be varied to meet the necessities of the particular right to be protected." It was distinctly re-affirmed in *Strauder* v. *West Virginia*, 100 U. S., 310 [*supra*], where we said that "A right or immunity created by the Constitution or only guarantied by it, even without any express delegation of power, may be protected by Congress." How then can it be claimed in view of the declarations of this court in former cases, that exemption of colored citizens, within their States, from race discrimination, in respect of the civil rights of citizens, is not an immunity created or derived from the National Constitution?

This court has always given a broad and liberal construction to the Constitution, so as to enable Congress, by legislation, to enforce rights secured by that instrument. The legislation which Congress may enact, in execution of its power to enforce the provisions of this Amendment, is such as may be appropriate to protect the right granted. The word "appropriate" was undoubtedly used with reference to its meaning, as established by repeated decisions of this court. Under given circumstances, that which the court characterizes as corrective legislation might be deemed by Congress appropriate and entirely sufficient. Under other circumstances primary direct legislation may be required. But it is for Congress, not the judiciary, to say that legislation is appropriate; that is, best adapted to the end to be attained. The judiciary may not, with safety to our institutions, enter the domain of legislative discretion, and dictate the means which Congress shall employ in the exercise of its granted powers. That would be sheer usurpation of the functions of a co-ordinate department, which, if often repeated, and permanently acquiesced in, would work a radical change in our system of government. In *United States* v. *Fisher,* 2 Cranch, 358, the court said that "Congress must possess the choice of means, and must be empowered to use any means which are in fact conducive to the exercise of a power granted by the Constitution." "The sound construction of the Constitution," said *Chief Justice* Marshall, "must allow to the National Legislature that discretion, with respect to the means by which the powers it confers are to be carried into execution, which will enable that body to perform the high duties assigned to it in the manner most beneficial to the people. Let the end be legitimate, let it be within the scope of the Constitution, and all means which are appropriate, which are plainly adapted to that end, which are not prohibited, but consist with the letter and spirit of the Constitution, are constitutional." *McCulloch* v. *Maryland,* 4 Wh., 421.

Must these rules of construction be now abandoned? Are the powers of the National Legislature to be restrained in proportion as the rights and privileges, derived from the Nation, are valuable? Are constitutional provisions, enacted to secure the dearest rights of freemen and citizens, to be subjected to that rule of construction, applicable to private instruments, which requires that the words to be interpreted must be taken most strongly against those who employ them? Or, shall it be remembered that "A constitution of government, founded by the people for themselves and their posterity, and for objects of the most momentous nature—for perpetual union, for the establishment of justice, for the general welfare, and for a perpetuation of the blessings of liberty—necessarily requires that every interpretation of its powers should have a constant reference to these objects? No interpretation of the words in which those powers are granted can be a sound one, which narrows down their ordinary import so as to defeat those objects." 1 Story, Const., sec. 422.

The opinion of the court, as I have said, proceeds upon the ground that the power of Congress to legislate for the protection of the rights and privileges secured by the 14th Amendment cannot be brought into activity except with the view, and as it may become necessary, to correct and annul state laws and state proceedings in hostility to such rights and privileges. In the absence of state laws or state action adverse to such rights and privileges, the Nation may not actively interfere for their protection and security, even against corporations and individuals exercising public or *quasi* public functions. Such I understand to be the position of my brethren. If the grant to colored citizens of the United States of citizenship in their respective States, imports exemption from race discrimination, in their States, in respect of such civil rights as belong to citizenship, then, to hold that the Amendment remits that right to the States for their protection, primarily, and stays the hands of the Nation, until it is assailed by state laws or state proceedings, is to adjudge that the Amendment, so far from enlarging the powers of Congress—as we have heretofore said it did—not only curtails them, but reverses the policy which the General Government has pursued from its very organization. Such an interpretation of the Amendment is a denial to Congress of the power, by appropriate legislation, to enforce one of its provisions. In view of the circumstances under which the recent Amendments were incorporated into the Constitution, and especially in view of the peculiar character of the new rights they created and secured, it ought not to be presumed that the General Government has abdicated its authority, by national legislation, direct and primary in its character to guard and protect privileges and immunities secured by that instrument. Such an interpretation of the Constitution ought not to be accepted if it be possible to avoid it. Its acceptance would lead to this anomalous result: that whereas, prior to the Amendments, Congress, with the sanction of this court, passed the most stringent laws—operating directly and primarily upon States and their offices and agents, as well as upon individuals—in vindication of slavery and the right of the master, it may not now, by legislation of a like primary and direct character, guard, protect and secure the freedom established, and the most essential right of the citizenship granted, by the constitutional amendments. With all respect for the opinion of others, I insist that the National Legislature may, without transcending the limits of the Constitution, do for human liberty and the fundamental rights of American citizenship, what it did, with the sanction of this court, for the protection of slavery and the rights of the masters of fugitive slaves. . . .

In every material sense applicable to the practical enforcement of the 14th Amendment, railroad corporations, keepers of inns and managers of places of public amusement are agents or instrumentalities of the State, because they are charged with duties to the public, and are amenable, in respect of their duties and functions, to governmental regulation. It seems to me that, within the principle settled in *Ex parte Virginia*, a denial, by these instrumentalities of the State, to the citizen, because of his race, of that equality of civil rights secured to him by law, is a denial by the State, within the meaning of the 14th Amendment. If it be not, then that race is left, in respect of the civil rights in question, practically at the mercy of corporations and individuals wielding power under the States.

But the court says that Congress did not, in the Act of 1866, assume, under the authority given by the 13th Amendment, to adjust what may be called the social rights of men and races in the community. I agree that government has nothing to do with social, as distinguished from technically legal, rights of individuals. No government ever has brought or ever can bring its people into social intercourse against their wishes. Whether one person will permit or maintain social relations with another is a matter with which government has no concern. I agree that if one citizen chooses not to hold social intercourse with another, he is not and cannot be made amenable to the law for his conduct in that regard; for even upon grounds of race, no legal right of a citizen is violated by the refusal of others to maintain merely social relations with him. What I affirm is that no State, nor the officers of any State, nor any corporation or individual wielding power under state authority for the public benefit or the public convenience, can, consistently either with the freedom established by the fundamental law, or with that equality of civil rights which now belongs to every citizen, discriminate against freemen or citizens, in those rights, because of their race, or because they once labored under the disabilities of slavery imposed upon them as a race. The rights which Congress, by the Act of 1875, endeavored to secure and protect, are legal, not social rights. The right, for instance, of a colored citizen to use the accommodations of a public highway, upon the same terms as are permitted to white citizens, is no more a social right than his right, under the law, to use the public streets of a city or a town, or a turnpike road, or a public market, or a postoffice, or his right to sit in a public building with others, of whatever race, for the purpose of hearing the political questions of the day discussed. Scarcely a day passes without our seeing in this court room citizens of the white and black races sitting side by side, watching the progress of our business. It would never occur to anyone that the presence of a colored citizen in a courthouse, or court room, was an invasion of the social rights of white persons who may frequent such places. And yet, such a suggestion would be quite as sound in law—I say it with all respect— as is the suggestion that the claim of a colored citizen to use, upon the same terms as is permitted to white citizens, the accommodations of public highways, or public inns, or places of public amusement, established under the license of the law, is an invasion of the social rights of the white race.

The court, in its opinion, reserves the question whether Congress, in the exercise of its power to regulate commerce amongst the several States, might or might not pass a law regulating rights in public conveyances passing from one State to another. I beg to suggest that that precise question was substantially presented here in the only one of these cases relating to railroads —*Robinson and Wife* v. *Memphis & Charleston Railroad Company.* In that case it appears that Mrs. Robinson, a citizen of Mississippi, purchased a railroad ticket entitling her to be carried from Grand Junction, Tennessee, to Lynchburg, Virginia. Might not the Act of 1875 be maintained in that case, as applicable at least to commerce between the States, notwithstanding it does not, upon its face, profess to have been passed in pursuance of the power of Congress to regulate commerce? Has it ever been held that the judiciary should overturn a statute, because the legislative department did not accurately recite therein the particular provision of the Constitution authorizing its enactment? We have often enforced municipal bonds in aid of railroad subscriptions, where they failed to recite the statute authorizing their issue, but recited one which did not sustain their validity. The inquiry in such cases has been: was there, in any statute, authority for the execution of the bonds? Upon this branch of the case, it may be remarked that the State of Louisiana, in 1869, passed a statute giving to passengers, without regard to race or color, equality of right in the accommodations of railroad and street cars, steamboats or other water crafts, stage-coaches, omnibuses or other vehicles. But in *Hall* v. *De Cuir*, 95 U. S., 487, that Act was pronounced unconstitutional so far as it related to commerce between the States, this court saying that "If the public good requires such legislation it must come from Congress, and not from the States." I suggest, that it may become a pertinent inquiry whether Congress may, in the exertion of its power to regulate commerce among the States, enforce among passengers on public conveyances, equality of right, without regard to race, color or previous condition of servitude, if it be true—which I do not admit—that such legislation would be an interference by government with the social rights of the people.

My brethren say, that when a man has emerged from slavery, and by the aid of beneficent legislation has shaken off the inseparable concomitants of that state, there must be some stage in the progress of his elevation when he takes the rank of a mere citizen, and ceases to be the special favorite of the laws, and when his rights as a citizen, or a man, are to be protected in the ordinary modes by which other men's rights are protected. It is, I submit, scarcely just to say that the colored race has been the special favorite of the laws. The Statute of 1875, now adjusted to be unconstitutional, is for the benefit of citizens of every race and color. What the Nation, through Congress, has sought to accomplish in reference to that race, is—what had already been done in every State of the Union for the white race—to secure and protect rights belonging to them as freemen and citizens; nothing more. It was not deemed enough "to help the feeble up, but to support him after." The one underlying purpose of congressional legislation has been to enable the black race to take the rank of mere citizens. The difficulty has been to compel a recognition of the legal right of the black race to take the rank of citizens, and to secure the enjoyment of privileges belonging, under the law, to them as a component part of the people for whose welfare and happiness government is ordained. At every step, in this direction, the Nation has been confronted with class tyranny, which a contemporary English historian says is, of all tyrannies, the most intolerable, "For it is ubiquitous in its operation, and weighs, perhaps, most heavily on those whose obscurity or distance would withdraw them from the notice of a single despot." Today, it is the colored race which is denied, by corporations and individuals wielding public authority, rights fundamental in their freedom and citizenship. At some future time, it may be that some other race will fall under the ban of race discrimination. If the constitutional Amendments be enforced, according to the intent with which, as I conceive, they were adopted, there cannot be in this Republic, any class of human beings in practical subjection to another class, with power in the latter to dole out to the former just such privileges as they may choose to grant. The supreme law of the land has decreed that no authority shall be exercised in this country upon the basis of discrimination, in respect of civil rights, against freemen and citizens because of their race, color or previous condition of servitude. To that decree—for the due enforcement of which, by appropriate legislation, Congress has been invested with express power—every one must bow, whatever may have been, or whatever now are, his individual views as to the wisdom or policy, either of the recent changes in the fundamental law, or of the legislation which has been enacted to give them effect.

For the reasons stated I feel constrained to withhold my assent to the opinion of the court.

22

Grover Cleveland and Laissez-Faire

The President Vetoes the Texas Seed Bill

Grover Cleveland (1837-1908) was chosen governor of New York in 1882, winning as a good-government Democrat over a machine Republican by a record majority; his victory was probably the chief single factor that converted Congressmen to vote for the Pendleton Act (see No. 20). As the merit system covered more and more of the Federal civil service, it became more difficult to sustain the political parties by spoils techniques. Party organizations relied increasingly on contributions from big business, and in business circles Grover Cleveland was regarded as a safe man. His conservatism won him election as President in 1884. The following veto, written under circumstances explained in the message, sets forth Cleveland's view of public policy in phrasing that became part of the cant of politicians: ". . . though the people support the Government the Government should not support the people." See Allan Nevins, *Grover Cleveland: A Study in Courage* (1933).

Grover Cleveland, Message of February 16, 1887, in James D. Richardson (ed.), *Messages and Papers of the Presidents,* vol. 8 (1900), pp. 557-558.

To the House of Representatives:
I return without my approval House bill No. 10203, entitled "An act to enable the Commissioner of Agriculture to make a special distribution of seeds in the drought-stricken counties of Texas, and making an appropriation therefor."
It is represented that a long-continued and extensive drought has existed in certain portions of the State of Texas, resulting in a failure of crops and consequent distress and destitution.

Though there has been some difference in statements concerning the extent of the people's needs in the localities thus affected, there seems to be no doubt that there has existed a condition calling for relief; and I am willing to believe that, notwithstanding the aid already furnished, a donation of seed grain to the farmers located in this region, to enable them to put in new crops, would serve to avert a continuance or return of an unfortunate blight.

And yet I feel obliged to withhold my approval of the plan, as proposed by this bill, to indulge a benevolent and charitable sentiment through the appropriation of public funds for that purpose.

I can find no warrant for such an appropriation in the Constitution, and I do not believe that the power and duty of the General Government ought to be extended to the relief of individual suffering which is in no manner properly related to the public service or benefit. A prevalent tendency to disregard the limited mission of this power and duty should, I think, be steadfastly resisted, to the end that the lesson should be constantly enforced that though the people support the Government the Government should not support the people.

The friendliness and charity of our countrymen can always be relied upon to relieve their fellow-citizens in misfortune. This has been repeatedly and quite lately demonstrated. Federal aid in such cases encourages the expectation of paternal care on the part of the Government and weakens the sturdiness of our national character, while it prevents the indulgence among our people of that kindly sentiment and conduct which strengthens the bonds of a common brotherhood.

It is within my personal knowledge that individual aid has to some extent already been extended to the sufferers mentioned in this bill. The failure of the proposed appropriation of $10,000 additional to meet their remaining wants will not necessarily result in continued distress if the emergency is fully made known to the people of the country.

It is here suggested that the Commissioner of Agriculture is annually directed to expend a large sum of money for the purchase, propagation, and distribution of seeds and other things of this description, two-thirds of which are, upon the request of

Senators, Representatives, and Delegates in Congress, supplied to them for distribution among their constituents.

The appropriation of the current year for this purpose is $100,000, and it will probably be no less in the appropriation for the ensuing year. I understand that a large quantity of grain is furnished for such distribution, and it is supposed that this free apportionment among their neighbors is a privilege which may be waived by our Senators and Representatives.

If sufficient of them should request the Commissioner of Agriculture to send their shares of the grain thus allowed them to the suffering farmers of Texas, they might be enabled to sow their crops, the constituents for whom in theory this grain is intended could well bear the temporary deprivation, and the donors would experience the satisfaction attending deeds of charity.

23

A Senator Discusses the Trust Problem

Orville Platt Speaks Against John Sherman's Bill

Orville H. Platt (1827-1905) was one of the quartet of Republicans who pretty much dominated the Senate for fifteen years. Much of their power derived from their seniority: William B. Allison (Iowa) entered the Senate in 1873; Platt (Connecticut) in 1879; Nelson W. Aldrich (Rhode Island) in 1881; John C. Spooner (Wisconsin) in 1885. But they also had varied abilities that supplemented each other, and Platt's specialty was his skill as a strategist of government. The following speech in 1890 against a much-amended antitrust bill sponsored by Senator John Sherman of Ohio illustrates the point, for it stakes out the next twenty years of the law's judicial history. Note the contentions that (1) excess capacity in many industries had resulted in "this deadly, brutal warfare which is called competition"; (2) Congress can constitutionally legislate only about transportation because manufacturing is not a part of interstate commerce, an argument that the Supreme Court accepted briefly in *United States* v. *E. C. Knight Company* (156 U.S. 1) in 1895; and (3) it is moral and should be legal for producers to combine to secure "fair and reasonable prices for their goods." The final doctrine emanated, in the Standard Oil and American Tobacco Cases of 1911, in the famous Rule of Reason by which the Sherman Anti-Trust Act was construed as outlawing only "unreasonable" restraints of trade. See Matthew Josephson, *The Politicos, 1865-1896* (1938), still the best overall analysis of national politics in the period. See also *United States* v. *E. C. Knight Company* (156 U.S. 1), 1895.

Speech by Orville H. Platt, March 27, 1890, *Congressional Record,* vol. 21, part 3, pp. 2729-2731.

M R. PLATT. MR. PRESIDENT, THE FIRST SECTION OF
this bill, which I am now commenting on, is complicated and involved, and I desire to read, leaving out some
things from this section, but leaving out nothing which in any
way changes the effect or the real intent and meaning of the
bill as applied to the persons of whom I am now speaking, and I
beg Senators to listen.

The bill provides that—

All arrangements, contracts, agreements between two or more
persons, which tend to prevent full and free competition in articles
of growth, production, or manufacture of any State or Territory of the
United States with similar articles of the growth, production, or
manufacture by any other State or Territory, and all arrangements
between such persons which tend to advance the cost to the consumer
of any such article are hereby declared to be against public policy,
unlawful, and void.

That is the real meaning of this bill. That is, all arrangements
whatever looking to the objects which are pointed out in the bill,
between any two or more persons, are unlawful. In other words,
this bill proceeds upon the false assumption that all competition
is beneficent to the country, and that every advance of price is an
injury to the country. That is the assumption upon which this
bill proceeds. There never was a greater fallacy in the world.
Competition, which this bill provides for as between any two
persons, must be full and free. Unrestricted competition is brutal
warfare, and injurious to the whole country. The great corporations of this country, the great monopolies of this country
are every one of them built upon the graves of weaker competitors that have been forced to their death by remorseless
competition. I am entirely sick of this idea that the lower the
prices are the better for the country, and that any effort to
advance prices, no matter how low they may be, and that any
arrangement between persons engaged in business to advance
prices, no matter how low they may be, is a wrong and ought
to be repressed and punished.

The true theory of this matter is that prices should be just
and reasonable and fair, that prices, no matter who is the

producer or what the article, should be such as will render a fair return to all persons engaged in its production, a fair profit on capital, on labor, and on everything else that enters into its production. When the price of any commodity, I do not care whether it is wheat or iron, I do not care whether it is corn or silverware—whenever the price of any commodity is forced below that standard, the whole country suffers. We have been running to bankruptcy and ruin and distress. But the theory of this bill is that, no matter how much the price may have been depressed, no matter how losing the business may be, the parties engaged in it must have no understanding between themselves by which they will come together and say that they will obtain a fair and a fairly remunerative price for the article which they produce. That is wicked, the bill says.

We have five thousand manufacturing establishments in the State of Connecticut, or had by the last census, and I think that gentlemen will hunt up and down that State and its borders without finding many of the trusts at which it is said this bill is aimed.

MR. GEORGE. Without finding any?

MR. PLATT. I said without finding "many" of the trusts.

MR. GEORGE. I thought the gentleman said "any."

MR. PLATT. Without finding many of the trusts at which this bill is aimed.

What I mean to say is that the great bulk of manufacturing in Connecticut, both as to the establishments and the amount of production, is carried on by men and associations of comparatively small capital, most of whom have sprung up from the ranks of labor themselves, and who have largely associated with laborers in engaging in their business. I do not deny that there may be some trusts there; but the bill which is aimed at those trusts reaches every arrangement, all arrangements, innocent or guilty, which those persons may make under any circumstances to preserve themselves from ruin and bankruptcy. It reaches more than that: every merchant in the State of Connecticut; all business in which persons who are engaged in this deadly, brutal warfare which is called competition think it for their advantage to come together and obtain fair prices for the articles in which they are dealing.

MR. HAWLEY. Will my colleague allow me to ask him a question? He says the bill reaches all those corporations and individuals. I want to know how it can reach every citizen in Connecticut whose bargain shall begin and be carried on and finally consummated in the midst of that State?

Mr. PLATT. I will show my colleague.

Mr. HAWLEY. How can it?

Mr. PLATT. I am not speaking about that. I find it is very unpopular here to refer to any proposed act as not being authorized by the Constitution of the United States.

Mr. GEORGE. And unfashionable.

Mr. PLATT. And I find that I am liable to considerable criticism if I make any argument against this bill because it transcends the constitutional power of Congress, and so I am taking the bill as it is on the face of it.

Mr. GEORGE. Will the Senator allow me just one word?

Mr. PLATT. Certainly.

Mr. GEORGE. I think the Senator ought to share the unpopularity of criticising the bill as being against the Constitution as well as some of the balance of us who have convictions that compel us to make those criticisms.

Mr. PLATT. I am not by any means a very strict constructionist of the Constitution; I think in a great many matters I am deemed to be extremely liberal in my views of the powers which Congress may exercise under the Constitution of the United States; but at the risk of unpopularity and of being declared to be unfashionable and of being criticised, I will say that in this whole bill, so far as I read it, there is but one constitutional provision, and that is that provision of the Senator from Texas [Mr. REAGAN] in his amendment which confines the bills to persons engaged in transportation—for that is the effect of his amendment—that uproots the interstate-commerce law, drives that by the board, repeals that law. If it be thought by the Senate that that is good policy, I do not object to that on the ground of unconstitutionality.

I am being diverted for the moment from the answer to the question asked by my colleague, but while I am diverted I desire to say this: It is not two years since this Senate was exercised over the idea that there must be something done to prevent the ruinous rate wars between railroads or that impending disaster was to be precipitated upon the country. And so we provided, in the interstate-commerce act, provisions which we thought would prevent these ruinous rate wars. We agreed then that ruinous competition among railroads was not for the interest of any portion of the people of this country. We provided that if they advanced rates in their joint tariffs they should give ten day's notice; that if they reduced rates by their joint tariffs they should give three days' notice. But here comes this amendment of the Senator from Texas, who has been godfather at least to the interstate-commerce act, and sweeps that all away and says that if those engaged in making joint tariffs shall ever advance a rate they shall go to State prison and pay $10,000 fine. That is the effect of the amendment of the Senator from Texas.

Now let me return to the question asked me by my colleague. He asked me how it could be done. I do not think it can, but I propose to deal with this bill as it reads. It seizes, lays hold of all articles of growth, production, or manufacture of any State which compete with similar articles of growth, production, or manufacture of any other State. That is what it attempts to lay its hand upon, and that is all-inclusive. It takes all articles. You can scarcely find an article of comerce, an article of merchandise in any State which does not compete with similar articles which are the growth, production, or manufacture of another State. So then, this bill sweeps in all business. It sweeps in the dealing in every article; it sweeps in the transactions of every merchant; it sweeps in the transactions of every manufacturer and of every producer. What does it say shall happen, what does it say is wrong with regard to such articles? for it includes all articles of trade. That all arrangements and agreements between two or more persons which tend to advance the cost to the consumer of any such article is "hereby declared to be against public policy, unlawful, and void."

Now, I want to illustrate a little. I have just received from the commissioner of labor in the State of Connecticut advance sheets of his forthcoming report. He has investigated a great many industries of the State of Connecticut. He has taken representative establishments in the State of Connecticut, and he has tabulated under different heads the result of their business operations in different years. By this report I want to show what the result was, during the year 1887, in eight representative woolen establishments in the State of Connecticut. They employed 1,967 persons. They had a capital of $2,904,404. The value of their manufactured goods was $3,299,871.21. The value of the stock and materials was $2,076,198.47. The cost of manufacture, less rent, interest, and taxes was $1,134,058.76. Rent and interest and taxes were $94,585.59. Superintendence, including all non-producers, was $96,696.66. Wages paid were $664,143.77. The gross profits were $89,613.98. There were no net profits, but a net loss of $4,971.61.

Mr. GEORGE. A loss of that much?

Mr. PLATT. The net loss in the eight establishments was $4,-971.61.

I allude to this for the purpose of showing that here were eight representative woolen establishments in the State of Connecticut that, not taking into account the matter of loss by bad debts, lost in that year's business in the aggregate $4,971.61—not a great loss I will agree.

Mr. GEORGE. Is that on the supposition that they collected every debt?

Mr. PLATT. That is upon the supposition that they collected every debt. Nothing is allowed here for loss by bad debts.

Mr. FRYE. Nothing for the depreciation of the property in the mill, either.

Mr. PLATT. No; and I think I am justified in saying that these concerns have since lost many thousand dollars by a failure in New York, but I speak of it for this: They are running their business at a loss; they are making articles to which this bill refers; and this bill says that if those eight men should combine to get a fair, living profit upon their manufacture, that contract, that agreement is against public policy, unlawful and void. That is but an illustration. It runs all through the business of my State and of the United States.

I do not like to vote against this bill. I believe that there are combinations in this country which are criminal, but I believe that every man in business—I do not care whether he is a farmer, a laborer, a miner, a sailor, a manufacturer, a merchant—has a right, a legal and a moral right, to obtain a fair profit upon his business and his work; and if he is driven by fierce competition to a spot where his business is unremunerative, I believe it is his right to combine for the purpose of raising prices until they shall be fair and remunerative. This bill makes no distinction. It says that every combination which has the effect in any way to advance prices is illegal and void. The Senator from Ohio in the first speech which he made here admitted that there were combinations in which there was no wrong, and yet he leveled his bill at them equally with the combinations which are doing wrong.

I do not believe there is in this country among any class of people a real desire that anybody shall do business without receiving a fair profit, without receiving a fair remuneration for the capital, skill, and work employed in carrying on the business, and I do not believe that there is any class of people in this country who, when they face this false assumption that cheap prices are the great, beneficent thing for the country and think of it, will agree to that proposition. Whenever the price of anything is below what it costs to produce it, it ought to be raised, and any combination for the purpose of raising it to a point where the price is fair and reasonable ought not to be condemned; it ought to be encouraged. It will not do, because a few concerns in this country are attempting to put prices where they are unreasonable, to enrich themselves beyond a fair compensation or equivalent for their capital, their skill, and their enterprise— it will not do to cast out your drag-net and bring within the condemnation of your law all the legitimate business enterprises of the country that are struggling along and trying to obtain only fair and reasonable prices for their goods, and who are giving life to labor, and peace and plenty to the whole land.

As I said, there is no greater fallacy than that the cheaper prices are the better it is for the community. It is not true. The farmer understands it when his wheat or his corn does not bring the cost of production, and this Senate is quick to see it and provide in this bill that there may be combinations in such cases. The farmer is not outside of the general economic principle. We do not raise wheat in the East, we consume it. Why should the Eastern man not be permitted to say, then, being a consumer of wheat, according to the theory of this bill, that as the price is down you must not raise it; you must not enhance the cost of flour to the consumer. We make no such contention as that. But there can not be two principles upon which a law shall stand. It must stand upon one principle. The theory of this bill is that prices must never be advanced by any two or more purposes, no matter how ruinously low they may be. That theory I denounce as utterly untenable, as immoral.

So, Mr. President, I can not vote for this bill in the shape in which I think it will come to a vote or in any shape in which I think it will be perfected. I am ready to go to the people of the State of Connecticut; I have faith and confidence in them; and when I tell them that here is a bill which, under the guise of dealing with trusts, would strike a cruel blow at their entire industries, I know that they will see it and understand it; and if there be a people anywhere in this country who can not understand it it is better for a Senator to answer to his judgment and his conscience than it is to answer to their misapprehension.

I am sorry, Mr. President, that we have not had a bill which had been carefully prepared, which had been thoughtfully prepared, which had been honestly prepared, to meet the object which we all desire to meet. The conduct of this Senate for the past three days—and I make no personal allusions—has not been in the line of the honest preparation of a bill to prohibit and punish trusts. It has been in the line of getting some bill with that title that we might go to the country with. The questions of whether a bill would be operative, of how it would operate, or whether it was within the power of Congress to enact it, have been whistled down the wind in this Senate as idle talk, and the whole effort has been to get some bill headed "A bill to punish trusts" with which to go to the country.

The distinguished author of the bill, the Senator in charge of it on this floor, when the Senator from Texas proposed his amendment, opposed it, and when the Senator from Kansas proposed his amendment opposed it and said that it ought to be voted down; and yet the moment they were put on the bill he seemed to be as thoroughly anxious for the passage of the bill with those amendments upon it as he had been of his own. We should legislate better than that. Every effort to refer this bill to any committee that would give it careful and honest consideration has been voted down in this Senate, and it is better to vote the bill down than it is to go to the people with a measure which shall resemble the apples which grow in the region of that fated plain on which once stood the city of Sodom. We may make this bill look like a beautiful remedy; we may call it a bill to punish trusts, but when you attempt to put it in operation it will be,

> Like that Dead Sea fruit,
> All ashes to the taste;

or it will be found to be a blow struck at the legitimate industries of the country such as they will not recover from in years and years.

24

Congress Legislates About Trusts

Text of the Sherman Anti-Trust Act

Although business combinations occurred in many ways, the one that captured the most attention and that gave its name in popular usage to the entire movement was the "trust." This legal device was first fully exploited by Standard Oil, and was soon copied by many other industrialists. Under its charter from Ohio, Standard Oil could not legally own plants in other states or stock in other corporations. So as it picked up out-of-state properties, control of each one was vested in three men acting as trustees, not for Standard Oil, but for its forty-one stockholders. At last, in 1882, some forty companies valued at $70 million were turned over to nine men named in the Standard Oil Trust Agreement, and 700,000 trust certificates (par $100) were issued to the Standard's stockholders. This octopus, which could act swiftly and secretly, stirred widespread fear and wrath, and at last in 1890 Congress felt compelled to make at least a gesture. The result was the following law; much of the phrasing is from the common law of various states or of England. See Hans B. Thorelli, *The Federal Antitrust Policy: Origination of an American Tradition* (1955).

From 26 *U.S. Statutes at Large* pp. 209-210.

CHAP. 647.—AN ACT TO PROTECT TRADE AND COMMERCE against unlawful restraints and monopolies.

Be it enacted by the Senate and House of Representatives of the United States of America in Congress assembled,

SEC. 1. Every contract, combination in the form of trust or otherwise, or conspiracy, in restraint of trade or commerce among the several States, or with foreign nations, is hereby declared to be illegal. Every person who shall make any such contract or engage in any such combination or conspiracy, shall be deemed guilty of a misdemeanor, and, on conviction thereof, shall be punished by fine not exceeding five thousand dollars, or by imprisonment not exceeding one year, or by both said punishments, in the discretion of the court.

Sec. 2. Every person who shall monopolize, or attempt to monopolize, or combine or conspire with any other person or persons, to monopolize any part of the trade or commerce among the several States, or with foreign nations, shall be deemed guilty of a misdemeanor, and, on conviction thereof, shall be punished by fine not exceeding five thousand dollars, or by imprisonment not exceeding one year, or by both said punishments, in the discretion of the court.

Sec. 3. Every contract, combination in form of trust or otherwise, or conspiracy, in restraint of trade or commerce in any Territory of the United States or of the District of Columbia, or in restraint of trade or commerce between any such Territory and another, or between any such Territory or Territories and any State or States or the District of Columbia, or with foreign nations, or between the District of Columbia and any State or States or foreign nations, is hereby declared illegal. Every person who shall make any such contract or engage in any such combination or conspiracy, shall be deemed guilty of a misdemeanor, and, on conviction thereof, shall be punished by fine not exceeding five thousand dollars, or by imprisonment not exceeding one year, or by both said punishments, in the discretion of the court.

Sec. 4. The several circuit courts of the United States are hereby invested with jurisdiction to prevent and restrain violations of this act; and it shall be the duty of the several district attorneys of the United States, in their respective districts, under the direction of the Attorney-General, to institute proceedings in equity to prevent and restrain such violations. Such proceedings may be by way of petition setting forth the case and praying that such violation shall be enjoined or otherwise prohibited. When the parties complained of shall have been duly notified of such petition the court shall proceed, as soon as may be, to the hearing and determination of the case; and pending such petition and before final decree, the court may at any time make such temporary restraining order or prohibition as shall be deemed just in the premises.

SEC. 5. Whenever it shall appear to the court before which any proceeding under section four of this act may be pending, that the ends of justice require that other parties should be brought before the court, the court may cause them to be summoned, whether they reside in the district in which the court is held or not; and subpoenas to that end may be served in any district by the marshal thereof.

SEC. 6. Any property owned under any contract or by any combination, or pursuant to any conspiracy (and being the subject thereof) mentioned in section one of this act, and being in the course of transportation from one State to another, or to a foreign country, shall be forfeited to the United States, and may be seized and condemned by like proceedings as those provided by law for the forfeiture, seizure, and condemnation of property imported into the United States contrary to law.

SEC. 7. Any person who shall be injured in his business or property by any other person or corporation by reason of anything forbidden or declared to be unlawful by this act, may sue therefor in any circuit court of the United States in the district in which the defendant resides or is found, without respect to the amount in controversy, and shall recover threefold the damages by him sustained, and the costs of suit, including a reasonable attorney's fee.

SEC. 8. That the word "person," or "persons," wherever used in this act shall be deemed to include corporations and associations existing under or authorized by the laws of either the United States, the laws of any of the Territories, the laws of any State, or the laws of any foreign country.

Approved, July 2, 1890.

25

Farmers Demand that the Government Help Them

The Populist Platform of 1892

The Farmers' Alliances, of varying official titles but all usually called by this name, were divided organizationally on both sectional and racial lines: one chiefly in the South, one in the North, and one Negro. But the three met jointly at Ocala, Florida, in December 1890 and issued the Ocala Demands, which resembled the following planks. (A notable difference was that the Ocala Demands called for government control of transportation and communication; only if that failed was government ownership and operation to be attempted.) This farmers' revolt resulted in the Peoples' Party of America. In reading the Populist platform, note (1) the portrayal of existing conditions; (2) the analysis of what ailed the country; (3) the characterization of prevailing political conditions; (4) the basic affirmations of the party; and (5) the demands for reform affecting money, transportation, and land. See John D. Hicks, *The Populist Revolt: A History of the Farmers' Alliance and the People's Party* (1931; 1961 reprint); George Harmon Knoles, *The Presidential Campaign and Election of 1892* (1942); and C. Vann Woodward, *Tom Watson: Agrarian Rebel* (1938).

From Edward Stanwood, *A History of the Presidency* (Boston: Houghton, Mifflin Company, 1898), pp. 509-512.

Assembled upon the 116th anniversary of the Declaration of Independence, the People's party of America, in their first national convention, invoking upon their action the blessing of Almighty God, puts forth, in the name and on behalf of the people of this country, the following preamble and declaration of principles:—

The conditions which surround us best justify our cooperation: we meet in the midst of a nation brought to the verge of moral, political, and material ruin. Corruption dominates the ballot-box, the legislature, the Congress, and touches even the ermine of the bench. The people are demoralized; most of the States have been compelled to isolate the voters at the polling-places to prevent universal intimidation or bribery. The newspapers are largely subsidized or muzzled; public opinion silenced; business prostrated; our homes covered with mortgages; labor impoverished; and the land concentrating in the hands of the capitalists. The urban workmen are denied the right of organization for self-protection; imported pauperized labor beats down their wages; a hireling standing army, unrecognized by our laws, is established to shoot them down, and they are rapidly degenerating into European conditions. The fruits of the toil of millions are boldly stolen to build up colossal fortunes for a few, unprecedented in the history of mankind; and the possessors of these, in turn, despise the republic and endanger liberty. From the same prolific womb of governmental injustice we breed the two great classes of tramps and millionaires.

The national power to create money is appropriated to enrich bondholders; a vast public debt, payable in legal tender currency, has been funded into gold-bearing bonds, thereby adding millions to the burdens of the people. Silver, which has been accepted as coin since the dawn of history, has been demonetized to add to the purchasing power of gold by decreasing the value of all forms of property as well as human labor; and the supply of currency is purposely abridged to fatten usurers, bankrupt enterprise, and enslave industry. A vast conspiracy against mankind has been organized on two continents, and it is rapidly taking possession of the world. If not met and overthrown at once, it forebodes terrible social convulsions, the destruction of civilization, or the establishment of an absolute despotism.

We have witnessed for more than a quarter of a century the struggles of the two great political parties for power and plunder, while grievous wrongs have been inflicted upon the suffering people. We charge that the controlling influences dominating both these parties have permitted the existing dreadful condition to develop without serious effort to prevent or restrain them. Neither do they now promise us any substantial reform. They have agreed together to ignore in the campaign every issue but one. They propose to drown the outcries of a plundered people with the uproar of a sham battle over the tariff, so that capitalists, corporations, national banks, rings, trusts, watered stock, the demonetization of silver, and the oppressions of the usurers may all be lost sight of. They propose to sacrifice our homes, lives, and children on the altar of mammon; to destroy the multitude in order to secure corruption funds from the millionaires.

Assembled on the anniversary of the birthday of the nation, and filled with the spirit of the grand general chief who established our independence, we seek to restore the government of the Republic to the hands of "the plain people," with whose class it originated. We assert our purposes to be identical with the purposes of the National Constitution, "to form a more perfect union and establish justice, insure domestic tranquillity, provide for the common defence, promote the general welfare, and secure the blessings of liberty for ourselves and our posterity." We declare that this republic can only endure as a free government while built upon the love of the whole people for each other and for the nation; that it cannot be pinned together by bayonets; that the civil war is over, and that every passion and resentment which grew out of it must die with it; and that we must be in fact, as we are in name, one united brotherhood of free men.

Our country finds itself confronted by conditions for which there is no precedent in the history of the world: our annual agricultural productions amount to billions of dollars in value, which must, within a few weeks or months, be exchanged for billions of dollars of commodities consumed in their production; the existing currency supply is wholly inadequate to make this exchange; the results are falling prices, the formation of combines and rings, the impoverishment of the producing class. We pledge ourselves, if given power, we will labor to correct these evils by wise and reasonable legislation, in accordance with the terms of our platform. We believe that the powers of government—in other words, of the people—should be expanded (as in the case of the postal service) as rapidly and as far as the good sense of an intelligent people and the teachings of experience shall justify, to the end that oppression, injustice, and poverty shall eventually cease in the land.

While our sympathies as a party of reform are naturally upon the side of every proposition which will tend to make men intelligent, virtuous, and temperate, we nevertheless regard these questions—important as they are—as secondary to the great issues now pressing for solution, and upon which not only our individual prosperity but the very existence of free institutions depends; and we ask all men to first help us to determine whether we are to have a republic to administer before we differ as to the conditions upon which it is to be administered; believing that the forces of reform this day organized will never cease to move forward until every wrong is remedied, and equal rights and equal privileges securely established for all the men and women of this country.

We declare, therefore,—

First. That the union of the labor forces of the United States this day consummated shall be permanent and perpetual; may its spirit enter all hearts for the salvation of the republic and and the uplifting of mankind!

Second. Wealth belongs to him who creates it, and every dollar taken from industry without an equivalent is robbery. "If any will not work, neither shall he eat." The interests of rural and civic labor are the same; their enemies are identical.

Third. We believe that the time has come when the railroad corporations will either own the people or the people must own the railroads; and, should the government enter upon the work of owning and managing all railroads, we should favor an amendment to the Constitution by which all persons engaged in the government service shall be placed under a civil service regulation of the most rigid character, so as to prevent the increase of the power of the national administration by the use of such additional government employees.

We demand,—

First, A national currency, safe, sound, and flexible, issued by the general government only, a full legal tender for all debts, public and private, and that, without the use of banking corporations, a just, equitable, and efficient means of distribution direct to the people, at a tax not to exceed two per cent. per annum, to be provided as set forth in the sub-treasury plan of the Farmers' Alliance, or a better system; also, by payments in discharge of its obligations for public improvements.

(a) We demand free and unlimited coinage of silver and gold at the present legal ratio of sixteen to one.

(b) We demand that the amount of circulating medium be speedily increased to not less than fifty dollars per capita.

(c) We demand a graduated income tax.

(d) We believe that the money of the country should be kept as much as possible in the hands of the people, and hence we demand that all state and national revenues shall be limited to the necessary expenses of the government economically and honestly administered.

(e) We demand that postal savings banks be established by the government for the safe deposit of the earnings of the people and to facilitate exchange.

Second, Transportation. Transportation being a means of exchange and a public necessity, the government should own and operate the railroads in the interest of the people.

(a) The telegraph and telephone, like the post-office system, being a necessity for the transmission of news, should be owned and operated by the government in the interest of the people.

Third, Land. The land, including all the natural sources of wealth, is the heritage of the people, and should not be monopolized for speculative purposes, and alien ownership of land should be prohibited. All land now held by railroads and other corporations in excess of their actual needs, and all lands now owned by aliens, should be reclaimed by the government and held for actual settlers only.

26

Silver-Tongued Orator on the Cross of Gold

Bryan's Speech to the Democratic National Convention of 1896

William Jennings Bryan (1860-1925) served in the House of Representatives from 1891 to 1895. Beaten then for reelection, he became a lecturer for free coinage of silver, on the payroll of the American Bimetallic League. He was a delegate from Nebraska to the Democratic national convention of 1896 in Chicago, and during the debate there on the platform he gave the following speech, which won for him the nomination for the Presidency. Note (1) Bryan's dramatization of the political contest of 1896; (2) his affirmations concerning rural and farm folk; (3) his definition of a business man; (4) the role Bryan assigned to the Democratic party; and (5) the character of the rhetoric used. See Henry Nash Smith, *Virgin Land: The American West as Symbol and Myth* (1950) for a brilliant discussion of the notion, which Bryan emphasizes here, that special virtue resided in the countryside and in farm folk, especially in the West. The latest book on this phase of Bryan's career is Paul W. Glad, *The Trumpet Soundeth: William Jennings Bryan and His Democracy, 1896-1912* (1960); for a more hostile view, see my *Six Days or Forever? Tennessee* v. *John Thomas Scopes* (1958; 1960 reprint). See also Harry Barnard, *Eagle Forgotten: The Life of John Peter Altgeld* (1933; 1962 reprint).

From William Jennings Bryan, *The First Battle: A Story of the Campaign of 1896* (Chicago: W. B. Conkey Company, 1897?), pp. 199-206.

208]

MR. CHAIRMAN AND GENTLEMEN OF THE CONVEN-
tion: I would be presumptuous, indeed, to present
myself against the distinguished gentlemen to whom you have
listened if this were a mere measuring of abilities; but this is not
a contest between persons. The humblest citizen in all the land,
when clad in the armor of a righteous cause, is stronger than all
the hosts of error. I come to speak to you in defense of a cause
as holy as the cause of liberty—the cause of humanity.

When this debate is concluded, a motion will be made to lay
upon the table the resolution offered in commendation of the administration, and also the resolution offered in condemnation of
the administration. We object to bringing this question down to
the level of persons. The individual is but an atom; he is born,
he acts, he dies; but principles are eternal; and this has been
a contest over a principle.

Never before in the history of this country has there been
witnessed such a contest as that through which we have just
passed. Never before in the history of American politics has
a great issue been fought out as this issue has been, by the voters
of a great party. On the fourth of March, 1895, a few Democrats,
most of them members of Congress, issued an address to the
Democrats of the nation, asserting that the money question was
the paramount issue of the hour; declaring that a majority of the
Democratic party had the right to control the action of the party
on this paramount issue; and concluding with the request that the
believers in the free coinage of silver in the Democratic party
should organize, take charge of, and control the policy of the
Democratic party. Three months later, at Memphis, an organization was perfected, and the silver Democrats went forth openly
and courageously proclaiming their belief, and declaring that,
if successful, they would crystallize into a platform the declaration which they had made. Then began the conflict. With a zeal
approaching the zeal which inspired the crusaders who followed
Peter the Hermit, our silver Democrats went forth from victory
unto victory until they are now assembled, not to discuss, not
to debate, but to enter up the judgment already rendered by the
plain people of this country. In this contest brother has been

arrayed against brother, father against son. The warmest ties of love, acquaintance and association have been disregarded; old leaders have ben cast aside when they have refused to give expression to the sentiments of those whom they would lead, and new leaders have sprung up to give direction to this cause of truth. Thus has the contest been waged, and we have assembled here under as binding and solemn instructions as were ever imposed upon representatives of the people.

We do not come as individuals. As individuals we might have been glad to compliment the gentleman from New York (Senator Hill), but we know that the people for whom we speak would never be willing to put him in a position where he could thwart the will of the Democratic party. I say it was not a question of persons; it was a question of principle, and it is not with gladness, my friends, that we find outselves brought into conflict with those who are now arrayed on the other side.

The gentleman who preceded me (ex-Governor Russell) spoke of the State of Massachusetts; let me assure him that not one present in all this convention entertains the least hostility to the people of the State of Massachusetts, but we stand here representing people who are the equals, before the law, of the greatest citizens in the State of Massachusetts. When you (turning to the gold delegates) come before us and tell us that we are about to disturb your business interests, we reply that you have disturbed our business interests by your course.

We say to you that you have made the definition of a business man too limited in its application. The man who is employed for wages is as much a business man as his employer; the attorney in a country town is as much a business man as the corporation counsel in a great metropolis; the merchant at the cross-roads store is as much a business man as the merchant of New York; the farmer who goes forth in the morning and toils all day—who begins in the spring and toils all summer—and who by the application of brain and muscle to the natural resources of the country creates wealth, is as much a business man as the man who goes upon the board of trade and bets upon the price of grain; the miners who go down a thousand feet into the earth, or climb two thousand feet upon the cliffs, and bring forth from their hiding places the precious metals to be poured into the channels of trade are as much business men as the few financial magnates who, in a back room, corner the money of the world. We come to speak for this broader class of business men.

Ah, my friends, we say not one word against those who live upon the Atlantic coast, but the hardy pioneers, who have braved all the dangers of the wilderness, who have made the desert to blossom as the rose—the pioneers away out there (pointing to the West), who rear their children near to Nature's heart, where they can mingle their voices with the voices of the birds—out there where they have erected schoolhouses for the education of their young, churches where they praise their Creator, and cemeteries where rest the ashes of their dead—these people, we say, are as deserving of the consideration of our party as any people in this country. It is for these that we speak. We do not come as aggressors. Our war is not a war of conquest; we are fighting in the defense of our homes, our families, and posterity. We have petitioned, and our petitions have been scorned; we have entreated, and our entreaties have been disregarded; we have begged, and they have mocked when our calamity came. We beg no longer; we entreat no more; we petition no more. We defy them.

The gentleman from Wisconsin has said that he fears a Robespierre. My friends, in this land of the free you need not fear that a tyrant will spring up from among the people. What we need is an Andrew Jackson to stand, as Jackson stood, against the encroachments of organized wealth.

They tell us that this platform was made to catch votes. We reply to them that changing conditions make new issues; that the principles upon which Democracy rests are as everlasting as the hills, but that they must be applied to new conditions as they arise. Conditions have arisen, and we are here to meet those conditions. They tell us that the income tax ought not to be brought in here; that it is a new idea. They criticise us for our criticism of the Supreme Court of the United States. My friends, we have not criticised; we have simply called attention to what you already know. If you want criticisms, read the dissenting opinions of the court. There you will find criticisms. They say that we passed an unconstitutional law; we deny it. The income tax law was not unconstitutional when it was passed; it was not unconstitutional when it went before the Supreme Court for the first time; it did not become unconstitutional until one of the judges changed his mind, and we cannot be expected to know when a judge will change his mind. The income tax is just. It simply intends to put the burdens of government justly upon the backs of the people. I am in favor of an income tax. When I find a man who is not willing to bear his share of the burdens of the government which protects him, I find a man who is unworthy to enjoy the blessings of a government like ours.

They say that we are opposing national bank currency; it is true. If you will read what Thomas Benton said, you will find he said that, in searching history, he could find but one parallel to Andrew Jackson; that was Cicero, who destroyed the conspiracy of Cataline and saved Rome. Benton said that Cicero only did for Rome what Jackson did for us when he destroyed the bank conspiracy and saved America. We say in our platform that we believe that the right to coin and issue money is a function of government. We believe it. We believe that it is a part of sovereignty, and can no more with safety be delegated to private individuals than we could afford to delegate to private individuals the power to make penal statutes or levy taxes. Mr. Jefferson, who was once regarded as good Democratic authority, seems to have differed in opinion from the gentleman who has addressed us on the part of the minority. Those who are opposed to this proposition tell us that the issue of paper money is a function of the bank, and the Government ought to go out of the banking business. I stand with Jefferson rather than with them, and tell them, as he did, that the issue of money is a function of government, and that the banks ought to go out of the governing business.

They complain about the plank which declares against life tenure in office. They have tried to strain it to mean that which it does not mean. What we oppose by that plank is the life tenure which is being built up in Washington, and which excludes from participation in official benefits the humbler members of society.

Let me call your attention to two or three important things. The gentleman from New York says that he will propose an amendment to the platform providing that the proposed change in our monetary system shall not affect contracts already made. Let me remind you that there is no intention of affecting those contracts which according to present laws are made payable in gold; but if he means to say that we cannot change our monetary system without protecting those who have loaned money before the change was made, I desire to ask him where, in law or in morals, he can find justification for not protecting the debtors when the act of 1873 was passed, if he now insists that we must protect the creditors.

He says he will also propose an amendment which will provide for the suspension of free coinage if we fail to maintain the parity within a year. We reply that when we advocate a policy which we believe will be successful, we are not compelled to raise a doubt as to our own sincerity by suggesting what we shall do if we fail. I ask him, if he would apply his logic to us, why he does not apply it to himself. He says he wants this country to try to secure an international agreement. Why does he not tell us what he is going to do if he fails to secure an international agreement? There is more reason for him to do that than there is for us to provide against the failure to maintain the parity. Our opponents have tried for twenty years to secure an international agreement, and those are waiting for it most patiently who do not want it at all.

And now, my friends, let me come to the paramount issue. If they ask us why it is that we say more on the money question than we say upon the tariff question, I reply that, if protection has slain its thousands, the gold standard has slain its tens of thousands. If they ask us why we do not embody in our platform all the things that we believe in, we reply that when we have restored the money of the Constitution all other necessary reforms will be possible; but that until this is done there is no other reform that can be accomplished.

Why is it that within three months such a change has come over the country? Three months ago, when it was confidently asserted that those who believe in the gold standard would frame our platform and nominate our candidates, even the advocates of the gold standard did not think that we could elect a president. And they had good reason for their doubt, because there is scarcely a State here today asking for the gold standard which is not in the absolute control of the Republican party. But note the change. Mr. McKinley was nominated at St. Louis upon a platform which declared for the maintenance of the gold standard until it can be changed into bimetallism by international agreement. Mr. McKinley was the most popular man among the Republicans, and three months ago everybody in the Republican party prophesied his election. How is [it] today? Why, the man who was once pleased to think that he looked like Napoleon—that man shudders today when he remembers that he was nominated on the anniversary of the battle of Waterloo. Not only that, but as he listens he can hear with ever-increasing distinctness the sound of the waves as they beat upon the lonely shores of St. Helena.

Why this change? Ah, my friends, is not the reason for the change evident to any one who will look at the matter? No private character, however pure, no personal popularity, however great, can protect from the avenging wrath of an indignant people a man who will declare that he is in favor of fastening the gold standard upon this country, or who is willing to surrender the right of self-government and place the legislative control of our affairs in the hands of foreign potentates and powers.

We go forth confident that we shall win. Why? Because upon the paramount issue of this campaign there is not a spot of ground upon which the enemy will dare to challenge battle. If they tell us that the gold standard is a good thing, we shall point to their platform and tell them that their platform pledges the party to get rid of the gold standard and substitute bimetallism. If the gold standard is a good thing, why try to get rid of it? I call your attention to the fact that some of the very people who are in this convention today and who tell us that we ought to declare in favor of international bimetallism—thereby declaring that the gold standard is wrong and that the principle of bimetallism is better—these very people four months ago were open and avowed advocates of the gold standard, and were then telling us that we could not legislate two metals together, even with the aid of all the world. If the gold standard is a good thing, we ought to declare in favor of its retention and not in favor of abandoning it; and if the gold standard is a bad thing why should we wait until other nations are willing to help us to let go? Here is the line of battle, and we care not upon which issue they force the fight; we are prepared to meet them on either issue or on both. If they tell us that the gold standard is the standard of civilization, we reply to them that this, the most enlightened of all the nations of the earth, has never declared for a gold standard and that both the great parties this year are declaring against it. If the gold standard is the standard of civilization, why, my friends, should we not have it? If they come to meet us on that issue we can present the history of our nation. More than that; we can tell them that they will search the pages of history in vain to find a single instance where the common people of any land have ever declared themselves in favor of the gold standard. They can find where the holders of fixed investments have declared for a gold standard, but not where the masses have.

Mr. Carlisle said in 1878 that this was a struggle between "the idle holders of idle capital" and "the struggling masses, who produce the wealth and pay the taxes of the country;" and, my friends, the question we are to decide is: Upon which side will the Democratic party fight; upon the side of "the idle holders of idle capital" or upon the side of "the struggling masses?" That is the question which the party must answer first, and then it must be answered by each individual hereafter. The sympathies of the Democratic party, as shown by the platform, are on the side of the struggling masses who have ever been the foundation of the Democratic party. There are two ideas of government. There are those who believe that, if you will only legislate to make the well-to-do prosperous, their prosperity will leak through on those below. The Democratic idea, however, has been that if you legislate to make the masses prosperous, their prosperity will find its way up through every class which rests upon them.

You come to us and tell us that the great cities are in favor of the gold standard; we reply that the great cities rest upon our broad and fertile prairies. Burn down your cities and leave our farms, and your cities will spring up again as if by magic; but destroy our farms and the grass will grow in the streets of every city in the country.

My friends, we declare that this nation is able to legislate for its own people on every question, without waiting for the aid or consent of any other nation on earth; and upon that issue we expect to carry every State in the Union. I shall not slander the inhabitants of the fair State of Massachusetts nor the inhabitants of the State of New York by saying that, when they are confronted with the proposition, they will declare that this nation is not able to attend to its own business. It is the issue of 1776 over again. Our ancestors, when but three millions in number, had the courage to declare their political independence of every other nation; shall we, their descendants, when we have grown to seventy millions, declare that we are less independent than our forefathers? No, my friends, that will never be the verdict of our people. Therefore, we care not upon what lines the battle is fought. If they say bimetallism is good, but that we cannot have it until other nations help us, we reply that, instead of having a gold standard because England has, we will restore bimetallism, and then let England have bimetallism because the United States has it. If they dare to come out in the open field and defend the gold standard as a good thing, we will fight them to the uttermost. Having behind us the producing masses of this nation and the world, supported by the commercial interests, the laboring interests, and the toilers everywhere, we will answer their demand for a gold standard by saying to them: You shall not press down upon the brow of labor this crown of thorns, you shall not crucify mankind upon a cross of gold.

27

New Legal Meanings of "Liberty" and "Property"

The Due Process Clause in *Allgeyer v. Louisiana*

Allgeyer v. *Louisiana* was complicated, but its facts can be stripped down. In 1894 the state of Louisiana banned firms within it from doing business with out-of-state marine insurance companies that had not complied with certain Louisiana laws. The Atlantic Mutual Insurance Company of New York had not done so. But E. Allgeyer & Co. of New Orleans signed a contract with this firm for an open policy of $200,000 of marine insurance. Allgeyer later mailed from Louisiana to Atlantic Mutual a request for a special policy, under the open policy, covering a specified transatlantic shipment of cotton. Action was brought by the state, and Allgeyer was fined. On appeal the conviction was unanimously upset by the U.S. Supreme Court. In the general Introduction above (p. 8), I noted the crucial passage changing the meanings of "liberty" and "property" in the Fourteenth Amendment. Perhaps nobody in 1897 foresaw where the new definitions would lead; but one place they led was to *Truax* v. *Corrigan* (257 U.S. 312). An Arizona statute of 1913 sought to regulate issuance of injunctions against peaceful picketing in labor disputes, but the Supreme Court in 1921 struck down the law, saying that it had reduced the earnings of the employer's business and deprived him of his "property" without due process of law within the meaning of the Fourteenth Amendment. In reading this decision note (1) the court's definition of liberty; (2) the grounds on which the court held the Louisiana statute invalid; (3) the limitations imposed on a state in exercising its police powers; and (4) the court's interpretation of contracts and property. See John Rogers Commons, *Legal Foundations of Capitalism* (1924), a classic, and Max Lerner's brilliant "The Supreme Court and American Capitalism," *Yale Law Journal*, XLII (1933), pp. 668-701.

From *Allgeyer* v. *Louisiana*, 165 U.S. 578 (1897).

M<small>R. JUSTICE PECKHAM DELIVERED THE OPINION OF</small> the court:

There is no doubt of the power of the state to prohibit foreign insurance companies from doing business within its limits. The state can impose such conditions as it pleases upon the doing of any business by those companies within its borders, and unless the conditions be complied with the prohibition may be absolute. The cases upon this subject are cited in the opinion of the court in *Hooper* v. *California*, 155 U. S. 648 . . .

The general contract contained in the open policy, as well as the special insurance upon each shipment of goods of which notice is given to the insurance company, being contracts made in New York and valid there, the state of Louisiana claims notwithstanding such facts that the defendants have violated the act of 1894, by doing an act in that state to effect for themselves insurance on their property then in that state in a marine insurance company which had not complied in all respects with the laws of that state, and that such violation consisted in the act of mailing a letter or sending a telegram to the insurance company in New York describing the cotton upon which the defendants desired the insurance under the open marine policy to attach. . . . In this case the only act which it is claimed was a violation of the statute in question consisted in sending the letter through the mail notifying the company of the property to be covered by the policy already delivered. We have then a contract which it is conceded was made outside and beyond the limits of the jurisdiction of the state of Louisiana, being made and to be performed within the state of New York, where the premiums were to be paid and losses, if any, adjusted. The letter of notification did not constitute a contract made or entered into within the state of Louisiana. It was but the performance of an act rendered necessary by the provisions of the contract already made between the parties outside of the state. It was a mere notification that the contract already in existence would attach to that particular property. In any event, the contract was made in New York, outside of the jurisdiction of

Louisiana, even though the policy was not to attach to the particular property until the notification was sent.

It is natural that the state court should have remarked that there is in this "statute an apparent interference with the liberty of defendants in restricting their rights to place insurance on property of their own whenever and in what company they desired." Such interference is not only apparent, but it is real, and we do not think that it is justified for the purpose of upholding what the state says is its policy with regard to foreign insurance companies which had not complied with the laws of the state for doing business within its limits. In this case the company did no business within the state, and the contracts were not therein made.

The supreme court of Louisiana says that the act of writing, within that state, the letter of notification, was an act therein done to effect an insurance on property then in the state, in a marine insurance company which had not complied with its laws, and such act was therefore prohibited by the statute. As so construed we think the statute is a violation of the 14th Amendment of the Federal Constitution, in that it deprives the defendants of their liberty, without due process of law. The statute which forbids such act does not become due process of law, because it is inconsistent with the provisions of the Constitution of the Union. The liberty mentioned in that amendment means, not only the right of the citizen to be free from the mere physical restraint of his person, as by incarceration, but the term is deemed to embrace the right of the citizen to be free in the enjoyment of all his faculties; to be free to use them in all lawful ways; to live and work where he will; to earn his livelihood by any lawful calling; to pursue any livelihood or avocation, and for that purpose to enter into all contracts which may be proper, necessary, and essential to his carrying out to a successful conclusion the purposes above mentioned.

It was said by Mr. Justice Bradley in *Butchers' Union S. H. & L. S. L. Co.* v. *Crescent City L. S. L. & S. H. Co.* 111 U. S. 746, 762, in the course of his concurring opinion in that case, that "the right to follow any of the common occupations of life is an inalienable right. It was formulated as such under the phrase 'pursuit of happiness' in the Declaration of Independence, which commenced with the fundamental proposition that 'all men are created equal that they are endowed by their Creator with certain inalienable rights; and among these are life, liberty, and the pursuit of happiness.' This right is a large ingredient in the civil liberty of the citizen." Again, on page 764, the learned justice said: "I hold that the liberty of pursuit—the right to follow any of the ordinary callings of life—is one of the privileges of a citizen of the United States." And again, on page 765: "But if it does not abridge the privileges and immunities of a citizen of the United States to prohibit him from pursuing his chosen calling, and giving to others the exclusive right of pursuing it, it certainly does deprive him, to a certain extent, of his liberty; for it takes from him the freedom of adopting and following the pursuit which he prefers; which, as already intimated, is a material part of the liberty of the citizen." It is true that these remarks were made in regard to questions of monopoly, but they well describe the rights which are covered by the word "liberty" as contained in the 14th Amendment.

Again, in *Powell* v. *Pennsylvania,* 127 U. S. 678, 684, Mr. Justice Harlan, in stating the opinion of the court, said: "The main proposition advanced by the defendant is that his enjoyment upon terms of equality with all others in similar circumstances of the privilege of pursuing an ordinary calling or trade, and of acquiring, holding, and selling property, is an essential part of his rights of liberty and property, as guaranteed by the 14th Amendment. The court assents to this general proposition as embodying a sound principle of constitutional law." It was there held, however, that the legislation under consideration in that case did not violate any of the constitutional rights of the plaintiff in error.

The foregoing extracts have been made for the purpose of showing what general definitions have been given in regard to the meaning of the word "liberty" as used in the amendment, but we do not intend to hold that in no such case can the state exercise its police power. When and how far such power may be legitimately exercised with regard to these subjects may be left for determination to each case as it arises.

Has not a citizen of a state, under the provisions of the Federal Constitution above mentioned, a right to contract outside of the state for insurance on his property—a right of which state legislation cannot deprive him? We are not alluding to acts done within the state by an insurance company or its agents doing business therein, which are in violation of the state statutes. Such acts come within the principle of *Hooper v. California,* 155 U. S. 648, and would be controlled by it. When we speak of the liberty to contract for insurance or to do an act to effectuate such a contract already existing, we refer to and have in mind the facts of this case, where the contract was made outside the state, and as such was a valid and proper contract. The act done within the limits of the state under the circumstances of this case and for the purpose therein mentioned, we hold a proper act, one which the defendants were at liberty to perform and which the state legislature had no right to prevent, at least with reference to the Federal Constitution. To deprive the citizen of such a right as herein described without due process of law is illegal. Such a statute as this in question is not due process of law, because it prohibits an act which under the Federal Constitution the defendants had a right to perform. This does not interfere in any way with the acknowledged right of the state to enact such legislation in the legitimate exercise of its police or other powers as to it may seem proper. In the exercise of such right, however, care must be taken not to infringe upon those other rights of the citizen which are protected by the Federal Constitution.

In the privilege of pursuing an ordinary calling or trade and of acquiring, holding, and selling property must be embraced the right to make all proper contracts in relation thereto, and although it may be conceded that this right to contract in relation to persons or property or to do business within the jurisdiction of the state may be regulated and sometimes prohibited when the contracts or business conflict with the policy of the state as contained in the statutes, yet the power does not and cannot extend to prohibiting the citizen from making contracts of the nature involved in this case outside of the limits and jurisdiction of the state, and which are also to be performed outside of such jurisdiction; nor can this state legally prohibit its citizens from doing such an act as writing this letter of notification, even though the property which is the subject of the insurance may at the time when such insurance attaches be within the limits of the state. The mere fact that a citizen may be within the limits of a particular state does not prevent his making a contract outside its limits while he himself remains within it. *Milliken* v. *Pratt*, 125 Mass. 374; *Tilden* v. *Blair*, 88 U. S. 21 Wall. 241.

The contract in this case was thus made. It was a valid contract, made outside of the state, to be performed outside of the state, although the subject was property temporarily within the state. As the contract was valid in the place where made and where it was performed, the party to the contract upon whom is devolved the right or duty to send the notification in order that the insurance provided for by the contract may attach to the property specified in the shipment mentioned in the notice, must have the liberty to do that act and to give that notification within the limits of the state, any prohibition of the state statute to the contrary notwithstanding. The giving of the notice is a mere collateral matter; it is not the contract itself, but is an act performed pursuant to a valid contract which the state had no right or jurisdiction to prevent its citizens from making outside the limits of the state.

The Atlantic Mutual Insurance Company of New York has done no business of insurance within the state of Louisiana and has not subjected itself to any provisions of the statute in question. It had the right to enter into a contract in New York with citizens of Louisiana for the purpose of insuring the property of its citizens, even if that property were in the state of Louisiana, and correlatively the citizens of Louisiana had the right without the state of entering into contract with an insurance company for the same purpose. Any act of the state legislature which should prevent the entering into such a contract, or the mailing within the state of Louisiana of such a notification as is mentioned in this case, is an improper and illegal interference with the conduct of the citizen, although residing in Louisiana, in his right to contract and to carry out the terms of a contract validly entered into outside and beyond the jurisdiction of the state. . . .

28

Muckraking as an Applied Art

Lincoln Steffens'
"Philadelphia: Corrupt and Contented"

Lincoln Steffens (1866-1936) was one of the most perceptive and eloquent American journalists of all time. After learning his craft on New York City newspapers, he became managing editor of *McClure's Magazine*. There he drifted into a project that helped to launch a sensationally successful style in American journalism—muckraking, the writing of detailed and careful studies of the corruption of city governments and corporations. The magazine printed one article on each of eight cities between October 1902 and November 1903, collected in 1904 as *The Shame of the Cities*. By that time Steffens was doing a similar series on state governments, collected as *The Struggle for Self-Government* in 1906. In reading the following article, note (1) the down-to-earth description of Philadelphia's corruption; (2) Steffens' analysis of reform as practiced in the United States; (3) the devices used by the machine to maintain power; (4) the relationship of the city and state political machines; (5) how the bosses used reform and reformers; (6) how Steffens accounted for Philadelphia's contentment with its corruption; and (7) the methods the bosses used to finance themselves and their machines. See *The Autobiography of Lincoln Steffens* (1931), and Ella Winter and Granville Hicks (eds.), *The Letters of Lincoln Steffens* (1938).

Lincoln Steffens, "Philadelphia: Corrupt and Contented," *McClure's Magazine*, vol. 21 (July 1903), pp. 249-263.

Oᴛʜᴇʀ ᴀᴍᴇʀɪᴄᴀɴ ᴄɪᴛɪᴇs, ɴᴏ ᴍᴀᴛᴛᴇʀ ʜᴏᴡ ʙᴀᴅ their own condition may be, all point with scorn to Philadelphia as worse—"the worst governed city in the country." St. Louis, Minneapolis, Pittsburg submit with some patience to the jibes of any other community; the most friendly suggestion from Philadelphia is rejected with contempt. The Philadelphians are "supine," "asleep"; hopelessly ring-ruled, they are "complacent." "Politically benighted," Philadelphia is supposed to have no light to throw upon a state of things that is almost universal. This is not fair. Philadelphia is, indeed, corrupt; but it is not without significance. Every city and town in the country can learn something from the typical political experience of this great representative city. New York is excused for many of its ills because it is the metropolis, Chicago because of its forced development; Philadelphia is our "third largest" city and its growth has been gradual and natural. Immigration has been blamed for our municipal conditions; Philadelphia, with 47 per cent. of the population native born of native born parents, is the most American of our greater cities. It is "good," too, and intelligent. I don't know how to measure the intelligence of a community, but a Pennsylvania college professor who declared to me his belief in education for the masses as a way out of political corruption, himself justified the "rake-off" of preferred contractors on public works on the ground of a "fair business profit." Another plea we have made is that we are too busy to attend to public business, and we have promised, when we come to wealth and leisure, to do better. Philadelphia has long enjoyed great and widely distributed prosperity; it is the city of homes; there is a dwelling house for every five persons,—men, women, and children,—of the population; and the people give one a sense of more leisure and repose than any community I ever dwelt in. Some Philadelphians account for their political state on the ground of their ease and comfort. There is another class of optimists whose hope is in an "aristocracy" that is to come by and by; Philadelphia is surer that it has a "real aristocracy" than any other place in the world, but its aristocrats with few exceptions are in the ring, with it, or of no political use. Then we hear that we are a young people and that when we are older and "have traditions," like some of the old countries, we also will be honest. Philadelphia is one of the oldest of our cities and treasures for us scenes and relics of some of the noblest traditions of our fair land. Yet I was told how once, for a joke, a party of boodlers counted out the "divvy" of their graft in unison with the ancient chime of Independence Hall.

Philadelphia is representative. This very "joke," told, as it was, with a laugh, is typical. All our municipal governments are more or less bad and all our people are optimists. Philadelphia is simply the most corrupt and the most contented. Minneapolis has cleaned up. Pittsburg has tried to, New York fights every other election, Chicago fights all the time. Even St. Louis has begun to stir (since the elections are over) and at the worst was only shameless. Philadelphia is proud; good people there defend corruption and boast of their machine. My college professor, with his philosophic view of "rake-offs," is one Philadelphia type. Another is the man, who, driven to bay with his local pride, says: "At least you must admit that our machine is the best you have ever seen."

Disgraceful? Other cities say so. But I say that if Philadelphia is a disgrace, it is a disgrace not to itself alone, nor to Pennsylvania, but to the United States and to American character. For this great city, so highly representative in other respects, is not behind in political experience, but ahead, with New York. Philadelphia is a city that has had its reforms. Having passed through all the typical stages of corruption, Philadelphia reached the period of miscellaneous loot with a boss for chief thief, under James McManes and the Gas Ring 'way back in the late sixties and seventies. This is the Tweed stage of corruption from which St. Louis, for example, is just emerging. Philadelphia, in two inspiring popular revolts, attacked the Gas Ring, broke it, and in 1885 achieved that dream of American cities—a good charter. The present condition of Philadelphia, therefore, is not that which precedes, but that which follows reform, and in this distinction lies its startling general significance. What has happened since the Bullitt Law or charter went into effect in Philadelphia may happen in any American city "after reform is over."

For reform with us is usually revolt, not government, and is soon over. Our people do not seek, they avoid self rule, and "re-

forms" are spasmodic efforts to punish bad rulers and get somebody that will give us good government or something that will
make it. A self-acting form of government is an ancient super-
stition. We are an inventive people and we all think that we
shall devise some day a legal machine that will turn out good
government automatically. The Philadelphians have treasured
this belief longer than the rest of us and have tried it more often.
Throughout their history they have sought this wonderful charter
and they thought they had it when they got the Bullitt Law,
which concentrates in the Mayor ample power, executive and
political, and complete responsibility. Moreover, it calls for very
little thought and action on the part of the people. All they expected to have to do when the Bullitt Law went into effect was
to elect as Mayor a good business man, who with his probity and
common sense would give them that good business administration
which is the ideal of many reformers.

The Bullitt Law went into effect in 1887. A committee of twelve
—four from the Union League, four from business organizations,
and four from the bosses—picked out the first man to run under
it on the Republican ticket, Edwin H. Fitler, an able, upright
business man, and he was elected. Strange to say, his administration was satisfactory to the citizens, who speak well of it to
this day, and to the politicians also; Boss McManes (the ring was
broken, not the boss) took to the next national convention from
Philadelphia a delegation solid for Fitler for President of the
United States. It was a farce, but it pleased Mr. Fitler, so Matthew S. Quay, the State boss, let him have a complimentary vote
on the first ballot. The politicians "fooled" Mr. Fitler, and they
"fooled" also the next business Mayor, Edwin S. Stuart, likewise
a most estimable gentleman. Under these two administrations
the foundation was laid for the present government of Philadelphia, the corruption to which Philadelphians seem so recon-
ciled, and the machine which is "at least the best you have ever
seen."

The Philadelphia machine isn't the best. It isn't sound, and I
doubt if it would stand in New York or Chicago. The enduring
strength of the typical American political machine is that it is
a natural growth—a sucker, but deep rooted in the people. The
New Yorkers vote for Tammany Hall. The Philadelphians do not

vote; they are disfranchised, and their disfranchisement is one anchor of the foundation of the Philadelphia organization.

This is no figure of speech. The honest citizens of Philadelphia have no more rights at the polls than the negroes down South. Nor do they fight very hard for this basic right. You can arouse their Republican ire by talking about the black Republican votes lost in the Southern States by white Democratic intimidation, but if you remind the average Philadelphian that he is in the same position, he will look startled, then say, "That's so, that's literally true, only I never thought of it in just that way." And it is literally true.

The machine controls the whole process of voting, and practices fraud at every stage. The assessor's list is the voting list, and the assessor is the machine's man. "The assessor of a division kept a disorderly house; he padded his lists with fraudulent names registered from his house; two of these names were used by election officers. . . . The constable of the division kept a disreputable house; a policeman was assessed as living there. . . . The election was held in the disorderly house maintained by the assessor. . . . The man named as judge had a criminal charge for a life offense pending against him. . . . Two hundred and fifty-two votes were returned in a division that had less than one hundred legal votes within its boundaries." These extracts from a report of the Municipal League suggest the election methods. The assessor pads the list with the names of dead dogs, children, and non-existent persons. One newspaper printed the picture of a dog, another that of a little four-year-old negro boy, down on such a list. A ring orator in a speech resenting sneers at his ward as "low down" reminded his hearers that that was the ward of Independence Hall, and, naming over signers of the Declaration of Independence, he closed his highest flight of eloquence with the statement that "these men, the fathers of American liberty, voted down here once. And," he added, with a catching grin, "they vote here yet." Rudolph Blankenburg, a persistent fighter for the right and the use of the right to vote, sent out just before one election a registered letter to each voter on the rolls of a certain selected division. Sixty-three per cent. were returned marked "not at," "removed," "deceased," etc. From one four-story house where forty-four voters were addressed, eighteen letters came back undelivered; from another of forty-eight voters, came back forty-one letters; from another sixty-one out of sixty-two; from another forty-four out of forty-seven. Six houses in one division were assessed at one hundred and seventy-two voters, more than the votes cast in the previous election in any one of two hundred entire divisions.

The repeating is done boldly, for the machine controls the election officers, often choosing them from among the fraudulent names; and when no one appears to serve, assigning the heeler ready for the expected vacancy. The police are forbidden by law to stand within thirty feet of the polls, but they are at the box and they are there to see that the machine's orders are obeyed and that repeaters whom they help to furnish are permitted to vote without "intimidation" on the names they, the police, have supplied. The editor of an anti-machine paper who was looking about for himself once told me that a ward leader who knew him well asked him into a polling place. "I'll shw you how it's done," he said, and he had the repeaters go round and round voting again and again on the names handed them on slips. "But," as the editor said, "that isn't the way it's done." The repeaters go from one polling place to another, voting on slips, and on their return rounds change coats, hats, etc. The business proceeds with very few hitches; there is more jesting than fighting. Intimidation in the past has had its effect; and is not often necessary now-a-days, but if it is needed the police are there to apply it. Several citizens told me that they had seen the police help to beat citizens or election officers who were trying to do their duty, then arrest the victim; and Mr. Clinton Rogers Woodruff, the executive counsel of the Municipal League, has published a booklet of such cases. But an official statement of the case is at hand in an announcement by John Weaver, the new machine Mayor of Philadelphia, that he is going to keep the police out of politics and away from the polls. "I shall see," he added, "that every voter enjoys the full right of suffrage and that ballots may be placed in the ballot box without fear of intimidation."

But many Philadelphians do not try to vote. They leave everything to the machine, and the machine casts their ballots for them. It is estimated that 150,000 voters did not go to the polls at the last election. Yet the machine rolled up a majority of 130,000 for

Weaver, with a fraudulent vote estimated all the way from forty to eighty thousand, and this in a campaign so machine-made that it was called "no contest." Francis Fisher Kane, the Democrat, got 32,000 votes out of some 204,000. "What is the use of voting?" these stay-at-homes ask. A friend of mine told me he was on the lists in the three wards in which he had successively dwelt. He votes personally in none, but the leader of his present ward tells him how he has been voted. Mr. J. C. Reynolds, the proprietor of the St. James Hotel, went to the polls at eleven o'clock last election day, only to be told that he had been voted. He asked how many others from his house had voted. An election officer took up a list, checked off twelve names, two down twice, and handed it to him. When Mr. Reynolds got home he learned that one of these had voted, the others had been voted. Another man said he rarely attempted to vote, but when he did, the officers let him, even though his name had already been voted on; and then the negro repeaters would ask if his "brother was coming 'round today." They were going to vote him, as they vote all good-natured citizens who stay away. "When this kind of man turns out," said a leader to me, "we simply have two repeaters extra—one to balance him and one more to the good." If necessary, after all this, the machine counts the vote "right," and there is little use appealing to the courts, since they have held that, excepting in one case, the ballot box is secret and cannot be opened. The only legal remedy lies in the purging of the assessors' lists, and when the Municipal League had this done in 1899, they reported that there was "wholesale voting on the very names stricken off."

Deprived of self-government, the Philadelphians haven't even self-governing machine government. They have their own boss, but he and his machine are subject to the State ring and take their orders from the State boss, Matthew S. Quay, who is the proprietor of Pennsylvania and the real ruler of Philadelphia, just as William Penn, the great proprietor, was. Philadelphians, especially the local bosses, dislike this description of their government, and they point for refutation to their charter. But this very Bullitt Law was passed by Quay, and he put it through the Legislature, not for reform reasons, but at the instance of David H. Lane, his Philadelphia lieutenant, as a check upon the power of Boss McManes. Later, when McManes proved hopelessly insubordinate, Quay decided to have done with him forever. He chose David Martin for boss, and from his seat in the United States Senate, Penn's successor raised up his man and set him over the people. Croker, who rose by his own strength to the head of Tammany Hall, has tried twice to appoint a successor; no one else could, and he failed. The boss of Tammany Hall is a growth. So Croker has attempted to appoint district leaders and failed: a Tammany district leader is a growth. Boss Martin, picked up and set down from above, was accepted by Philadelphia and the Philadelphia machine, and he removed old ward leaders and appointed new ones. Some leaders in Philadelphia own their wards, of course, but Martin and, after him, Durham have sent men into a ward to lead it, and they have led it.

The Philadelphia organization is upside down. It has its root in the air, or, rather, like the banyan tree, it sends its roots from the center out both up and down and all around, and there lies its peculiar strength. For when I said it was dependent and not sound, I did not mean that it was weak. It is dependent as a municipal machine, but the organization that rules Philadelphia is, as we have seen, not a mere municipal machine, but a city, State, and national organization. The people of Philadelphia are Republicans in a Republican city in a Republican State in a Republican nation, and they are bound ring on ring on ring. The President of the United States and his patronage; the National Cabinet and their patronage; the Congress and the patronage of the Senators and the Congressmen from Pennsylvania; the Governor of the State and the State Legislature with their powers and patronage; and all that the Mayor and City Councils have of power and patronage;—all these bear down upon Philadelphia to keep it in the control of Quay's boss and his little ring. This is the ideal of party organization, and, possibly, is the end toward which our democratic republic is tending. If it is, the end is absolutism. Nothing but a revolution could overthrow this obligarchy, and there is its danger. With no outlet at the polls for public feeling, the machine cannot be taught anything it does not know excepting at the cost of annihilation.

But the Philadelphia machine-leaders know their business. As

I said in a previous article ("Tweed Days in St. Louis"), the politicians will learn, if the people won't, from exposure and reform. The Pennsylvania bosses learned the "uses of reform"; we have seen Quay applying it to discipline McManes, and he since has turned reformer himself, to punish local bosses. The bosses have learned also the danger of combination between citizens and the Democrats. To prevent this, Quay and his friends have spread sedulously the doctrine of "reform within the party," and, from the Committee of One Hundred on, the reformers have stuck pretty faithfully to this principle. But lest the citizens should commit such a sin against their party, Martin formed a permanent combination of the Democratic with the Republican organization, using to that end a goodly share of the Federal and county patronage. Thus the people of Philadelphia were "fixed" so that they couldn't vote if they wanted to, and if they should want to, they couldn't vote for a Democrat, except of Republican or independent choosing. In other words, having taken away their ballot, the bosses took away also the choice of parties.

But the greatest lesson learned and applied was that of conciliation and "good government." The people must not want to vote or rebel against the ring. This ring, like any other, was formed for the exploitation of the city for private profit, and the cementing force is the "cohesive power of public plunder." But McManes and Tweed had proved that miscellaneous larceny was dangerous, and why should a lot of cheap politicians get so much and the people nothing at all? The people had been taught to expect but little from their rulers: good water, good light, clean streets well paved, fair transportation, the decent repression of vice, public order and public safety, and no scandalous or open corruption. It would be good business and good politics to give them these things. Like Chris Magee, who studied out the problem with him, Martin took away from the rank and file of the party and from the ward leaders and office holders the privilege of theft, and he formed companies and groups to handle the legitimate public business of the city. It was all graft, but it was to be all lawful, and, in the main, it was. Public franchises, public works, and public contracts were the principal branches of the business, and Martin adopted the dual boss idea

which we have seen worked out by Magee and Flinn in Pitts-
burg. In Philadelphia it was Martin and Porter, and just as
Flinn had a firm, Booth & Flinn, Ltd., so Porter was Filbert and
Porter.

Filbert and Porter got all the public contracts they could
handle, and the rest went to other contractors friendly to them
and to the ring. Sometimes the preferred contractor was the
lowest bidder, but he did not have to be. The law allowed awards
to be "lowest and best," and the courts held that this gave the
officials discretion. But since public criticism was to be considered, the ring, to keep up appearances, resorted to many
tricks. One was to have fake bids made above the favorite.
Another was to have the favorite bid high but set an impossible
time limit; the department or the City Councils could extend the
time afterwards. Still another was to arrange for specifications
which would make outsiders bid high, then either openly alter
the plans or let the ring firm perform work not up to requirements.

Many of Martin's deals and jobs were scandals, but they
were safe; they were in the direction of public service; and the
great mass of the business was done quietly. Moreover, the
public was getting something for its money,—not full value, but
a good percentage. In other words, there was a limit to the "rake-
off," and some insiders have told me that it had been laid down
as a principle with the ring that the people should have in value
(that is in work or benefit, including fair profit) ninety-five cents
out of every dollar. In some of the deals I investigated, the
"rake-off" over and above profit was as high as twenty-five per
cent. Still, even at this, there was "a limit," and the public was
getting, as one of the leaders told me, "a run for its money."
Cynical as it all sounds, this view is taken by many Philadelphians almost if not quite as intelligent as my college professor.

But there was another element in the policy of conciliation
which is a potent factor in the contentment of Philadelphia, and
I regard it as the key to that "apathy" which has made the community notorious. We have seen how Quay had with him the
Federal resources and those of the State, and the State ring, and
we have seen how Martin, having the city, Mayor, and Councils,
won over the Democratic city leaders. Here they had under pay

in office, at least 15,000 men and women. But each of these 15,000 persons was selected for office because he could deliver votes, either by organizations, by parties, or by families. These must represent pretty near a majority of the city's voters. But this is by no means the end of the ring's reach. In the State ring are the great corporations, the Standard Oil Company, Cramp's Ship Yard, and the steel companies, with the Pennsylvania Railroad at their head, and all the local transportation and other public utility companies following after. They get franchises, privileges, exemptions, etc.; they have helped finance Quay through deals: the Pennsylvania paid Martin, Quay said once, a large yearly salary; the Cramps get contracts to build United States ships, and for years have been begging for a subsidy on home-made ships. The officers, directors, and stockholders of these companies, with their friends, their bankers, and their employees are of the organization. Better still, one of the local bosses of Philadelphia told me he could always give a worker a job with these companies, just as he could in a city department, or in the mint, or post-office. Then there are the bankers who enjoy, or may some day enjoy, public deposits; those that profit on loans to finance political financial deals; the promoting capitalists who share with the bosses on franchises; and the brokers who deal in ring securities and speculation on ring tips. Through the exchange the ring financiers reach the investing public, which is a large and influential body. The traction companies, which bought their way from beginning to end by corruption, which have always been in the ring, and whose financiers have usually shared in other big ring deals, adopted early the policy of bribing the people with "small blocks of stock." Dr. Frederick W. Speirs, in his "The Street Railway System of Philadelphia," came upon transactions which "indicate clearly that it is the policy of the Union Company to get the securities into the hands of a large number of small holders, the plain inference being that a wide distribution of securities will fortify the company against possible attacks by the public." In 1895 he found a director saying: "Our critics have engaged the Academy of Music, and are to call an assemblage of people opposed to the street railways as now managed. It would take eight Academies of Music to hold the stockholders of the Union Traction Company."

But we are not yet through. Quay has made a specialty all his life of reformers, and he and his local bosses have won over so many that the list of former reformers is very, very long. Martin drove down his roots through race and religion, too. Philadelphia was one of the hot-beds of "know-nothingism." Martin recognized the Catholic, and the Irish-Irish, and so drew off into the Republican party the great natural supply of the Democrats; and his successors have given high places to representative Jews. "Surely this isn't corruption!" No, and neither is that corruption which makes the heads of great educational and charity institutions "go along," as they say in Pennsylvania, in order to get appropriations for their institutions from the State and land from the city. They know what is going on, but they do not join reform movements. The provost of the University of Pennsylvania declined to join in a revolt because, he said, it might impair his usefulness to the University. And so it is with others, and with clergymen who have favorite charities; with Sabbath associations and City Beautiful clubs; with lawyers who want briefs; with real estate dealers who like to know in advance about public improvements, and real estate owners who appreciate light assessments; with shopkeepers who don't want to be bothered with strict inspections.

If there is no other hold for the ring on a man there always is the protective tariff. "I don't care," said a manufacturer. "What if they do plunder and rob us, it can't hurt me unless they raise the tax rates, and even that won't ruin me. Our party keeps up the tariff. If they should reduce that, my business would be ruined."

Such, then, are the ramifications of this machine, such is its strength. No wonder Martin could break his own rules, as he did, and commit excesses. Martin's doom was proclaimed not in Philadelphia, but in the United States Senate, and his offence was none of this business of his, but his failure to nominate as successor to Mayor Stuart the man, Boies Penrose, whom Matt Quay chose for that place. Martin had consented, but at the last moment he ordered the nomination of Charles F. Warwick instead. The day that happened Mr. Quay arose on the floor of the Senate and, in a speech so irrelevant to the measure under consideration that nobody out of Pennsylvania understood it, said that there was in his town a man who had given as his reason for not doing what he had promised to do, the excuse that he was "under a heavy salary from a great corporation (the Pennsylvania Railroad) and was compelled to do what the corporation wished him to do. And," added Senator Quay, "men in such a position with high power for good or evil ought . . . to go about . . . with the dollar mark of the corporation on their foreheads." Quay named as the new boss Israel W. Durham, a ward leader under Martin.

Martin having the city through Mayor Warwick fought Quay in the State, with Chris Magee for an ally, but Quay beat them both there and then prepared to beat them in their own cities. His cry was Reform, and he soon had the people shouting for it.

Quay responded with a Legislative committee to investigate abuses in the cities, but this so-called "Lexow" was called off before it amounted to much more than a momentary embarrassment to Martin. Martin's friends, on the other hand, caught Quay and nearly sent him to prison. The People's Bank, James Mc-Manes, president, failed. The cashier, John S. Hopkins, had been speculating and letting Quay and other politicians have bank funds without collateral for stock gambling. In return, Quay and the State Treasurer left heavy State deposits with the bank. Hopkins lost his nerve and shot himself. McManes happened to call in friends of Martin to advise him, and these suggested a Martin man for receiver. They found among the items money lent to Quay without security, except the State funds, and telegrams asking Hopkins to buy "1000 Met" (Metropolitan) and promising in return to "shake the plum tree." Quay, his son, Richard R., and Benjamin J. Haywood, the State Treasurer, were indicted for conspiracy, and every effort was made to have the trial precede the next election for the Legislature which was to elect a successor to Quay in the United States Senate; but Quay got stays and postponements in the hope that a more friendly District Attorney could be put in that office. Martin secured the election of Peter F. Rothermel, who was eager to try the case, and Quay had to depend on other resources. The trial came in due course, and failed; Judge Biddle ruled out the essential evidence on the ground that it was excluded by the statute of limitation. Rothermel went on with the trial, but it was hopeless; Quay was acquitted and the other cases were abandoned.

Popular feeling was excited by this exposure of Quay, but there was no action till the factional fighting suggested a use for it. Quay had refused the second United States Senatorship to John Wanamaker, and Wanamaker led through the State and in Philadelphia a fight against the boss, which has never ceased. It took the form of a reform campaign, and Quay's methods were made plain, but the boss beat Wanamaker at every point, had Penrose made Senator, and through Penrose and Durham was gradually getting possession of Philadelphia. The final triumph came with the election of Samuel H. Ashbridge as Mayor.

"Stars-and-stripes Sam," as Ashbridge is sometimes called, was a speech-maker and a "joiner." That is to say, he made a practice of going to lodges, associations, brotherhoods, Sunday-schools, and all sorts of public and private meetings, joining some, but making at all speeches patriotic and sentimental. He was very popular. Under the Bullitt Law, as I have said, all that is necessary to a good administration and complete, though temporary reform, is a good mayor. The politicians feel that they must nominate a man in whom the people as well as themselves have faith. They had had faith in Warwick, both the ring and the people, and Warwick had found it impossible to satisfy two such masters. Now they put their faith in Ashbridge, and so did Durham and so did Martin. All interests accepted him, therefore, and all watched him with hope and more or less assurance; none more than the good people. And, indeed, no man could have promised more or better public service than Ashbridge. The result, however, was distracting.

Mr. Ashbridge "threw down" Martin, and he recognized Quay's man, "Is" Durham, as the political boss. Durham is a high type of boss, candid, but of few words; generous, but businesslike; complete master of himself, and a genius at organization. For Pennsylvania politics he is a conservative leader, and there would have been no excesses under him, as there have been few "rows." But Mr. Durham has not been the master of the Philadelphia situation. He bowed to Quay and he could not hold Ashbridge. Philadelphians say that if it should come to a fight,

Durham could beat Quay in Philadelphia, but it doesn't come
to a fight. Another thing Philadelphians say is that he "keeps
his word," yet he broke it (with notice) when Quay asked
him to stand for Pennypacker for Governor. As I said before,
however, Philadelphia is so constituted that it apparently cannot
have self-government, not even its own boss, so that the al-
legiance paid to Quay is comprehensible. But the submission of
the boss to the Mayor was extraordinary, and it seemed to some
sagacious politicians dangerous.

For Mr. Ashbridge broke through all the principles of moderate
grafting developed by Martin. Durham formed his ring—taking
in James P. McNichol as co-ruler and preferred contractor; John
M. Mack as promoter and financier; and he widened the inside
circle to include more individuals. But while he was more liberal
toward his leaders, and not inclined "to grab off everything for
himself," as one leader told me, he maintained the principle of
concentration and strict control as good politics and good
business. So, too, he adopted Martin's program of public improvements, the filtration, boulevards, etc., and added to it. When
Ashbridge was well settled in office, these schemes were all
started, and the Mayor pushed them with a will. According to
the "Philadelphia Plan," the Mayor should not be in the ring.
He should be an ambitious man, and his reward promotion, not
riches. If he is "out for the stuff," he is likely to be hurried by the
fretful thought that his term is limited to four years, and since
he cannot succeed himself as Mayor, his interest in the future
of the machine is less than that of a boss, who goes on forever.

When he was nominated, Ashbridge had debts of record
amounting to some $40,000. Before he was elected these were
satisfied. Soon after he took office he declared himself in an
interview with former Postmaster Thomas L. Hicks. Here is Mr.
Hicks's account of the incident:

"At one of the early interviews I had with the Mayor in his
office, he said to me: 'Tom, I have been elected Mayor of Philadelphia. I have four years to serve. I have no further ambitions.
I want no other office when I am out of this one, and I shall get
out of this office all there is in it for Samuel H. Ashbridge.'

"I remarked that this was a very foolish thing to say. 'Think
how that could be construed,' I said.

" 'I don't care anything about that,' he declared. 'I mean to get out of this office everything there is in it for Samuel H. Ashbridge.' "

When he retired from office last April, he became the president of a bank, and was reputed to be rich. Here is the summary published by the Municipal League at the close of his labors:

"The four years of the Ashbridge administration have passed into history, leaving behind them a scar on the fame and reputation of our city which will be a long time healing. Never before, and let us hope never again, will there be such brazen defiance of public opinion, such flagrant disregard of public interest, such abuse of powers and responsibilities for private ends. These are not generalizations, but each statement can be abundantly proved by numerous instances."

These "numerous instances" are notorious in Philadelphia; some of them were reported all over the country. One of them was the attempted blackmailing of John Wanamaker. Thomas B. Wanamaker, John Wanamaker's son, bought the *North American,* a newspaper which had been and still is exposing the abuses and corruption of the political ring. Abraham L. English, Mr. Ashbridge's Director of the Department of Public Safety, called on Mr. John Wanamaker, said he had been having him watched, and was finally in a position to demand that the newspaper stop the attacks. The merchant exposed the attempt, and a committee appointed to investigate reported that: "Mr. English has practically admitted that he attempted to intimidate a reputable citizen and unlawfully threatened him in an effort to silence criticism of a public newspaper: that from the Mayor's refusal to order an investigation of the conduct of Mr. English on the request of a town meeting of representative citizens, the community is justified in regarding him as aiding and abetting Mr. English in the corrupt act committed, and that the Mayor is therefore to be equally censured by the community."

The other "instances of brazen abuse of power" were the increase of protected vice—the importation from New York of the "white slavery system of prostitution," the growth of "speak-easies," and the spread of gambling and of policy playing until it took in the school children. This last the *North American* exposed, but in vain till it named police officers who had refused when asked to interfere. Then a Judge summoned the editors and reporters of the paper, the Mayor, Director English, school children, and police officers to appear before him. The Mayor's personal attorney spoke for the police during the inquiry, and it looked black for the newspaper till the children began to tell their stories. When the hearing was over the Judge said:

"The evidence shows conclusively that our public school system in this city is in danger of being corrupted at its fountain; that in one of the schools over one hundred and fifty children were buyers of policy, as were also a large number of scholars in other schools. It was first discovered about eighteen months ago, and for about one year has been in full operation." The police officers were not punished, however.

That corruption had reached the public schools and was spreading rapidly through the system, was discovered by the exposure and conviction of three school directors of the twenty-eighth ward. It was known before that teachers and principals, like any other office holders, had to have a "pull" and pay assessments for election expenses. "Voluntary contributions" was the term used, but over the notices in blue pencil was written "2 per cent.," and teachers who asked directors and ward bosses what to do, were advised that they would "better pay." Those that sent less than the amount suggested, got receipts: "check received: shall we hold for balance or enter on account?" But the exposure in the twenty-eighth ward brought it home to the parents of the children that the teachers were not chosen for fitness but for political reasons, and that the political reasons had become cash.

Miss Rena A. Haydock, testified as follows: "I went to see Mr. Travis, who was a friend of mine, in reference to getting a teacher's certificate. He advised me to see all of the directors, especially Mr. Brown. They told me that it would be necessary for me to pay $120 to get the place. They told me of one girl who had offered $250, and her application had been rejected. That was before they broached the subject of money to me. I said that I didn't have $120 to pay, and they replied that it was customary for teachers to pay $40 a month out of their first three months' salary. The salary was $47. They told me they didn't want the money for themselves, but that it was necessary to buy the other faction. Finally I agreed to the proposition, and they told me that I must be careful not to mention it to anybody or it would injure my reputation. I went with my brother to pay the money to Mr. Johnson. He held out a hat, and when my brother handed the money to him he took it behind the hat."

The regular business of the ring was like that of Pittsburg, but more extensive. I have space only for one incident of one phase of it: Widener and Elkins, the national franchise buyers, are Philadelphians, and they were in the old Martin ring. They had combined all the street railways of the city before 1900, and they were withdrawing from politics, with their traction system. But the Pennsylvania rings will not let' corporations that have risen in corruption reform and retire, and, besides, it was charged that in the Martin-Quay fight, the street railways had put up money to beat Quay for the United States Senate. At any rate, plans were laid to "mace" the street railways.

"Macing" is a form of high blackmail. When they have sold out all they have, the politicians form a competing company and compel the old concern to buy out or sell out. While Widener and Elkins were at sea, in 1901, the Philadelphia ring went to the Legislature and had introduced there two bills, granting a charter to practically all the streets and alleys not covered by tracks in Philadelphia, and to run short stretches of the old companies' tracks to make connections. Clinton Rogers Woodruff, who was an Assemblyman, has told the story. Without notice the bills were introduced at 3 P.M. on Monday, May 29th; they were reported from committee in five minutes; by 8:50 P.M. they were printed and on the members' desks, and by 9 P.M. were passed on first reading. The bills passed second reading the next day, Memorial Day, and on the third day were passed from the Senate to the House, where they were "jammed through" with similar haste and worse trickery. In six legislative days the measures were before Governor Stone, who signed them June 7th, at midnight, in the presence of Quay, Penrose, Congressman Foerderer, Mayor Ashbridge's banker, James P. McNichol, John M. Mack, and other capitalists and politicians. Under the law, one hundred charters were applied for the next morning—thirteen for Philadelphia. The charters were granted on June 5th, and that same day a special meeting of the Philadelphia Select Council was called for Monday. There the citizens of Philadelphia met the oncoming charters, but their hearing was brief. The charters went through without a hitch, and were sent to Mayor Ashbridge on June 13th.

The Mayor's secretary stated authoritatively in the morning that the Mayor would not sign that day. But he did. John Wanamaker sent him an offer of $2,500,000 for the franchises about to be given away. Ashbridge threw the letter into the street, unread. Mr. Wanamaker had deposited $250,000 as a guarantee of good faith and his action was becoming known. The ordinances were signed by midnight, and the city lost at least two and one-half millions of dollars; but the ring made it and much more. When Mr. Wanamaker's letter was published, Congressman Foerderer, an incorporator of the company, answered for the machine. He said the offer was an advertisement; that it was late, and that they were sorry they hadn't had a chance to "call the bluff." Mr. Wanamaker responded with a renewal of the offer of $2,500,000 to the city, and, he said, "I will add $500,000 as a bonus to yourself and your associates personally for the conveyance of the grants and corporate privileges you now possess." That ended the controversy.

But the deal went on. Two more bills, called "Trolley Chasers," were put through, to finish off the legislation, too hurriedly done to be perfect. One was to give the company the right to build either elevated or underground, or both; the second to forbid all further such grants without a hearing before a board consisting of the Governor, the Secretary of the Commonwealth, and the Attorney-General. With all these franchises and exclusive privileges, the new company made the old one lease their plant in operation to the company which had nothing but "rights," or, in Pennsylvania slang, a "good, husky mace."

Ashbridgeism put Philadelphia and the Philadelphia machine to a test which candid ring leaders did not think they would stand. What did the Philadelphians do? Nothing. They have their reformers: they have men like Francis B. Reeves, who fought with every straight reform movement from the days of the Committee of One Hundred; they have men like Rudolph Blankenburg, who have fought with every reform that promised any kind of relief; there are the Municipal League, with an organization by wards, the Citizens' Municipal League, the Allied Reform League, and the Law and Order Society; there are young men and veterans; there are disappointed politicians and ambitious men who are not advanced fast enough by the machine. There is discontent in a good many hearts, and some men are ashamed. But "the people" won't follow. One would think the Philadelphians would follow any leader: what should they care whether he is pure white or only gray? But they do care. "The people" seem to prefer to be ruled by a known thief than an ambitious reformer. They will make you convict their Tweeds, McManeses, Butlers, and Shepherds, and even then they may forgive them and talk of monuments to their precious memory, but they take delight in the defeat of John Wanamaker because they suspect that he wants to go to the United States Senate.

All the stout-hearted reformers made a campaign to reëlect Rothermel, the District Attorney who had dared to try Quay. Surely there was an official to support! But no, Quay was against him. The reformers used money, some $250,000, I believe— fighting the devil with fire,—but the machine used more money, $700,000, from the teachers, "speak-easies," office holders, bankers, and corporations. The machine handled the ballot, Rothermel was beaten by John Weaver. There have been other campaigns, before and since, led by the Municipal League, which is managed with political sense, but each successive defeat was by a larger majority for the machine, and against good government.

There is no check upon this machine excepting the chance of a mistake, the imminent fear of treachery, and the remote danger of revolt. To meet this last, the machine, as a State organization, has set about throttling public criticism. Ashbridge proved that blackmail was ineffective. Durham, Quay, and Governor Penny-packer have passed a libel law which, if it stands, may muzzle the press. The Governor was actuated apparently only by his sufferings from cartoons and comments during his campaign; the Philadelphia ring has boodling plans ahead which exposure might make exasperating to the people. The *Philadelphia Press,* the leading Republican organ in the State, puts it right: "The Governor wanted it (the law) in the hope of escaping from the unescapable cartoon. The gang wanted it in the hope of muzzling the opposition to jobs. . . . The act is distinctly designed to gag the press in the interest of the plunderers and against the interest of the people."

Disfranchised, without a choice of parties, denied, so the Municipal League declares, the ancient right of petition, and now to lose "free speech,"—is there no hope for Philadelphia? Yes, the Philadelphians have a very present hope. It is in their new Mayor, John Weaver. There is nothing in his record to inspire faith in an outsider. He speaks himself of two notorious "miscarriages of justice" during his term as District Attorney; he was the nominee of the ring; and the ring men have confidence in him. But so have the people, and Mr. Weaver makes fair promises. So did Ashbridge. There is this difference, however: Mr. Weaver has made a good start. He compromised with the machine on his appointments, but he declared against the protection of vice, for free voting, and he stopped some "wholesale grabs" or "maces" that appeared in the Legislature, just before he took office.

One was a bill to enable (ring) companies to "appropriate, take, and use all water within this commonwealth and belonging either to public or to private persons as it may require for its private purposes." This was a scheme to sell out the water works of Philadelphia, and all other such plants in the State. Another bill was to open the way to a seizure of the light and power of the city and of the State. Martin and Warwick "leased" the city gas works. Durham and his crowd wanted a whack at it. "It shall be lawful," the bill read, "for any city, town, or borough owning any gas works or electric light plant for supplying light, heat, and power, to sell, lease or otherwise dispose of the same to individuals or corporations, and in order to obtain the best possible returns therefor, such municipal body may . . . vest in the lessees or purchasers the exclusive right, both as against such municipal corporations and against any and all other persons and corporations, to supply gas or electricity. . . ." As in St. Louis the public property of Philadelphia is to be sold off. These schemes are to go through later, I am told, but on Mr. Weaver's declarations that he would not "stand for them," they were laid over.

It looks as if the Philadelphians were right about Mr. Weaver, but what if they are? Think of a city putting its whole faith in one man, in the *hope* that John Weaver, an Englishman by birth, will *give* them good government! And why should he do that? Why should he serve the people and not the ring? The ring can make or break him; the people of Philadelphia can neither reward nor punish him. For even if he restores to them their ballots and proves himself a good Mayor, he cannot succeed himself; the good charter forbids.

29

How to Make Money in Politics

George Washington Plunkitt
Talks About Honest Graft

Accustomed to England, where the "professional politicians" numbered only 4,000, James Bryce was astonished at the "hundreds of thousands" in the United States pursuing politics as a means of livelihood. Such a man was George Washington Plunkitt of Tammany Hall, and he made a good living too, becoming a millionaire. His monologues that follow were taken down by a newspaperman. In reading this selection, note (1) the author's distinction between honest and dishonest graft; (2) his firsthand lessons concerning "unearned increments" in real estate; (3) his means of gaining and maintaining political support; and (4) his criticism of Steffens. An engaging account by a Tammany mayor is Harold C. Syrett (ed.), *The Gentleman and the Tiger: The Autobiography of George B. McClellan, Jr.* (1956). On Chicago, see my *Altgeld's America* (1958).

From William L. Riordan (ed.), *Plunkitt of Tammany Hall* (New York: McClure, Phillips & Co., 1905), pp. 3-10, 46-61.

Honest Graft and Dishonest Graft

Everybody is talkin' these days about Tammany men growin' rich on graft, but nobody thinks of drawin' the distinction between honest graft and dishonest graft. There's all the difference in the world between the two. Yes, many of our men have grown rich in politics. I have myself. I've made a big fortune out of the game, and I'm gettin' richer every day, but I've not gone in for dishonest graft—blackmailin' gamblers, saloon-keepers, disorderly people, etc.—and neither has any of the men who have made big fortunes in politics.

"There's an honest graft, and I'm an example of how it works. I might sum up the whole thing by sayin': 'I seen my opportunities and I took 'em.'

"Just let me explain by examples. My party's in power in the city, and it's goin' to undertake a lot of public improvements. Well, I'm tipped off, say, that they're going to lay out a new park at a certain place.

"I see my opportunity and I take it. I go to that place and I buy up all the land I can in the neighborhood. Then the board of this or that makes its plan public, and there is a rush to get my land, which nobody cared particular for before.

"Ain't it perfectly honest to charge a good price and make a profit on my investment and foresight? Of course, it is. Well, that's honest graft.

"Or, supposin' it's a new bridge they're goin' to build. I get tipped off and I buy as much property as I can that has to be taken for approaches. I sell at my own price later on and drop some more money in the bank.

"Would n't you? It's just like lookin' ahead in Wall Street or in the coffee or cotton market. It's honest graft, and I'm lookin' for it every day in the year. I will tell you frankly that I've got a good lot of it, too.

"I'll tell you of one case. They were goin' to fix up a big park, no matter where. I got on to it, and went lookin' about for land in that neighborhood.

"I could get nothin' at a bargain but a big piece of swamp, but I took it fast enough and held on to it. What turned out was just what I counted on. They could n't make the park complete with Plunkitt's swamp, and they had to pay a good price for it. Anything dishonest in that?

"Up in the watershed I made some money, too. I bought up several bits of land there some years ago and made a pretty good guess that they would be bought up for water purposes later by the city.

"Somehow, I always guessed about right, and should n't I enjoy the profit of my foresight? It was rather amusin' when the condemnation commissioners came along and found piece after piece of the land in the name of George Plunkitt of the Fifteenth Assembly District, New York City. They wondered how I knew just what to buy. The answer is—I seen my opportunity and I took it. I have n't confined myself to land; anything that pays is in my line.

"For instance, the city is repavin' a street and has several hundred thousand old granite blocks to sell. I am on hand to buy, and I know just what they are worth.

"How? Never mind that. I had a sort of monopoly of this business for a while, but once a newspaper tried to do me. It got some outside men to come over from Brooklyn and New Jersey to bid against me.

"Was I done? Not much. I went to each of the men and said: 'How many of these 250,000 stones do you want?' One said 20,000, and another wanted 15,000, and another wanted 10,000. I said: 'All right, let me bid for the lot, and I'll give each of you all you want for nothin'.

"They agreed, of course. Then the auctioneer yelled: 'How much am I bid for these 250,000 fine pavin' stones?'

" 'Two dollars and fifty cents,' says I.

" 'Two dollars and fifty cents!' screamed the auctioneer. 'Oh, that's a joke! Give me a real bid.'

"He found the bid was real enough. My rivals stood silent. I got the lot for $2.50 and gave them their share. That's how the attempt to do Plunkitt ended, and that's how all such attempts end.

"I've told you how I got rich by honest graft. Now, let me tell you that most politicians who are accused of robbin' the city get rich the same way.

"They did n't steal a dollar from the city treasury. They just seen their opportunities and took them. That is why, when a reform administration comes in and spends a half million dollars in tryin' to find the public robberies they talked about in the campaign, they don't find them.

"The books are always all right. The money in the city treasury is all right. Everything is all right. All they can show is that the Tammany heads of departments looked after their friends, within the law, and gave them what opportunities they could to make honest graft. Now, let me tell you that's never goin' to hurt Tammany with the people. Every good man looks after his friends, and any man who does n't is n't likely to be popular. If I have a good thing to hand out in private life, I give it to a friend. Why should n't I do the same in public life?

"Another kind of honest graft. Tammany has raised a good many salaries. There was an awful howl by the reformers, but don't you know that Tammany gains ten votes for every one it lost by salary raisin'?

"The Wall Street banker thinks it shameful to raise a department clerk's salary from $1500 to $1800 a year, but every man who draws a salary himself says: 'That's all right. I wish it was me.' And he feels very much like votin' the Tammany ticket on election day, just out of sympathy.

"Tammany was beat in 1901 because the people were deceived into believin' that it worked dishonest graft. They did n't draw a distinction between dishonest and honest graft, but they saw that some Tammany men grew rich, and supposed they had been robbin' the city treasury or levyin' blackmail on disorderly houses, or workin' in with the gamblers and lawbreakers.

"As a matter of policy, if nothing else, why should the Tammany leaders go into such dirty business, when there is so much honest graft lyin' around when they are in power? Did you ever consider that?

"Now, in conclusion, I want to say that I don't own a dishonest dollar. If my worst enemy was given the job of writin' my epitaph when I'm gone, he could n't do more than write:

" 'George W. Plunkitt. He Seen His Opportunities, and He Took Em.' "

To Hold Your District—Study Human Nature and Act Accordin'

"There's only one way to hold a district; you must study human nature and act accordin'. You can't study human nature in books. Books is a hindrance more than anything else. If you have been to college, so much the worse for you. You'll have to unlearn all you learned before you can get right down to human nature, and unlearnin' takes a lot of time. Some men can never forget what they learned at college. Such men may get to be district leaders by a fluke, but they never last.

"To learn real human nature you have to go among the people, see them and be seen. I know every man, woman, and child in the Fifteenth District, except them that's been born this summer— and I know some of them, too. I know what they like and what they don't like, what they are strong at and what they are weak in, and I reach them by approachin' at the right side.

"For instance, here's how I gather in the young men. I hear of a young feller that's proud of his voice, thinks that he can sing fine. I ask him to come around to Washington Hall and join our Glee Club. He comes and sings, and he's a follower of Plunkitt for life. Another young feller gains a reputation as a base-ball player in a vacant lot. I bring him into our base-ball club. That fixes him. You'll find him workin' for my ticket at the polls next election day. Then there's the feller that likes rowin' on the river, the young feller that makes a name as a waltzer on his block, the young feller that's handy with his dukes—I rope them all in by givin' them opportunities to show themselves off. I don't trouble them with political arguments. I just study human nature and act accordin'.

"But you may say this game won't work with the high-toned fellers, the fellers that go through college and then join the Citizens' Union. Of course it would n't work. I have a special treatment for them. I ain't like the patent medicine man that gives the same medicine for all diseases. The Citizens' Union kind of a young man! I love him! He's the daintiest morsel of the lot, and he don't often escape me.

"Before telling you how I catch him, let me mention that before the election last year, the Citizens' Union said they had four hundred or five hundred enrolled voters in my district. They had a lovely headquarters, too, beautiful roll-top desks and the cutest rugs in the world. If I was accused of havin' contributed to fix up the nest for them, I would n't deny it under oath. What do I mean by that? Never mind. You can guess from the sequel, if you're sharp.

"Well, election day came. The Citizens' Union's candidate for Senator, who ran against me, just polled five votes in the district, while I polled something more than 14,000 votes. What became of the 400 or 500 Citizens' Union enrolled voters in my district? Some people guessed that many of them were good Plunkitt men all along and worked with the Cits just to bring them into the Plunkitt camp by election day. You can guess that way, too, if you want to. I never contradict stories about me, especially in hot weather. I just call your attention to the fact that on last election day 395 Citizens' Union enrolled voters in my district were missin' and unaccounted for.

"I tell you frankly, though, how I have captured some of the Citizens' Union's young men. I have a plan that never fails. I watch the City Record to see when there's civil service examinations for good things. Then I take my young Cit in hand, tell him all about the good thing and get him worked up till he goes and takes an examination. I don't bother about him any more. It's a cinch that he comes back to me in a few days and asks to join Tammany Hall. Come over to Washington Hall some night and I'll show you a list of names on our rolls marked 'C.S.' which means, 'bucked up against civil service.'

"As to the older voters, I reach them, too. No, I don't send them campaign literature. That's rot. People can get all the political stuff they want to read—and a good deal more, too—in the papers. Who reads speeches, nowadays, anyhow? It's bad enough to listen to them. You ain't goin' to gain any votes by stuffin' the letter boxes with campaign documents. Like as not you'll lose votes, for there's nothin' a man hates more than to hear the letter-carrier ring his bell and go to the letter-box expectin' to find a letter he was lookin' for, and find only a lot of printed politics. I met a man this very mornin' who told me he voted the Democratic State ticket last year just because the Republicans kept crammin' his letter-box with campaign documents.

"What tells in holdin' your grip on your district is to go right down among the poor families and help them in the different ways they need help. I've got a regular system for this. If there's a fire in Ninth, Tenth, or Eleventh Avenue, for example, any hour of the day or night, I'm usually there with some of my election district captains as soon as the fire-engines. If a family is burned out I don't ask whether they are Republicans or Democrats, and I don't refer them to the Charity Organization Society, which would investigate their case in a month or two and decide they were worthy of help about the time they are dead from starvation. I just get quarters for them, buy clothes for them if their clothes were burned up, and fix them up till they get things runnin' again. It's philanthropy, but it's politics, too—mighty good politics. Who can tell how many votes one of these fires bring me? The poor are the most grateful people in the world, and, let me tell you, they have more friends in their neighborhoods than the rich have in theirs.

"If there's a family in my district in want I know it before the charitable societies do, and me and my men are first on the ground. I have a special corps to look up such cases. The consequence is that the poor look up to George W. Plunkitt as a father, come to him in trouble—and don't forget him on election day.

"Another thing, I can always get a job for a deservin' man. I make it a point to keep on the track of jobs, and it seldom happens that I don't have a few up my sleeve ready for use. I know every big employer in the district and in the whole city, for that matter, and they ain't in the habit of sayin' no to me when I ask them for a job.

"And the children—the little roses of the district! Do I forget them? Oh, no! They know me, every one of them, and they know that a sight of Uncle George and candy means the same thing. Some of them are the best kind of vote-getters. I'll tell you a case. Last year a little Eleventh Avenue rosebud whose father is a Republican, caught hold of his whiskers on election day and said she would n't let go till he'd promise to vote for me. And she did n't.

On "The Shame of the Cities"

"I've been readin' a book by Lincoln Steffens on 'The Shame of the Cities.' Steffens means well but, like all reformers, he don't know how to make distinctions. He can't see no difference between honest graft and dishonest graft and, consequent, he gets things all mixed up. There's the biggest kind of a difference between political looters and politicians who make a fortune out of politics by keepin' their eyes wide open. The looter goes in for himself alone without considerin' his organization or his city. The politician looks after his own interests, the organization's interests, and the city's interests all at the same time. See the distinction? For instance, I ain't no looter. The looter hogs it. I never hogged. I made my pile in politics, but, at the same time, I served the organization and got more big improvements for New York City than any other livin' man. And I never monkeyed with the penal code.

"The difference between a looter and a practical politician is the difference between the Philadelphia Republican gang and Tammany Hall. Steffens seems to think they're both about the same; but he's all wrong. The Philadelphia crowd runs up against the penal code. Tammany don't. The Philadelphians ain't satisfied with robbin' the bank of all its gold and paper money. They stay to pick up the nickels and pennies and the cop comes and nabs them. Tammany ain't no such fool. Why, I remember, about fifteen or twenty years ago, a Republican superintendent of the Philadelphia almshouse stole the zinc roof off the buildin' and sold it for junk. That was carryin' things to excess. There's a limit to everything, and the Philadelphia Republicans go beyond the limit. It seems like they can't be cool and moderate like real politicians. It ain't fair, therefore, to class Tammany men with the Philadelphia gang. Any man who undertakes to write political books should never for a moment lose sight of the distinction between honest graft and dishonest graft, which I explained in full in another talk. If he puts all kinds of graft on the same level, he'll make the fatal mistake that Steffens made and spoil his book.

"A big city like New York or Philadelphia or Chicago might be compared to a sort of Garden of Eden, from a political point of view. It's an orchard full of beautiful apple-trees. One of them has got a big sign on it, marked: 'Penal Code Tree—Poison.' The other trees have lots of apples on them for all. Yet, the fools go to the Penal Code Tree. Why? For the reason, I guess, that a cranky child refuses to eat good food and chews up a box of matches with relish. I never had any temptation to touch the Penal Code Tree. The other apples are good enough for me, and O Lord! how many of them there are in a big city!

"Steffens made one good point in his book. He said he found that Philadelphia, ruled almost entirely by Americans, was more corrupt than New York, where the Irish do almost all the governin'. I could have told him that before he did any investigatin' if he had come to me. The Irish was born to rule, and they 're the honestest people in the world. Show me the Irishman who would steal a roof off an almshouse! He don't exist. Of course, if an Irishman had the political pull and the roof was much worn, he might get the city authorities to put on a new one and get the contract for it himself, and buy the old roof at a bargain—but that's honest graft. It's goin' about the thing like a gentleman—and there's more money in it than in tearin' down an old roof and cartin' it to the junkman's—more money and no penal code.

"One reason why the Irishman is more honest in politics than many Sons of the Revolution is that he is grateful to the country and the city that gave him protection and prosperity when he was driven by oppression from the Emerald Isle. Say, that sentence is fine, ain't it? I'm goin' to get some literary feller to work it over into poetry for next St. Patrick's Day dinner.

"Yes, the Irishman is grateful. His one thought is to serve the city which gave him a home. He has this thought even before he lands in New York, for his friends here often have a good place in one of the city departments picked out for him while he is still in the old country. Is it any wonder that he has a tender spot in his heart for old New York when he is on its salary list the mornin' after he lands?

"Now, a few words on the general subject of the so-called shame of cities. I don't believe that the government of our cities is any worse, in proportion to opportunities, than it was fifty years ago. I'll explain what I mean by 'in proportion to opportunities.' A half a century ago, our cities were small and poor. There was n't many temptations lyin' around for politicians. There was hardly anything to steal, and hardly any opportunities for even honest graft. A city could count its money every night before goin' to bed, and if three cents was missin', all the fire-bells would be rung. What credit was there in bein' honest under them circumstances? It makes me tired to hear of old codgers back in the thirties or forties boastin' that they retired from politics without a dollar except what they earned in their profession or business. If they lived to-day, with all the existin' opportunities, they would be just the same as twentieth century politicians. There ain't any more honest people in the world just now than the convicts in Sing Sing. Not one of them steals anything. Why? Because they can't. See the application?

"Understand, I ain't defendin' politicians of to-day who steal. The politician who steals is worse than a thief. He is a fool. With the grand opportunities all around for the man with a political pull, there's no excuse for stealin' a cent. The point I want to make is that if there is some stealin' in politics, it don't mean that the politicians of 1905 are, as a class, worse than them of 1835. It just means that the old-timers had nothin' to steal, while the politicians now are surrounded by all kinds of temptations and some of them naturally—the fool ones—buck up against the penal code."

Part IV. History of Foreign Relations]

30

Justification of the Big Navy Policy

Theodore Roosevelt Reviews Mahan's
The Influence of Sea Power upon History

Theodore Roosevelt (1858-1919), prior to his futile race for the Presidency in 1912, had lost only one campaign for elective office— for the mayoralty of New York in 1886, when he ran behind both the Democrat and the Labor candidate Henry George. He served in the state assembly from 1881 to 1884. Thereafter he held only appointive jobs until the Spanish-American War. Then his spectacular heroism with the Rough Riders in Cuba, plus an assassin's bullet, brought him incredibly swift advances: he was elected governor of New York in 1898; Vice President in 1900; and with the death of McKinley in 1901 he moved into the White House. One of his most significant efforts as President was to build up American naval power. But he had embraced that policy more than a decade earlier, and his chief mentor had been Captain Alfred Thayer Mahan, head of the naval war college at Newport from 1886 to 1889. Roosevelt's enthusiasm is already apparent in the following review of Mahan's great *The Influence of Sea Power upon History, 1660-1783* (1890). In reading Roosevelt's review, note (1) what he says concerning Mahan's qualifications for writing on seapower in history; (2) how Mahan differed from other historians who wrote on similar subjects; and (3) what lessons Theodore Roosevelt saw in Mahan's book. Mahan's book was republished in paperback in 1957. See also Henry F. Pringle, *Theodore Roosevelt* (1931); William E. Livezey, *Mahan on Seapower* (1947); and Harold and Margaret Sprout, *The Rise of American Naval Power, 1766-1918* (1946).

Theodore Roosevelt, review of A. T. Mahan's *The Influence of Sea Power upon History, Atlantic Monthly,* vol. 66 (October 1890), pp. 563-567.

Captain Mahan has written distinctively the best and most important, and also by far the most interesting, book on naval history which has been produced on either side of the water for many a long year. Himself an officer who has seen active service and borne himself with honor under fire, he starts with an advantage that no civilian can possess. On the other hand, he does not show the shortcomings which make the average military man an exasperatingly incompetent military historian. His work is in every respect scholarly, and has not a trace of the pedantry which invariably mars mere self-conscious striving after scholarship. He is thoroughly conversant with his subject, and has prepared himself for it by exhaustive study and research, and he approaches it in, to use an old-fashioned phrase, an entirely philosophical spirit. He subordinates detail to mass-effects, trying always to grasp and make evident the essential features of a situation; and he neither loses sight of nor exaggerates the bearing which the history of past struggles has upon our present problems.

One of his merits is the use of French authorities. For the last three centuries England has been the central and commanding figure in naval history, and, naturally, her writers, followed by our own, have acted blandly on the belief that they themselves wrote the only books on the subject worth reading. As a matter of fact, the French historians and essayists form a school of marked excellence in many ways. It would, for instance, be difficult to match in English such writings as those of Admiral Jurien de la Gravière. Only by a study of the French authors is it possible to arrive at the true facts in the history of the gigantic sea struggle, lasting for over a century, which began at Bantry Bay and Beachy Head and ended at Trafalgar.

In his Introduction, Captain Mahan shows very clearly the practical importance of the study of naval history in the past to those who wish to estimate and use aright the navies of the present. He dwells on the fact that not only are the great principles of strategy much the same as they ever were, but that also many of the underlying principles of the tactics of the past are applicable to the tactics of the present; or, at least, that the tacticians of to-day can with advantage study the battles of the past. He does not fall into the mistake of trying to make forced analogies, but he does prove, for one thing, that the school which professes the *mêlée* or "never-mind-manoeuvring" principles, no less than the other school, which tends to turn manoeuvring into an end instead of a means, and to develop mere timid tactical trifling, may study the fleet actions and naval campaigns of the last two centuries to good purpose. There are plenty of naval authorities who believe that an encounter between squadrons of modern ironclads, with their accompanying rams and torpedo-boats, can be nothing but a huge bloody scramble, in which each ship fights for its own hand. This belief may be true as an estimate of probabilities; but if it be, it will only show that as yet the nineteenth century does not know how to wield with proper skill the wonderful weapons it has forged. Similarly, the early sea fights between fleets of sailing-ships were mere mêlées; men knowing nothing more of tactics than that one-sided view of the "shock" principle which consists in running headlong at an adversary,—a system whereof the success depends entirely upon the nature of the adversary. But as time went on a change took place, and there arose great admirals, who differed as much from the rough fleet-leaders who preceded them as Alexander differed from Alaric. Sea war grew into an art, and the fleet that conquered had to pay heed to such considerations as unity of action and intelligent direction of force quite as much as to the valor of the seaman and the fighting capacity of the individual ships.

Captain Mahan's effort is to show the tremendous effect which sea power has had upon the development of certain of the great nations of the world, especially at momentous crises of their history. In his introductory chapter he gives one striking illustration, for he shows that it was the sea power of Rome, during the second Punic war, which was one of the chief determining factors in bringing about the failure of Hannibal's campaign in Italy, and the consequent overthrow of Carthage. He makes this point so clear that it is difficult to see how it can be controverted successfully. The second Punic war was one of the all-important world struggles, and has been described again and again by every kind of writer for the past twenty centuries, yet Captain Mahan is the first who has given proper prominence to one of the main causes by which the result was determined. This is a fair example of Captain Mahan's acute historic insight, and it is characteristic of the way his book is written. Hitherto, historians of naval matters, at least so far as English and American writers are concerned, have completely ignored the general strategic bearing of the struggles which they chronicle; they have been for the most part mere annalists, who limited themselves to describing the actual battles and the forces on each side. On the other hand, the general historian sees but dimly how much and in what way the net outcome of a conflict has been influenced by the might of the contestants on the sea, and in consequence pay but vague and unsubstantial heed to the really vital cause by which the result was accomplished. Captain Mahan, however, never loses sight of the deep, underlying causes and of the connection between events. His discussion of the campaigns and battles, of the strategy and tactics, is full and clear, and written in a perfectly scientific and dispassionate spirit. But this is not his greatest merit. He never for a moment loses sight of the relations which the struggles by sea bore to the history of the time; and, for the period which he covers, he shows, as no other writer has done, the exact points and the wonderful extent of the influence of the sea power of the various contending nations upon their ultimate triumph or failure, and upon the futures of the mighty races to which they belonged.

In the first chapter after the Introduction, he discusses the various elements which go to make up sea power, writing always, as elsewhere throughout the book, with especial heed to the circumstances of the United States at the present time. He shows how sea power is affected by the geographical position, physical conformation, extent, and density of population of a country no less than by the character of the people and of the government. He points out the need of adequate fortifications and navy yards on all the coast, and incidentally specifies the need at some point on the Gulf coast, preferably the mouth of the Mississippi; and he lays stress on the necessity of a large commercial marine, if we wish the sea population which alone furnishes a secure base for naval power. He draws one or two instructive lessons from the sudden rise and no less sudden fall of the French sea power during the reign of Louis XIV., and shows how that monarch undid the work of his great minister Colbert. One of the most interesting points he makes is when he deals with the inherent wrongheadedness of the French policy of hostility to Holland. As he shows, Holland's greatness lay on the sea, and her real rival, the rival before whom she ultimately succumbed, was England. France, also, strove for development by sea only to be steadily thwarted and finally worsted by the island kingdom; while on land Holland had no territory which France was able to gain. It was, therefore, clearly the true wisdom of both nations to make common cause against the people who, in the end, triumphed over both. A policy of steady alliance between France and Holland, from the days of De Ruyter, Tromp, Duquesne, and Tourville onward, might have changed the fate of the world; and, if so, would probably have changed it much for the worse. The spread of the mighty English-speaking race, their rise to world-dominion, was greatly helped by the jealous division between its two most formidable foes during the critical years when the possession of the North American continent hinged largely on the control of the Atlantic Ocean.

Captain Mahan's second and third chapters treat of the wars waged by Holland against England and France, separately or united. Undoubtedly the greatest figure in these wars was the Dutch Admiral De Ruyter; and the series of long and exhausting struggles between Holland and England are especially noteworthy because they afford the only instance where any naval power has striven for the mastery with England, on equal terms, through a succession of wars wherein victory and defeat alternated in campaign after campaign and battle after battle. On the whole, the superiority remained with the English, and the net result left them ahead. But no other nation ever gave England such a tussle for the dominion of the seas; and no admiral, not even Nelson, accomplished more for his country than De Ruyter did in the battles terminating with the battle of the Texel, wherein, with much inferior forces, he held at bay the combined French and English fleet, and thus saved Holland from an invasion which meant destruction. The old hero himself perished, a couple of years later, in the Mediterranean, at the battle of Stromboli. He was then in command of a mixed squadron, part Dutch and part Spanish, and was opposed by a superior French fleet under the able Huguenot Duquesne, who stood in France much as, a century before, Lord Howard stood in England. The first fight between these two redoubtable antagonists was a draw; in the second the Spanish ships fled, and De Ruyter was overcome and slain. The Spanish fleets, from the time of Drake to that of Nelson, won hardly a single victory; and even when they formed part of a coalition, their presence in a given battle rarely did more than swell the adversary's triumph.

In all these seventeenth-century fights fire-ships played an important part, and our author draws one or two curious and interesting comparisons between them and their modern analogues, the torpedo-boats. He then describes the war in which, at the end of the seventeenth cntury, the French were first pitted against the combined forces of the English and Dutch. The English at that date had no admiral who can be considered the equal of the Frenchman Tourville, though Tourville himself cannot rank with such men as Suffren, Tegethof, or Farragut, not to speak of Nelson. For the first three years of the war Tourville cruised with his fleet off the shores of England and Ireland, and kept the upper hand of his opponents, defeating them twice. In one of these battles, at Beachy Head, he destroyed a dozen Dutch and English ships, but, through overcaution, failed to strike a decisive blow at the enemy, though much his superior in strength. Two years later he was beaten by an overwhelming force at the obstinate battle of the Hague. Disheartened by this defeat, the French gave up trying to contend for the supremacy, and turned their attention to privateering, or commerce-destroying, on a colossal scale. They inflicted thereby much damage on the English, but the damage was not of a kind that materially affected the issue of the war.

The next four chapters deal with the maritime history of Europe up to the outbreak of the American Revolution; that is, with the first three quarters of the eighteenth century. At the very beginning of this period, in the war of the Spanish succession, England established her overwhelming preponderance at sea, which has lasted, with but one or two partial interruptions, to our own time. Until this period she had shown no such preponderance. During the seventeenth century, though on the whole she established her superiority, she did so only by a long series of desperate and doubtful struggles with the Dutch and French; and she was defeated again and again by both these rivals. She produced one or two noted admirals, like Blake and Monk, but none who stood above the sea chiefs of her adversaries.

All this was changed after the year 1700. From the time when Gibraltar was taken to the beginning of the war for American independence, England possessed the undisputed supremacy of the ocean. It was this, more than anything else, which gave her North America and India, and paved the way for her taking possession of Australia and South Africa. But the very extent of her superiority prevented any serious efforts to overcome it, and the campaigns and battles of this period possess but little interest in themselves.

When, however, England, in the midst of her struggle with the revolted colonies, was struck by the combined navies of France and Spain, both of them, but especially that of France, having been sedulously cared for and built up in the interval, the fight became most interesting, for it was waged on equal terms. Captain Mahan's account of this war is excellent. Among other things, he shows clearly the harm wrought to France by the system of tactical timidity in naval warfare which her rulers adopted and instilled into the minds of their sea commanders. The English always tried to destroy their opponent's navies, and it was their cue to attack, which they always did with great courage, though often with so little skill as to neutralize their efforts. The French, on the other hand, had been cowed by repeated defeat, and, except when led by some born fighter, like the Bailli de Suffren, rarely took the offensive or pressed home a blow, though they fought with great skill when attacked; and their strategy was fatally defective, in that they conducted their campaigns, not with the purpose of destroying the enemy's fighting power, his war fleets, but with the purpose of neutralizing or evading it, while some island or outpost was secured or conquered. It must be said, nevertheless, that our author does not give sufficient weight to the military operations on land, and to the effect produced by the American privateers.

This war of the American Revolution brought to the front two great admirals, Rodney and Suffren; and two of the best chapters in Captain Mahan's book are those in which he describes the deeds of these men. The military analysis in these two chapters is really very fine; no previous writer has approached it, in dealing with either the Frenchman or the Englishman. In particular, Suffren's campaign in the Indian Ocean has never before been treated with such clearness of perception and appreciation. Indeed, to most English writers he has hitherto been little but a name; and it was hardly possible for a Frenchman to write of him as justly as Captain Mahan has done.

One or two of the points which Captain Mahan brings out have a very important bearing on our present condition, especially in view of the increased interest which is felt in the navy and coast defense. There is a popular idea that we could accomplish wonders by privateering,—or rather by commerce-destroying, as Captain Mahan calls it. He shows very clearly, on the other hand, that commerce-destroying can never be more than a secondary factor—even though of very considerable importance—in bringing to a conclusion a war with a powerful foe. He shows also that, for the most successful kind of commerce-destroying, there must be a secure base of operations near the line of the enemy's commerce, and some kind of line of battle to fall back on,—and the United States possesses neither. Doubtless, in event of a war, we might cause annoyance and loss to an enemy's commerce; but we could not by this method accomplish anything like as much as the people at large, and not a few of our naval officers also, believe. It is beyond all comparison more important to cripple the enemy's fighting-ships than to harass his merchantmen.

Again, as Captain Mahan shows, our experience in the Civil War is worthless as a test of what we could do against a foreign sea power. It is impossible to imagine a more foolish state of mind than that which accepts the belief in our capacity to improvise means of resistance against the sea power of Europe, ready equipped and armed at all points, because we were successful in overcoming with our makeshifts an enemy even more unprepared than we were ourselves. It is true that at the end of four years' warfare we had developed a formidable fleet; but in the event of a European contest, it is not likely that we should be allowed as many weeks before the fatal blow fell. There is a loose popular idea that we could defend ourselves by some kind of patent method, invented on the spur of the moment. This is sheer folly. There is no doubt that American ingenuity could do something, but not enough to prevent the enemy from ruining our coasting-trade and threatening with destruction half our coast towns. Proper forts, with heavy guns, could do much; but our greatest need is the need of a fighting-fleet. Forts alone could not prevent the occupation of any town or territory outside the range of their guns, or the general wasting of the seaboard; while a squadron of heavy battle-ships, able to sail out and attack the enemy's vessels as they approached, and possessing the great advantage of being near their own base of supplies, would effectually guard a thousand miles of coast. Passive defense, giving the assailant complete choice of the time and place for attack, is always a most dangerous expedient. Our ships should be the best of their kind,—this is the first desideratum; but, in addition, there should be plenty of them. We need a large navy, composed not merely of cruisers, but containing also a full proportion of powerful battle-ships, able to meet those of any other nation. It is not economy—it is niggardly and foolish short-sightedness—to cramp our naval expenditures, while squandering money right and left on everything else, from pensions to public buildings.

In conclusion, it must be said that Captain Mahan's style is clear, simple, and terse. His book is as interesting as it is valuable; and in writing it he has done a real service.

31

United States Hegemony
in Latin America

Richard Olney Discusses the
Venezuela Boundary Dispute

Richard Olney (1835-1917), a prosperous and forceful railroad lawyer, entered the second cabinet of Grover Cleveland in 1893 as Attorney General. In that post he played a leading role in smashing the Pullman boycott of 1894. In May 1895 Secretary of State Gresham died, and Olney was promoted to the job. Although no friend of the Big Navy policy, he soon showed himself capable of a decided truculence in foreign relations. Great Britain had possessed British Guiana since 1814, and its boundary with Venezuela had never been determined. In the seventy-two years of its existence, no one had ever claimed that the Monroe Doctrine required compulsory arbitration of every boundary dispute in Latin America involving a European power, yet Olney made that claim in the following dispatch of July 20, 1895, to the American ambassador in London. The dispatch was brash and often inaccurate, but President Cleveland thought it "the best thing of the kind that I have ever read. . . ." In reading this dispatch, note (1) Olney's review of what the Monroe Doctrine meant; (2) the characteristic nineteenth-century attitude toward the relationship of the United States and Europe; (3) what the mission of America mean to Olney; (4) the threat that Olney saw to American security; (5) the precise issue involved in the dispute; and (6) what action was contemplated should Great Britain refuse to arbitrate the dispute. Dexter Perkins' standard *The Monroe Doctrine, 1865-1907* (1937) is still useful but needs to be corrected by Walter LaFeber's two fine articles: "The American Business Community and Cleveland's Venezuela Message," *Business History Review*, vol. 34 (1960), pp. 392-402, and "The Background of Cleveland's Venezuelan Policy: A Reinterpretation," *American Historical Review*, vol. 66 (1960-1961), pp. 947-967.

... THAT AMERICA IS IN NO PART OPEN TO COLONI-
zation, though the proposition was not universally
admitted at the time of its first enunciation, has long been universally conceded. We are now concerned, therefore, only with
that other practical application of the Monroe doctrine the
disregard of which by an European power is to be deemed an
act of unfriendliness towards the United States. The precise
scope and limitations of this rule cannot be too clearly apprehended. It does not establish any general protectorate by the
United States over other American states. It does not relieve any
American state from its obligations as fixed by international law
nor prevent any European power directly interested from en-
forcing such obligations or from inflicting merited punishment
for the breach of them. It does not contemplate any interference
in the internal affairs of any American state or in the relations
between it and other American states. It does not justify any
attempt on our part to change the established form of government of any American state or to prevent the people of such
state from altering that form according to their own will and
pleasure. The rule in question has but a single purpose and
object. It is that no European power or combination of European powers shall forcibly deprive an American state of the
right and power of self-government and of shaping for itself
its own political fortunes and destinies.

That the rule thus defined has been the accepted public law
of this country ever since its promulgation cannot fairly be
denied. Its pronouncement by the Monroe administration at that
particular time was unquestionably due to the inspiration of
Great Britain, who at once gave to it an open and unqualified
adhesion which has never been withdrawn. But the rule was
decided upon and formulated by the Monroe administration as
a distinctively American doctrine of great import to the safety

From Richard Olney to Thomas F. Bayard, July 20, 1895, *Papers
Relating to the Foreign Relations of the United States . . . 1895,*
House of Representatives Document No. 1, 54th Cong., 1st
Sess., Part I, vol. 1 (Washington, D.C.: Government Printing
Office, 1896), pp. 554-562.

and welfare of the United States after the most careful consideration by a Cabinet which numbered among its members John Quincy Adams, Calhoun, Crawford, and Wirt, and which before acting took both Jefferson and Madison into its counsels. Its promulgation was received with acclaim by the entire people of the country irrespective of party. Three years after, Webster declared that the doctrine involved the honor of the country. "I look upon it," he said, "as part of its treasures of reputation, and for one I intend to guard it," and he added,

I look on the message of December, 1823, as forming a bright page in our history. I will help neither to erase it nor to tear it out; nor shall it be by any act of mine blurred or blotted. It did honor to the sagacity of the Government, and I will not diminish that honor.

Though the rule thus highly eulogized by Webster has never been formally affirmed by Congress, the House in 1864 declared against the Mexican monarchy sought to be set up by the French as not in accord with the policy of the United States, and in 1889 the Senate expressed its disapproval of the connection of any European power with a canal across the Isthmus of Darien or Central America. It is manifest that, if a rule has been openly and uniformly declared and acted upon by the executive branch of the Government for more than seventy years without express repudiation by Congress, it must be conclusively presumed to have its sanction. Yet it is certainly no more than the exact truth to say that every administration since President Monroe's has had occasion, and sometimes more occasions than one, to examine and consider the Monroe doctrine and has in each instance given it emphatic endorsement. Presidents have dwelt upon it in messages to Congress and Secretaries of State have time after time made it the theme of diplomatic representation. Nor, if the practical results of the rule be sought for, is the record either meager or obscure. Its first and immediate effect was indeed most momentous and far reaching. It was the controlling factor in the emancipation of South America and to it the independent states which now divide that region between them are largely indebted for their very existence. Since then the most striking single achievement to be credited to the rule is the evacuation of Mexico by the French upon the termination of the civil war. But we are also indebted to it for the provisions of the Clayton-Bulwer treaty, which both neutralized any inter-oceanic canal across Central America and expressly excluded Great Britain from occupying or exercising any dominion over any part of Central America. It has been used in the case of Cuba as if justifying the position that, while the sovereignty of Spain will be respected, the island will not be permitted to become the possession of any other European power. It has been influential in bringing about the definite relinquishment of any supposed protectorate by Great Britain over the Mosquito Coast. . . .

The foregoing enumeration not only shows the many instances wherein the rule in question has been affirmed and applied, but also demonstrates that the Venezuelan boundary controversy is in any view far within the scope and spirit of the rule as uniformly accepted and acted upon. A doctrine of American public law thus long and firmly established and supported could not easily be ignored in a proper case for its application, even were the considerations upon which it is founded obscure or questionable. No such objection can be made, however, to the Monroe doctrine understood and defined in the manner already stated. It rests, on the contrary, upon facts and principles that are both intelligible and incontrovertible. That distance and three thousand miles of intervening ocean make any permanent political union between an European and an American state unnatural and inexpedient will hardly be denied. But physical and geographical considerations are the least of the objections to such a union. Europe, as Washington observed, has a set of primary interests which are peculiar to herself. America is not interested in them and ought not to be vexed or complicated with them. Each great European power, for instance, to-day maintains enormous armies and fleets in self-defense and for protection against any other European power or powers. What have the states of America to do with that condition of things, or why should they be impoverished by wars or preparations for wars with whose causes or results they can have no direct concern? If all Europe were to suddenly fly to arms over the fate of Turkey, would it not be preposterous that any American state should find itself inextricably involved in the miseries and burdens of the contest? If it were, it would prove to be a partnership in the cost and losses of the struggle but not in any ensuing benefits.

What is true of the material, is no less true of what may be termed the moral interests involved. Those pertaining to Europe are peculiar to her and are entirely diverse from those pertaining and peculiar to America. Europe as a whole is monarchical, and, with the single important exception of the Republic of France, is committed to the monarchical principle. America, on the other hand, is devoted to the exactly opposite principle—to the idea that every people has an inalienable right of self-government—and, in the United States of America, has furnished to the world the most conspicuous and conclusive example and proof of the excellence of free institutions, whether from the standpoint of national greatness or of individual happiness. It can not be necessary, however, to enlarge upon this phase of the subject—whether moral or material interests be considered, it can not but be universally conceded that those of Europe are irreconcilably diverse from those of America, and that any European control of the latter is necessarily both incongruous and injurious. If, however, for the reasons stated the forcible intrusion of European powers into American politics is to be deprecated—if, as it is to be deprecated, it should be resisted and prevented—such resistance and prevention must come from the United States. They would come from it, of course, were it made the point of attack. But, if they come at all, they must also come from it when any other American state is attacked, since only the United States has the strength adequate to the exigency.

Is it true, then, that the safety and welfare of the United States are so concerned with the maintenance of the independence of every American state as against any European power as to justify and require the interposition of the United States whenever that independence is endangered? The question can be candidly answered in but one way. The states of America, South as well as North, by geographical proximity, by natural sympathy, by similarity of governmental constitutions, are friends and allies, commercially and politically, of the United States. To allow the subjugation of any of them by an European power is, of course, to completely reverse that situation and signifies the loss of all the advantages incident to their natural relations to us. But that is not all. The people of the United States have a vital interest in the cause of popular self-government. They have secured the right for themselves and their posterity at the cost of infinite blood and treasure. They have realized and exemplified its beneficent operation by a career unexampled in point of national greatness or individual felicity. They believe it to be for the healing of all nations, and that civilization must either advance or retrograde accordingly as its supremacy is extended or curtailed. Imbued with these sentiments, the people of the United States might not impossibly be wrought up to an active propaganda in favor of a cause so highly valued both for themselves and for mankind. But the age of the Crusades has passed, and they are content with such assertion and defense of the right of popular self-government as their own security and welfare demand. It is in that view more than in any other that they believe it not to be tolerated that the political control of an American state shall be forcibly assumed by an European power.

The mischiefs apprehended from such a source are none the less real because not immediately imminent in any specific case, and are none the less to be guarded against because the combination of circumstances that will bring them upon us cannot be predicted. The civilized states of Christendom deal with each other on substantially the same principles that regulate the conduct of individuals. The greater its enlightenment, the more surely every state perceives that its permanent interests require it to be governed by the immutable principles of right and justice. Each, nevertheless, is only too liable to succumb to the temptations offered by seeming special opportunities for its own aggrandizement, and each would rashly imperil its own safety were it not to remember that for the regard and respect of other states it must be largely dependent upon its own strength and power. To-day the United States is practically sovereign on this continent, and its fiat is law upon the subjects to which it confines its interposition. Why? It is not because of the pure friendship or good will felt for it. It is not simply by reason of its high character as a civilized state, nor because wisdom and justice and equity are the invariable characteristics of the dealings of the United States. It is because, in addition to all other grounds, its infinite resources combined with its isolated position render it master of the situation and practically invulnerable as against any or all other powers.

All the advantages of this superiority are at once imperiled if the principle be admitted that European powers may convert American states into colonies or provinces of their own. The principle would be eagerly availed of, and every power doing so would immediately acquire a base of military operations against us. What one power was permitted to do could not be denied to another, and it is not inconceivable that the struggle now going on for the acquisition of Africa might be transferred to South America. If it were, the weaker countries would unquestionably be soon absorbed, while the ultimate result might be the partition of all South America between the various European powers. The disastrous consequences to the United States of such a condition of things are obvious. The loss of prestige, of authority, and of weight in the councils of the family of nations, would be among the least of them. Our only real rivals in peace as well as enemies in war would be found located at our very doors. Thus far in our history we have been spared the burdens and evils of immense standing armies and all the other accessories of huge warlike establishments, and the exemption has largely contributed to our national greatness and wealth as well as to the happiness of every citizen. But, with the powers of Europe permanently encamped on American soil, the ideal conditions we have thus far enjoyed can not be expected to continue. We too must be armed to the teeth, we too must convert the flower of our male population into soldiers and sailors, and by withdrawing them from the various pursuits of peaceful industry we too must practically annihilate a large share of the productive energy of the nation.

How a greater calamity than this could overtake us it is difficult to see. Nor are our just apprehensions to be allayed by suggestions of the friendliness of European powers—of their good will towards us—of their disposition, should they be our neighbors, to dwell with us in peace and harmony. The people of the United States have learned in the school of experience to what extent the relations of states to each other depend not upon sentiment nor principle, but upon selfish interest. They will not soon forget that, in their hour of distress, all their anxieties and burdens were aggravated by the possibility of demonstrations against their national life on the part of powers with whom they had long maintained the most harmonious relations. They have yet in mind that France seized upon the apparent opportunity of our civil war to set up a monarchy in the adjoining state of Mexico. They realize that had France and Great Britain held important South American possessions to work from and to benefit, the temptation to destroy the predominance of the Great Republic in this hemisphere by furthering its dismemberment might have been irresistible. From that grave peril they have been saved in the past and may be saved again in the future through the operation of the sure but silent force of the doctrine proclaimed by President Monroe. To abandon it, on the other hand, disregarding both the logic of the situation and the facts of our past experience, would be to renounce a policy which has proved both an easy defense against foreign aggression and a prolific source of internal progress and prosperity.

There is, then, a doctrine of American public law, well founded in principle and abundantly sanctioned by precedent, which entitles and requires the United States to treat as an injury to itself the forcible assumption by an European power of political control over an American state. The application of the doctrine to the boundary dispute between Great Britain and Venezuela remains to be made and presents no real difficulty. Though the dispute relates to a boundary line, yet, as it is between states, it necessarily imports political control to be lost by one party and gained by the other. The political control at stake, too, is of no mean importance, but concerns a domain of great extent— the British claim, it will be remembered, apparently expanded in two years some 33,000 square miles—and, if it also directly involves the command of the mouth of the Orinoco, is of immense consequence in connection with the whole river navigation of the interior of South America. It has been intimated, indeed, that in respect of these South American possessions Great Britain is herself an American state like any other, so that a controversy between her and Venezuela is to be settled between themselves as if it were between Venezuela and Brazil or between Venezuela and Colombia, and does not call for or justify United States intervention. If this view be tenable at all, the logical sequence is plain.

Great Britain as a South American state is to be entirely differentiated from Great Britain generally, and if the boundary question cannot be settled otherwise than by force, British Guiana, with her own independent resources and not those of the British Empire, should be left to settle the matter with Venezuela—an arrangement which very possibly Venezuela might not object to. But the proposition that an European power with an American dependency is for the purposes of the Monroe doctrine to be classed not as an European but as an American state will not admit of serious discussion. If it were to be adopted, the Monroe doctrine would be too valueless to be worth asserting. Not only would every European power now having a South American colony be enabled to extend its possessions on this continent indefinitely, but any other European power might also do the same by first taking pains to procure a fraction of South American soil by voluntary cession.

The declaration of the Monroe message—that existing colonies or dependencies of an European power would not be interfered with by the United States—means colonies or dependencies then existing, with their limits as then existing. So it has been invariably construed, and so it must continue to be construed unless it is to be deprived of all vital force. Great Britain cannot be deemed a South American state within the purview of the Monroe doctrine, nor, if she is appropriating Venezuelan territory, is it material that she does so by advancing the frontier of an old colony instead of by the planting of a new colony. The difference is matter of form and not of substance and the doctrine if pertinent in the one case must be in the other also. It is not admitted, however, and therefore cannot be assumed, that Great Britain is in fact usurping dominion over Venezuelan territory. While Venezuela charges such usurpation, Great Britain denies it, and the United States, until the merits are authoritatively ascertained, can take sides with neither. But while this is so—while the United States may not, under existing circumstances at least, take upon itself to say which of the two parties is right and which wrong—it is certainly within its right to demand that the truth shall be ascertained. Being entitled to resent and resist any sequestration of Venezuelan soil by Great Britain, it is necessarily entitled to know whether such sequestration has occurred or is now going on. Otherwise, if the United States is without the right to know and have it determined whether there is or is not British aggression upon Venezuelan territory, its right to protest against or repel such aggression may be dismissed from consideration.

The right to act upon a fact the existence of which there is no right to have ascertained is simply illusory. It being clear, therefore, that the United States may legitimately insist upon the merits of the boundary question being determined, it is equally clear that there is but one feasible mode of determining them, viz., peaceful arbitration. The impracticability of any conventional adjustment has been often and thoroughly demonstrated. Even more impossible of consideration is an appeal to arms—a mode of settling national pretensions unhappily not yet wholly obsolete. If, however, it were not condemnable as a relic of barbarism and a crime in itself, so one-sided a contest could not be invited nor even accepted by Great Britain without distinct disparagement to her character as a civilized state. Great Britain, however, assumes no such attitude. On the contrary, she both admits that there is a controversy and that arbitration should be resorted to for its adjustment. But, while up to that point her attitude leaves nothing to be desired, its practical effect is completely nullified by her insistence that the submission shall cover but a part of the controversy—that, as a condition of arbitrating her right to a part of the disputed territory, the remainder shall be turned over to her. If it were possible to point to a boundary which both parties had ever agreed or assumed to be such either expressly or tacitly, the demand that territory conceded by such line to British Guiana should be held not to be in dispute might rest upon a reasonable basis. But there is no such line. The territory which Great Britain insists shall be ceded to her as a condition of arbitrating her claim to other territory has never been admitted to belong to her. It has always and consistently been claimed by Venezuela.

Upon what principle—except her feebleness as a nation—is

she to be denied the right of having the claim heard and passed upon by an impartial tribunal? No reason nor shadow of reason appears in all the voluminous literature of the subject. "It is to be so because I will it to be so" seems to be the only justification Great Britain offers. It is, indeed, intimated that the British claim to this particular territory rests upon an occupation, which, whether acquiesced in or not, has ripened into a perfect title by long continuance. But what prescription affecting territorial rights can be said to exist as between sovereign states? Or, if there is any, what is the legitimate consequence? It is not that all arbitration should be denied, but only that the submission should embrace an additional topic, namely, the validity of the asserted prescriptive title either in point of law or in point of fact. No different result follows from the contention that as matter of principle Great Britain cannot be asked to submit and ought not to submit to arbitration her political and sovereign rights over territory. This contention, if applied to the whole or to a vital part of the possessions of a sovereign state, need not be controverted. To hold otherwise might be equivalent to holding that a sovereign state was bound to arbitrate its very existence.

But Great Britain has herself shown in various instances that the principle has no pertinency when either the interests or the territorial area involved are not of controlling magnitude and her loss of them as the result of an arbitration cannot appreciably affect her honor or her power. Thus, she has arbitrated the extent of her colonial possessions twice with the United States, twice with Portugal, and once with Germany, and perhaps in other instances. The Northwest Water Boundary arbitration of 1872 between her and this country is an example in point and well illustrates both the effect to be given to long-continued use and enjoyment and the fact that a truly great power sacrifices neither prestige nor dignity by reconsidering the most emphatic rejection of a proposition when satisfied of the obvious and intrinsic justice of the case. By the award of the Emperor of Germany, the arbitrator in that case, the United States acquired San Juan and a number of smaller islands near the coast of Vancouver as a consequence of the decision that the term "the channel which separates the continent from Vancouver's Island," as used in the treaty of Washington of 1846, meant the Haro channel and not the Rosario channel. Yet a leading contention of Great Britain before the arbitrator was that equity required a judgment in her favor because a decision in favor of the United States would deprive British subjects of rights of navigation of which they had had the habitual enjoyment from the time when the Rosario Strait was first explored and surveyed in 1798. So, though by virtue of the award the United States acquired San Juan and the other islands of the group to which it belongs, the British Foreign Secretary had in 1859 instructed the British Minister at Washington as follows:

Her Majesty's Government must, therefore, under any circumstances, maintain the right of the British Crown to the Island of San Juan. The interests at stake in connection with the retention of that Island are too important to admit of compromise and Your Lordship will consequently bear in mind that, whatever arrangement as to the boundary line is finally arrived at, no settlement of the question will be accepted by Her Majesty's Government which does not provide for the Island of San Juan being reserved to the British Crown.

Thus, as already intimated, the British demand that her right to a portion of the disputed territory shall be acknowledged before she will consent to an arbitration as to the rest seems to stand upon nothing but her own *ipse dixit*. She says to Venezuela, in substance: "You can get none of the debatable land by force, because you are not strong enough; you can get none by treaty, because I will not agree; and you can take your chance of getting a portion by arbitration, only if you first agree to abandon to me such other portion as I may designate." It is not perceived how such an attitude can be defended nor how it is reconcilable with that love of justice and fair play so eminently characteristic of the English race. It in effect deprives Venezuela of her free agency and puts her under virtual duress. Territory acquired by reason of it will be as much wrested from her by the strong hand as if occupied by British troops or covered by British fleets. It seems therefore quite impossible that this position of Great Britain should be assented to by the United States, or that, if such position be adhered to with the result of enlarging the bounds of British Guiana, it should not be regarded as amounting, in substance, to an invasion and conquest of Venezuelan territory.

In these circumstances, the duty of the President appears to him unmistakable and imperative. Great Britain's assertion of title to the disputed territory combined with her refusal to have that title investigated being a substantial appropriation of the territory to her own use, not to protest and give warning that the transaction will be regarded as injurious to the interests of the people of the United States as well as oppressive in itself would be to ignore an established policy with which the honor and welfare of this country are closely identified. While the measures necessary or proper for the vindication of that policy are to be determined by another branch of the Government, it is clearly for the Executive to leave nothing undone which may tend to render such determination unnecessary.

You are instructed, therefore, to present the foregoing views to Lord Salisbury by reading to him this communication (leaving with him a copy should he so desire), and to reinforce them by such pertinent considerations as will doubtless occur to you. They call for a definite decision upon the point whether Great Britain will consent or will decline to submit the Venezuelan boundary question in its entirety to impartial arbitration. It is the earnest hope of the President that the conclusion will be on the side of arbitration, and that Great Britain will add one more to the conspicuous precedents she has already furnished in favor of that wise and just mode of adjusting international disputes. If he is to be disappointed in that hope, however—a result not to be anticipated and in his judgment calculated to greatly embarrass the future relations between this country and Great Britain—it is his wish to be made acquainted with the fact at such early date as will enable him to lay the whole subject before Congress in his next annual message.

32

Religion and the Philippines

President McKinley Talks to
His Methodist Brethren

William McKinley (1843-1901) served more than four years in the Union Army. Entering politics, he was elected to the House of Representatives in 1877 and served there continuously, save for a year, until 1891. His defeat in 1890 came after he had sponsored the McKinley Tariff Act, which raised import duties to record highs. Public memory proved short, and he was elected governor of Ohio in 1891 and reelected in 1893. The shrewd campaign of the Cleveland, Ohio, businessman Mark Hanna won McKinley the Republican nomination for the Presidency in 1896; he defeated Bryan in the election. Although not a war hawk, McKinley in the spring of 1898 at last yielded to the furor over the sinking of the U.S.S. *Maine* and to the frenzy to "free Cuba." In the following interview, the President explains how he decided that the United States should keep the Philippines; he also reveals much about the type of religion that helped to motivate his decision. See Margaret Leech, *In the Days of McKinley* (1959); Ernest R. May, *Imperial Democracy: The Emergence of America as a Great Power* (1961); Julius W. Pratt, *Expansionists of 1898: The Acquisition of Hawaii and the Spanish Islands* (1936); and Walter LeFeber, *The New Empire: An Interpretation of American Expansion, 1860–1898* (1963).

General James F. Rusling, "Interview with President McKinley," *The Christian Advocate*, vol. 78 (January 22, 1903), pp. 137-138.

Very interesting and appropriate to the second
celebration of President McKinley's birthday since
his martyrdom, is the following account of an interview with the
late President.

It was my good fortune to be present at a memorable interview with President McKinley, at the White House, Washington, D. C., on Tuesday, Nov. 21, 1899, and at the request of
many friends I beg to give the facts as follows:

The General Missionary Committee of the Methodist Episco-
pal Church had met in Washington the previous week, and was
still in session there. The President had given us a handsome
reception at the White House, assisted by his Cabinet and their
wives, and Admiral Dewey and his wife, and a committee was
appointed to draft a resolution expressive of our thanks for his
courtesy, and present the same to him. The committee consisted of Bishops Bowman and Hurst, Drs. Upham and Buckley,
and myself, and it fell to my lot to write said resolution, which
was submitted to the other members for criticism, few changes
being made. We chose Dr. Upham as our chairman, and re-
paired to the White House by appointment on said day, where
we were received by the President in his private office.

His desk was covered with books and papers, and evidently
he had been busily engaged on his message or in official correspondence, when we were ushered in. But he laid everything
aside, and rising stood at his desk while Dr. Upham addressed
him, with his usual felicity, stating the object of our visit and
reading said resolution. The President replied briefly, and then
as we were about to depart added:

"Gentlemen, just a moment. I have something I would like
to say. And, first, just a word with you, esteemed Bishops. Last
winter Congress increased the army by several regiments, but
provided no chaplains for them. Now I believe in army chaplains, and in my next message am going to recommend that
chaplains be authorized for all these new regiments; and I want
the Methodist Church to have its fair share of these, but no
more; and I want the very best men for these chaplaincies I can
get. Now won't you help me out with these chaplains? I don't

want any man under thirty years, nor over fifty years. No untried preacher. No worn-out preacher. But able-bodied, good chaplains. Now can't you Bishops devise some plan to give me good candidates? The Catholics manage to do that. When one of their men comes before me he has passed what is really a thorough Civil Service examination, and a moral and physical examination as well, and is indorsed by his responsible bishop and archbishop; and when I appoint him I know what I am doing, and get a good chaplain as a rule.

"But some time ago I appointed a Methodist chaplain, who came to me with letters and recommendations from half a dozen presiding elders, doctors of divinity, etc., as well as members of Congress and senators, and recently they have had to court-martial him for various misconduct, and I suppose we shall have to cashier him—greatly to my regret as a brother Methodist. Now I appeal to you, beloved Bishops, cannot you save me from such a thing hereafter? Why can't we arrange so that every Methodist application shall first be referred to your board or a committee of your board, and approved? And then I shall know where I stand when I appoint a Methodist chaplain."

Bishops Bowman and Hurst assented to this—the rest concurring—and we turned to leave. But again President McKinley earnestly said:

"Hold a moment longer! Not quite yet, gentlemen! Before you go I would like to say just a word about the Philippine business. I have been criticised a good deal about the Philippines, but don't deserve it. The truth is I didn't want the Philippines, and when they came to us, as a gift from the gods, I did not know what to do with them. When the Spanish war broke out Dewey was at Hongkong, and I ordered him to go to Manila and to capture or destroy the Spanish fleet, and he had to; because, if defeated, he had no place to refit on that side of the globe, and if the Dons were victorious they would likely cross the Pacific and ravage our Oregon and California coasts. And so he had to destroy the Spanish fleet, and did it! But that was as far as I thought then.

"When next I realized that the Philippines had dropped into our laps I confess I did not know what to do with them. I sought counsel from all sides—Democrats as well as Republicans—but, got little help. I thought first we would take only Manila; then Luzon; then other islands perhaps also. I walked the floor of the White House night after night until midnight; and I am not ashamed to tell you, gentlemen, that I went down on my knees and prayed Almighty God for light and guidance more than one night. And one night late it came to me this way—I don't know how it was, but it came: (1) That we could not give them back to Spain—that would be cowardly and dishonorable; (2) that we could not turn them over to France or Germany—our commercial rivals in the Orient—that would be bad business and discreditable; (3) that we could not leave them to themselves—they were unfit for self-government—and they would soon have anarchy and misrule over there worse than Spain's was; and (4) that there was nothing left for us to do but to take them all, and to educate the Filipinos, and uplift and civilize and Christianize them, and by God's grace do the very best we could by them, as our fellow-men for whom Christ also died. And then I went to bed, and went to sleep, and slept soundly, and the next morning I sent for the chief engineer of the War Department (our map-maker), and I told him to put the Phillippines on the map of the United States [pointing to a large map on the wall of his office], and there they are, and there they will stay while I am President!"

He said all this with great earnestness and impressiveness, as if he wanted us to remember it forever, and as only a great states-man and ruler like George Washington or Abraham Lincoln would have said it. And thinking he was now through, we all said good-bye, and turned again to leave—not wanting to take his time unnecessarily. But again President McKinley exclaimed:

"Don't go yet, please! Just a word more, friends; there's no hurry! It is not likely that we six gentlemen will ever meet again in this world—considering the chances of human life and the changes of time. No, it isn't at all likely! And before we part I just want to say to you, whatever men may think about me, or not think, I am a Methodist, and nothing but a Methodist—a Christian, and nothing but a Christian. When I was a little child my dear old mother used to take me to Methodist prayer meeting and class meeting. When I grew older I early joined the Methodist Church and Sunday school, and then became a Sunday school teacher, and afterward a Sunday school superintendent, and member of the Epworth League." Here he paused briefly, and solemnly, but presently resumed with much feeling: "And by the blessing of heaven, I mean to live and die, please God, in the faith of my mother!"

And then, indeed, we said good-bye, and shaking hands all around finally departed—never to meet again on this planet. But let me cast this passing tribute as a wreath of roses upon his grave, and place this record here to his credit forever: We Americans are certainly fortunate in our great ideals and great Presidents.

It goes without saying that I was deeply impressed by this interview, and have often referred to it since both publicly and privately. Some other things were spoken of, but these three were the chief things, and I have given much of the President's language (*ipissima verba* substantially), as I verily believe. It is submitted to the reader, and the men and times to come, as the very truth of passing American history.

Trenton, N. J.

[It should be added that General Rusling was appointed to draft the resolution presented to President McKinley on that occasion, which, however, was submitted to the other members for criticism, few changes being made.

The conversation was quite general for a few minutes before the President requested the committee, as it was about to depart, to remain a few moments, during which several things were said sufficient to form the materials for another interesting account.

The account given by General Rusling on the important subjects mentioned is substantially correct, as much so as any conversation could be made unless every word were taken down stenographically.

Concerning what President McKinley said with respect to army chaplains, we asked him on that occasion whether he would authorize the publication of his remarks in THE CHRISTIAN ADVOCATE, and he said that he would do so.

In addition to what he above reported of his remarks upon the Philippine Islands, President McKinley placed in our hands and allowed us to read the original instructions given to the commission for guidance in making a final settlement with the Spanish government. These instructions, which had not been made public at that time, made a profound impression upon the committee.

It has been the good fortune of General Rusling to be present at two important conversations, the first being the famous one which President Lincoln had with General Sickles, about which as the result of various interivews of General Rusling and General Sickles there was much discussion, resulting in substantial agreement. The other was this, on which there will be no disagreement among the five who were addressed by President McKinley on that occasion.—[EDITOR CHRISTIAN ADVOCATE.]

33

No Colonies for the United States

Carl Schurz Attacks Expansion after the Spanish-American War

Carl Schurz (1829-1906) was forced to flee his native Germany because of his participation in the revolution of 1848, and he arrived in the United States in 1852. After serving as a brigadier general in the Union army, he spent a term in the United States Senate. In 1876 he supported the regular Republican candidate for President, Rutherford B. Hayes, and then became Secretary of the Interior in 1877. But while these last actions made many Liberal Republicans think him an apostate, he was an exemplar of that faith throughout his career: he opposed Radical Reconstruction and government corruption, he fought for civil service reform, and, finally, he fought against the acquisition of any overseas colonies. In the following speech delivered in 1899, note (1) Schurz's understanding of the mission of America; (2) his view of the war against Spain; (3) the contrasts he saw between earlier American expansion and post-Spanish American War expansion; (4) what prospects he saw of Americanizing the new possessions; (5) dangers to the practice of democracy at home in overseas expansion; (6) the effect of expansion upon foreign relations; and (7) his answers to those advocating an expansionist policy. The quoted Social Darwinian statement by Representative Sulloway should be viewed in the perspective not only of Richard Hofstadter's *Social Darwinism in American Thought, 1860-1915* (1945) but also of Irvin G. Wyllie, *The Self-Made Man in America: The Myth of Rags to Riches* (1954) and Wyllie's "Social Darwinism and the Businessman," *Proceedings of the American Philosophical Society*, vol. 103 (1959), pp. 629-635.

From Carl Schurz, *American Imperialism: The Convocation Address Delivered on the Occasion of the Twenty-Seventh Convocation of the University of Chicago, Jan. 4, 1899* (Boston: Dana Estes & Company, 1899), pp. 3-31 (pamphlet in Boston Public Library).

. . . IF EVER, IT BEHOOVES THE AMERICAN PEOPLE TO think and act with calm deliberation, for the character and future of the republic and the welfare of its people now living and yet to be born are in unprecedented jeopardy. To form a candid judgment of what this republic has been, what it may become, and what it ought to be, let us first recall to our minds its condition before the recent Spanish War.

Our government was, in the words of Abraham Lincoln, "the government of the people, by the people, and for the people." It was the noblest ambition of all true Americans to carry this democratic government to the highest degree of perfection in justice, in probity, in assured peace, in the security of human rights, in progressive civilization; to solve the problem of popular self-government on the grandest scale, and thus to make this republic the example and guiding star of mankind.

We had invited the oppressed of all nations to find shelter here, and to enjoy with us the blessings of free institutions. They came by the millions. Some were not so welcome as others, but under the assimilating force of American life in our temperate climate, which stimulates the working energies, nurses the spirt of orderly freedom, and thus favors the growth of democracies, they became good Americans, most in the first, all in the following generations. And so with all the blood-crossings caused by the motley immigration, we became a substantially homogeneous people, united by common political beliefs and ideals, by common interests, laws, and aspirations,—in one word, a nation. Indeed, we were not without our difficulties and embarrassments, but only one of them, the race antagonism between the negroes and the whites, especially where the negroes live in mass, presents a problem which so far has baffled all efforts at practical solution in harmony with the spirit of our free institutions, and thus threatens complications of grave character.

We gloried in the marvellous growth of our population, wealth, power, and civilization, and in the incalculable richness of the resources of our country, a country capable of harboring three times our present population, and of immeasurable further material development. Our commerce with the world abroad, although we had no colonies, and but a small navy, spread with unprecedented rapidity, capturing one foreign market after another, not only for the products of our farms, but also for many of those manufacturing industries, with prospect of indefinite extension.

Peace reigned within our borders, and there was not the faintest shadow of danger of foreign attack. Our voice, whenever we chose to speak in the councils of nations, was listened to with respect, even the mightiest sea-power on occasion yielding to us a deference far beyond its habit in its intercourse with others. We were considered ultimately invincible, if not invulnerable, in our continental stronghold. It was our boast, not that we possessed great and costly armies and navies, but that we did not need any. This exceptional blessing was our pride, as it was the envy of the world. We looked down with pitying sympathy on other nations which submissively groaned under the burden of constantly increasing armaments, and we praised our good fortune for having saved us from so wretched a fate.

Such was our condition, such our beliefs and ideals, such our ambition and our pride, but a short year ago. Had the famous peace message of the Czar of Russia, with its protest against growing militarism, and its plea for disarmament, reached us then, it would have been hailed with enthusiasm by every American as a triumph of our example. We might have claimed only that to our republic, and not to the Russian monarch, belonged the place of leadership in so great an onward step in the progress of civilization.

Then came the Spanish War. A few vigorous blows laid the feeble enemy helpless at our feet. The whole scene seemed to have suddenly changed. According to the solemn proclamation of our government, the war had been undertaken solely for the liberation of Cuba, as a war of humanity and not of conquest. But our easy victories had put conquest within our reach, and when our arms occupied foreign territory, a loud demand arose that, pledge or no pledge to the contrary, the conquests should be kept, even the Philippines on the other side of the globe, and that as to Cuba herself, independence would only be a provisional formality. Why not? was the cry. Has not the career of the republic almost from its very beginning been one of territorial expansion? Has it not acquired Louisiana, Florida, Texas, the vast countries that came to us through the Mexican War, and Alaska, and has it not digested them well? Were not those acquisitions much larger than those now in contemplation? If the republic could digest the old, why not the new? What is the difference?

Only look with an unclouded eye, and you will soon discover differences enough, warning you to beware. There are five of decisive importance.

1. All the former acquisitions were on this continent, and, excepting Alaska, contiguous to our borders.

2. They were situated, not in the tropical, but in the temperate zone, where democratic institutions thrive, and where our people could migrate in mass.

3. They were but very thinly peopled,—in fact, without any population that would have been in the way of new settlement.

4. They could be organized as territories in the usual manner, with the expectation that they would presently come into the Union as self-governing States, with populations substantially homogeneous to our own.

5. They did not require a mateiral increase of our army or navy, either for their subjection to our rule, or for their defense against any probable foreign attack that might be provoked by being in our possession.

Acquisitions of that nature we might, since the slavery trouble has been allayed, make indefinitely without in any dangerous degree imperilling our great experiment of democratic institutions on the grandest scale; without putting the peace of the republic in jeopardy, and without depriving us of the inestimable privilege of comparative unarmed security on a compact continent which may, indeed, by an enterprising enemy, be scratched on its edges, but is, with a people like ours, virtually impregnable. Even of our far-away Alaska it can be said that, although at present a possession of doubtful value, it is at least mainly on this continent, and may at some future time, when the inhabitants of the British possessions happily wish to unite with us, be within our uninterrupted boundaries.

Compare now with our old acquisitions as to all these important points those at present in view.

They are not continental, not contiguous to our present domain, but beyond seas, the Philippines many thousand miles distant from our coast. They are all situated in the tropics, where people of the northern races, such as Anglo-Saxons, or, generally speaking, people of Germanic blood, have never migrated in mass to stay; and they are more or less densely populated, parts of them as densely as Massachusetts, their populations consisting almost exclusively of races to whom the tropical climate is congenial,— Spanish creoles mixed with negroes in the West Indies, and Malays, Tagals, Filipinos, Chinese, Japanese, Negritos, and various more or less barbarous tribes in the Philippines.

When the question is asked whether we may hope to adapt those countries and populations to our system of government, the advocates of annexation answer cheerily, that when they belong to us, we shall soon "Americanize" them. This may mean that Americans in sufficiently large numbers will migrate there to determine the character of those populations so as to assimilate them to our own.

This is a delusion of the first magnitude. We shall, indeed, be able, if we go honestly about it, to accomplish several salutary things in those countries. But one thing we cannot do. We cannot strip the tropical climate of those qualities which have at all times deterred men of the northern races, to which we belong, from migrating to such countries in mass, and to make their homes there, as they have migrated and are still migrating to countries in the temperate zone. This is not a mere theory, but a fact of universal experience.

It is true, you will find in tropical regions a sprinkling of persons of Anglo-Saxon or other northern origin,—merchants, railroad builders, speculators, professional men, miners, and mechanics; also here and there an agriculturist. But their number is small, and most of them expect to go home again as soon as their money-making purpose is more or less accomplished.

Thus we observe now that business men with plenty of means are casting their eyes upon our "new possessions" to establish mercantile houses there, or manufactories to be worked with native labor; and moneyed syndicates and "improvement companies" to exploit the resources of those countries; and speculators and promoters to take advantage of what may turn up,—the franchise grabber, as reported, is already there,—many having perfectly legitimate ends in view, others ends not so legitimate, and all expecting to be more or less favored by the power of our government; in short, *the capitalist* is thinking of going there, or to send his agents, his enterprises in most cases to be directed from these more congenial shores. But you will find that laboring men of the northern races, as they have never done so before, will not now go there in mass to do the work of the country, agricultural or industrial, and to found there permanent homes; and this is not merely because the rate of wages in such countries is, owing to native competition, usually low, but because they cannot thrive there under the climatic conditions.

But it is the working-masses, those laboring in agriculture and the industries, that everywhere form the bulk of the population; and they are the true constituency of democratic government. And as the northern races cannot do the work of the tropical zone, they cannot furnish such constituencies. It is an incontestable and very significant fact that the British, the best colonizers in history, have, indeed, established in tropical regions governments, and rather absolute ones, but they have never succeeded in establishing there democratic commonwealths of the Anglo-Saxon type, like those in America or Australia.

The scheme of Americanizing our "new possesions" in that sense is therefore absolutely hopeless. The immutable forces of nature are against it. Whatever we may do for their improvement, the people of the Spanish Antilles will remain in overwhelming numerical predominance, Spanish creoles and negroes, and the people of the Philippines, Filipinos, Malays, Tagals, and so on,— some of them quite clever in their way, but the vast majority utterly alien to us, not only in origin and language, but in habits, traditions, ways of thinking, principles, ambitions,—in short, in most things that are of the greatest importance in human intercourse and especially in political coöperation. And under the influences of their tropical climate they will prove incapable of becoming assimilated to the Anglo-Saxon. They would, therefore, remain in the population of this republic a hopelessly heterogeneous element,—in some respects more hopeless even than the colored people now living among us.

What, then, shall we do with such populations? Shall we,

according, not indeed to the letter, but to the evident spirit of our constitution, organize those countries as territories with a view to their eventual admission as States? If they become States on an equal footing with the other States they will not only be permitted to govern themselves as to their home concerns, but they will take part in governing the whole republic, in governing us, by sending Senators and Representatives into our Congress to help make our laws, and by voting for President and Vice-President to give our national government its executive. The prospect of the consequences which would follow the admission of the Spanish creoles and the negroes of West India islands, and of the Malays and Tagals of the Philippines, to participation in the conduct of our government is so alarming that you instinctively pause before taking the step.

But this may be avoided, it is said, by governing the new possessions as mere dependencies, or subject provinces. I will waive the constitutional question and merely point out that this would be a most serious departure from the rule that governed our former acquisitions, which are so frequently quoted as precedents. It is useless to speak of the District of Columbia and Alaska as proof that we have done such things before and can do them again. Every candid mind will at once admit the vast difference between those cases and the *permanent* establishment of substantially arbitrary government, over large territories with many millions of inhabitants, and with a prospect of their being many more of the same kind, if we once launch out on a career of conquest. The question is not merely whether we *can* do such things, but whether, having the public good at heart, we *should* do them.

If we adopt such a system, then we shall, for the first time since the abolition of slavery, again have two kinds of Americans: Americans of the first class, who enjoy the privilege of taking part in the government in accordance with our old constitutional principles, and Americans of the second class, who are to be ruled in a substantially arbitrary fashion by the Americans of the first class, through congressional legislation and the action of the national executive,—not to speak of individual "masters" arrogating to themselves powers beyond the law.

This will be a difference no better—nay, rather somewhat

worse—than that which a century and a quarter ago still existed between Englishmen of the first and Englishmen of the second class, the first represented by King George and the British Parliament, and the second by the American colonists. The difference called forth that great paean of human liberty, the American Declaration of Independence,—a document which, I regret to say, seems, owing to the intoxication of conquest, to have lost much of its charm among some of our fellow citizens. Its fundamental principle was that "governments derive their just powers from the consent of the governed." We are now told that we have never fully lived up to that principle, and that, therefore, in our new policy we may cast it aside altogether. But I say to you that, if we are true believers in democratic government, it is our duty to move in the direction toward the full realization of that principle, and not in the direction away from it. If you tell me that we cannot govern the people of those new possessions in accordance with that principle, then I answer that this is a good reason why this democracy should not attempt to govern them at all.

If we do, we shall transform the government of the people, for the people, and by the people, for which Abraham Lincoln lived, into a government of one part of the people, the strong, over another part, the weak. Such an abandoment of a fundamental principle as a permanent policy may at first seem to bear only upon more or less distant dependencies. but it can hardly fail in its ultimate effects to disturb the rule of the same principle in the conduct of democratic government at home. And I warn the American people that a democracy cannot so deny its faith as to the vital conditions of its being, it cannot long play the king over subject populations, without creating within itself ways of thinking and habits of action most dangerous to its own vitality,—most dangerous especially to those classes of society which are the least powerful in the assertion, and the most helpless in the defence of their rights. Let the poor and the men who earn their bread by the labor of their hands pause and consider well before they give their assent to a policy so deliberately forgetful of the equality of rights.

I do not mean to say, however, that all of our new acquisitions would be ruled as subject provinces. Some of them, the Philippines, would probably remain such but some others would doubtless become States. In Porto Rico, for instance, politicians of lively ambition are already clamoring for the speedy organization of that island as a regular territory, soon to be admitted as a State of the Union. You may say that they will have a long wait. Be not so sure of that. Consult your own experience. Has not more than one territory, hardly fitted for statehood, been precipitated into the Union as a State when the majority party in Congress thought that, by doing so, its party strength could be augmented in the Senate, and in the House, and in the electoral college? Have our parties become so unselfishly virtuous that this may not happen again? So we may see Porto Rico admitted before we have had time to rub our eyes.

You may say that little Porto Rico would not matter much. But can any clear-thinking man believe that, when we are once fairly started in the course of indiscriminate expansion, we shall stop there? Will not the same reasons which induced us to take Porto Rico also be used to show that the two islands of San Domingo with Hayti, and of Cuba, which separate Porto Rico from our coast, would, if they were in foreign hands, be a danger to us, and that we *must* take them? Nothing could be more plausible. Why, the necessity of annexing San Domingo is already freely discussed, and agencies to bring this about are actually at work. And as to Cuba, every expansionist will tell you that it is only a matter of time. And does any one believe that those islands, if annexed, will not become States of this Union? That would give us at least three, perhaps four new States, with about 3,500,000 inhabitants, Spanish and French creoles and negroes, with six or eight Senators, and from fifteen to twenty Representatives in Congress, and a corresponding number of votes in the electoral college.

Nor are we likely to stop there. If we build and own the Nicaragua Canal, instead of neutralizing it, we shall easily persuade ourselves that our control of that canal will not be safe unless we own all the country down to it, so that it be not separated from our borders by any foreign, and possibly hostile power. Is this too adventurous an idea to become true? Why, it is not half as adventurous and extravagant as the idea of uniting to this republic the Philippines, nine thousand miles away. It is already proposed to acquire in some way strips of territory several miles wide on each side of that canal for its military protection. But that will certainly be found insufficient, if foreign countries lie between. We must, therefore, have those countries. That means Mexico and various small Central American republics, with a population in all of about fourteen millions, mostly Spanish-Indian mixture,—making at least fifteen States, entitled to thirty Senators and scores of Representatives and presidential electors. . . . You may think that the introduction of more than thirty men in our Senate, over eighty in the lower house of our Congress, and much over one hundred votes in our electoral college, to speak and act for the mixture of Spanish, French, and negro blood on the West India Islands, and for the Spanish and Indian mixture on the continent south of us—for people utterly alien and mostly incapable of assimilation to us in their tropical habitation—to make our laws and elect our Presidents, and incidentally to help us lift up the Philippines to a higher plane of civlization—is too shocking a proposition to be entertained for a moment, and that our people will resist it to the bitter end. No, they will not resist it, if indiscriminate expansion has once become the settled policy of the republic. They will be told, as they are told now, that we are in it and cannot get honorably out of it; that destiny, and Providence, and duty demand it; that it would be cowardly to shrink from our new responsibilities; that those populations cannot take care of themselves, and that it is our mission to let them have the blessing of our free institutions; that we must have new markets for our products; that those countries are rich in re-sources, and that there is plenty of money to be made by taking them; that the American people can whip anybody and do any-thing they set out to do; and that "Old Glory" should float over every land on which we can lay our hands.

Those who have yielded to such cries once, will yield to them again. Conservative citizens will tell them that thus the homo-geneousness of the people of the republic, so essential to the working of our democratic institutions, will be irretrievably lost; that our race troubles, already dangerous, will be infinitely ag-gravated, and that the government of, by, and for the people will be in imminent danger of fatal demoralization. They will be cried down as pusillanimous pessimists, who are no longer American patriots. The American people will be driven on and on by the force of events as Napoleon was when started on his career of limitless conquest. This is imperialism as now advocated. Do we wish to prevent its excesses? Then we must stop at the beginning, before taking Porto Rico. If we take that island, not even to speak of the Philippines, we shall have placed ourselves on the inclined plane, and roll on and on, no longer masters of our own will, until we have reached bottom. And where will that bottom be? Who knows?

Our old acquisitions did not require a material increase of our army and navy. What of the new? It is generally admitted that we need very considerable additions to our armaments on land and sea to restore and keep order on the islands taken from Spain, and then to establish our sovereignty there. This is a ticklish business. In the first place, Spain has never been in actual control and possession of a good many of the Philippine islands, while on others the insurgent Filipinos had well-nigh destroyed the Spanish power when the treaty of Paris was made. The people of those islands will either peaceably submit to our rule or they will not. If they do not, and we must conquer them by force of arms, we shall at once have war on our hands.

What kind of a war will that be? The Filipinos fought against Spain for their freedom and independence, and unless they abandon their recently proclaimed purpose, it is for their freedom and independence that they will fight against us. To be sure, we promise them all sorts of good things if they will consent to become our subjects. But they may, and probably will, prefer independence to foreign rule, no matter what fair promises the foreign invader makes. For to the Filipinos the American is essentially a foreigner, more foreign in some respects than even the Spaniard was. Now, if they resist, what shall we do? Kill them? Let soldiers marching under the stars and stripes shoot them down? . . . However, this is imperialism. It bids us not to be squeamish. Indeed, some of our fellow citizens seem already to be full of its spirit. The Hon. Cyrus A. Sulloway, a member of Congress from New Hampshire, is reported to have said in a recent interview: "The Anglo-Saxon advances into the new regions with a Bible in one hand and a shotgun in the other. The inhabitants of those regions that he cannot convert with the aid of the Bible and bring into his markets, he gets rid of with the

shotgun. It is but another demonstration of the survival of the
the fittest." In other words, unless you worship as we command
you, and give us a profitable trade, we shall have to shoot you
down. The bloodiest of the old Spanish conquerors, four centuries ago, could not have spoken better. It has a strange sound
in free America. Let us hope that the spread of this hideous
brutality of sentiment will prove only a temporary epidemic, like
the influenza, and will yield again when the intoxication of victory
subsides and our heads become cool once more. If it does not,
more shotguns will be needed than Mr. Sulloway may now
anticipate.

If we take those new regions, we shall be well entangled in
that contest for territorial aggrandizement, which distracts other
nations and drives them far beyond their original design. So it
will be inevitably with us. We shall want new conquests to protect
that which we already possess. The greed of speculators, working
upon our government, will push us from one point to another,
and we shall have new conflicts on our hands, almost without
knowing how we got into them. It has always been so under
such circumstances, and always will be. This means more and
more soldiers, ships, and guns.

A singular delusion has taken hold of the minds of otherwise
clear-headed men. It is that our new friendship with England will
serve firmly to secure the world's peace. Nobody can hail that
friendly feeling between the two nations more warmly than I do,
and I fervidly hope it will last. But I am profoundly convinced
that if this friendship results in the two countries setting out to
grasp "for the Anglo-Saxon," as the phrase is, whatever of the
earth may be attainable,—if they hunt in couple,—they will surely
soon fall out about the game, and the first serious quarrel, or at
least one of the first, we shall have, will be with Great Britain.
. . . British friendship is a good thing to have, but, perhaps, not
so good a thing to need. If we are wise we shall not put ourselves
in the situation in which we shall need it. British statesmanship
has sometimes shown great skill in making other nations fight
its battles. This is very admirable from its point of view, but it
is not so pleasant for the nations so used. I should be loath to
see this republic associated with Great Britain in apparently joint
concerns as a junior partner with a minority interest, or the

American navy in the situation of a mere squadron of the British fleet. This would surely lead to trouble in the settling of accounts. Lord Salisbury was decidedly right when, at the last lord mayor's banquet, he said that the appearance of the United States as a factor in Asiatic affiairs was likely to conduce to the interest of Great Britain, but might "not conduce to the interest of peace." Whether he had eventual quarrels with this republic in mind, I do not know. But it is certain that the expression of British sentiment I have just quoted shows us a Pandora box of such quarrels.

Ardently desiring the maintenance of the friendship between England and this republic, I cannot but express the profound belief that this friendship will remain most secure if the two nations do not attempt to accomplish the same ends in the same way and on the same field, but continue to follow the separate courses prescribed by their peculiar conditions and their history.

The history of England is that of a small island, inhabited by a vigorous, energetic, and rapidly multiplying race, with the sea for its given field of action. Nothing could be more natural than that, as the population presssed against its narrow boundaries, Englishmen should have swarmed out, founding colonies and gradually building up an empire of possessions scattered all over the globe. England now *must* have the most powerful fleet in the world, not only for the protection of her distant possessions, but because if any other sea power, or combination of sea powers, could effectually blockade her coasts, her people, as they now are, might be starved in a few months. England must be the greatest sea power in order to be a great power at all.

The American people began their career as one of the colonial offshoots of the English stock. They found a great continent to occupy and to fill with democratic commonwealths. Our country is large enough for several times our present population. Our home resources are enormous, in great part not yet touched. We need not fear to be starved by the completest blockade of our coasts, for we have enough of everything and to spare. On the contrary, such a blockade might rather result in starving others that need our products. We are to-day one of the greatest powers on earth, without having the most powerful fleet, and without stepping beyond our continent. We are sure to be by far the greatest power of all, as our homogenous, intelligent, and patriotic population multiplies, and our resources are developed, without firing a gun or sacrificing a life for the sake of conquest, —far more powerful than the British Empire with all its Hindoos, and than the Russian Empire with all its Mongols. We can exercise the most beneficent influences upon mankind, not by forcing our rule or our goods upon others that are weak at the point of the bayonet, but through the moral power of our example, in proving how the greatest as well as the smallest nation can carry on the government of the people, by the people, and for the people in justice, liberty, order, and peace without large armies and navies.

Let this republic and Great Britain each follow the course which its conditions and its history have assigned to it, and their ambitions will not clash, and their friendships can be maintained for the good of all. And if our British cousins should ever get into serious stress, American friendship may stand behind them; but then Britain would depend on our friendship, which, as an American, I should prefer, and not America on British friendship, as our British friends who so impatiently urge us to take the Philippines, would have it. But if we do take the Philippines, and thus entangle ourselves in the rivalries of Asiatic affairs, the future will be, as Lord Salisbury predicted, one of wars and rumors of wars, and the time will be forever past when we could look down with condescending pity on the nations of the old world groaning under militarism with all its burdens.

We are already told that we should need a regular army of at least one hundred thousand men, three-forths of whom are to serve in our "new possessions." The question is whether this necessity is only to be temporary or permanent. Look at the cost. Last year the support of the army proper required about $23,000,000. It is computed that, taking the increased costliness of the service in the tropics into account, the army under the new dispensation will require about $150,000,000; that is, $127,000,000 a year more. It is also officially admitted that the possession of the Philippines would render indispensable a much larger increase of the navy than would otherwise be necessary, costing untold millions for the building and equipment of ships, and untold millions every year for their maintenance and for the increased number of officers and men. What we shall have to spend for fortifications and the like cannot now be computed. But there is a burden upon us which in like weight no other nation has to bear. To-day, thirty-three years after the Civil War, we have a pension roll of very nearly one million names. And still they come. We paid to pensioners over $145,000,000 last year, a sum larger than the annual cost of the whole military peace establishment of the German Empire, including its pension roll. Our recent Spanish War will, according to a moderate estimate, add at least $20,000,000 to our annual pension payments. But if we send troops to the tropics and keep them there, we must look for a steady stream of pensioners from that quarter, for in the tropics soldiers are "used up" very fast, even if they have no campaigning to do.

But all such estimates are futile. There may, and probably will be, much campaigning to do to keep our new subjects in obedience, or even in conflicts with other powers. And what military and naval expeditions will then cost, with our extravagant habits, and how the pension roll then will grow, we know to be incalculable. Moreover, we shall then be in the situation of those European powers, the extent of whose armaments are determined, not by their own wishes, but by the armaments of their rivals. We, too, shall nervously watch reports from abroad telling us that this power is augmenting the number of its warships, or that another is increasing its battalions, or strengthening its colonial garrisons in the neighborhood of our far-away possessions; and we shall have to follow suit. Not we ourselves, but our rivals and possible enemies will decide how large our armies and navies must be, and how much money we must spend for them. And all that money will have to come out of the pockets of our people, the poor as well as the rich. Our taxpaying capacity and willingness are indeed very great. But set your policy of imperialism in full swing, as the acquisition of the Philippines will do, and the time will come, and come quickly, when every American farmer and workingman, when going to his toil, will, like his European brother, have "to carry a fully armed soldier on his back.". . .

It would seem, therefore, that the new territorial acquisitions in view are after all very different from those we have made before. But something more is to be said. When the Cuban affair approached a crisis, President McKinley declared in his message that "forcible annexation cannot be thought of," for "it would, by our code of morals, be criminal aggression." And in resolving upon the war against Spain, Congress, to commend that war to the public opinion of mankind, declared with equal emphasis and solemnity that the war was, from a sense of duty and humanity, made specifically for the liberation of Cuba, and that Cuba "is, and of right ought to be, free and independent." If these declarations were not sincere, they were base and disgraceful acts of hypocrisy. If they were sincere at the time, would they not be turned into such disgraceful acts of hypocrisy by subsequently changing the war, professedly made from motives of duty and humanity, into a war of conquest and self-aggrandizement? It is pretended that these virtuous promises referred to Cuba only. But if President McKinley had said that, while the forcible annexation of Cuba would be criminal aggression, the forcible annexation of anything else would be perfectly right, and if Congress had declared that as to Cuba the war would be one of mere duty, humanity, and liberation, but that we would take by conquest whatever else we could lay our hands on, would not all mankind have broken out in a shout of scornful derision?

I ask in all candor, taking President McKinley at his word: Will the forcible annexation of the Philippines by our code of morals not be criminal aggression,—a self-confessed crime? I ask further, if the Cubans, as Congress declared, are *and of right ought to be* free and independent, can anybody tell me why the Porto Ricans and the Filipinos ought not *of right* to be free and independent? Can you sincerely recognize the right to freedom and independence of one and refuse the same right to another in the same situation, and then take his land? Would not that be double-dealing of the most shameless sort? . . .

The cry suddenly raised that this great country has become too small for us is too ridiculous to demand an answer, in view of that fact that our present population may be tripled and still have ample elbow-room, with resources to support many more. But we are told that our industries are gasping for breath; that we are suffering from overproduction; that our products must have new outlets, and that we need colonies and dependencies the world over to give us more markets. More markets? Certainly. But do we, civilized beings, indulge in the absurd and barbarous notion that we must own the countries with which we wish to trade? Here are our official reports before us, telling us that of late years our export trade has grown enormously, not only of farm products, but of the products of our manufacturing industries; in fact, that "our sales of manufactured goods have continued to extend with a facility and promptitude of results which have excited the serious concern of countries that, for generations, had not only controlled their home markets, but had practically monopolized certain lines of trade in other lands."

There is a distinguished Englishman, the Right Hon. Charles T. Ritchie, President of the Board of Trade, telling a British Chamber of Commerce that "we (Great Britain) are being rapidly overhauled in exports by other nations, especially the United States and Germany," their exports fast advancing, while British exports are declining. What? Great Britain, the greatest colonial power in the world, losing in competition with two nations, one of which had, so far, no colonies or dependencies at all, and the other none of any commercial importance? What does this mean? It means that, as proved by the United States and Germany, colonies are not necessary for the expansion of trade, and that, as proved by Great Britain, colonies do not protect a nation against a loss of trade. Our trade expands, without colonies or big navies, because we produce certain goods better and in proportion cheaper than other people do. British trade declines, in spite of immense dependencies and the strongest navy, because it does not successfully compete with us in that respect. Trade follows, not the flag, but the best goods for the price. Expansion of export trade and new markets! We do not need foreign conquests to get them, for we have them, and are getting them more and more in rapidly increasing growth.

"But the Pacific Ocean," we are mysteriously told, "will be the great commercial battle-field of the future, and we must quickly use the present opportunity to secure our position on it. The visible presence of great power is necessary for us to get our share of the trade of China. Therefore, we must have the Philippines." Well, the China trade is worth having, although for a time out of sight the Atlantic Ocean will be an infinitely more important battle-field of commerce than the Pacific, and one European customer is worth more than twenty or thirty Asiatics. But does the trade of China really require that we should have the Philippines and make a great display of power to get our share? Read the consular reports, and you will find that in many places in China our trade is rapidly gaining, while in some British trade is declining, and this while Great Britain has on hand the greatest display of power imaginable and we have none. And in order to increase our trade there, our consuls advise us to improve our commercial methods, saying nothing of the necessity of establishing a base of naval operations, and of our appearing there with war-ships and heavy guns. Trade is developed, not by the best guns, but by the best merchants. But why do other nations prepare to fight for the Chinese trade? Other nations have done many foolish things which we have been, and I hope will remain, wise enough not to imitate. If it should come to fighting for Chinese customers, the powers engaged in that fight are not unlikely to find out that they pay too high a price for what can be gained, and that at last the peaceful and active *neutral* will have the best bargain. At any rate, to launch into all the embroilments of an imperialistic policy by annexing the Philippines in order to snatch something more of the Chinese trade would be for us the foolishest game of all.

Generally speaking, nothing could be more irrational than all the talk about losing commercial or other opportunities which "will never come back if we fail to grasp them now." Why, we are so rapidly growing in all the elements of power ahead of all other nations that, not many decades hence, unless we demoralize ourselves by a reckless policy of adventure, not one of them will be able to resist our will if we choose to enforce it. This the world knows, and is alarmed at the prospect. Those who are most alarmed may wish that we should give them now, by some rash enterprise, an occasion for dealing us a damaging blow, while we are less irresistible.

"But we must have coaling stations for our navy!" Well, can we not get as many coaling stations as we need without owning populous countries behind them that would entangle us in dangerous political responsibilities and complications? Must Great Britain own the whole of Spain in order to hold Gibraltar?

"But we must civilize those poor people!" Are we not ingenious and charitable enough to do much for their civilization without subjugating and ruling them by criminal aggression?

The rest of the pleas for imperialism consist mostly of those high-sounding catch-words of which a free people, when about to decide a great question, should be especially suspicious. We are admonished that it is time for us to become a "world power." Well, we *are* a world power now, and have been for many years. What is a world power? A power strong enough to make its voice listened to with deference by the world whenever it chooses to speak. Is it necessary for a world power, in order to be such, to have its finger in every pie? Must we have the Philippines in order to become a world power? To ask the question is to answer it.

The American flag, we are told, whenever once raised, must never be hauled down. Certainly, every patriotic citizen will always be ready, if need be, to fight and to die under his flag, wherever it may wave in justice, and for the best interests of the country. But I say to you, woe to the republic if it should ever be without citizens patriotic and brave enough to defy the demagogues' cry, and to haul down the flag wherever it may be raised not in justice, and not for the best interests of the country. Such a republic would not last long.

But, they tell us, we have been living in a state of contemptible isolation which must be broken so that we may feel and conduct ourselves "as a full-grown member of the family of nations." What is that so-called isolation? Is it commercial? Last year our foreign trade amounted to nearly two thousand million dollars, and is rapidly growing. Is that commercial isolation? Or are we politically isolated? Remember our history. Who was it that early in this century broke up the piracy of the Barbary States? Who was it that took a leading part in delivering the world's commerce of the Danish Sound dues? Who was it that first opened Japan to communication with the Western world? And what power has in this century made more valuable contributions to international law than the United States? Do you call that contemptible isolation? It is true, we did not meddle much with foreign affairs that did not concern us. But if the circle of our interests widens, and we wish to meddle more, must we needs have the Philippines in order to feel and conduct ourselves as a member of the family of nations?

We are told that, having grown so great and strong, we must at last cast off our childish reverence for the teachings of Washington's farewell address—those "nursery rhymes that were sung around the cradle of the republic." I apprehend that many of those who now so flippantly scoff at the heritage the Father of his Country left us in his last words of admonition have never read that venerable document. I challenge those who have, to show me a single sentence of general import in it that would not, as a wise rule of national conduct, apply to the circumstances of to-day! What is it that has given to Washington's farewell address an authority that was revered by all until our recent victories made so many of us drunk with wild ambitions? Not only the prestige of Washington's name, great as that was and should ever remain. No, it was the fact that, under a respectful observance of those teachings, this republic has grown from the most modest beginnings into a Union spanning this vast continent; our people have multiplied from a handful to seventy-five millions; we have risen from poverty to a wealth the sum of which the imagination can hardly grasp; this American nation has become one of the greatest and most powerful on earth, and, continuing in the same course, will surely become the greatest and most powerful of all. Not Washington's name alone gave his teachings their dignity and weight. It was the practical results of his policy that secured to it, until now, the intelligent approbation of the American people. And unless we have completely lost our senses, we shall never despise and reject as mere "nursery rhymes" the words of wisdom left us by the greatest of Americans, following which the American people have achieved a splendor of development without parallel in the history of mankind.

You may tell me that this is all very well, but that by the acts of our own government we are now in this annexation business, and how can we get decently out of it? I answer that the difficulties of getting out of it may be great, but that they are infinitely less great than the difficulties we shall have to contend with if we stay in it.

Looking them in the face, let us first clear our minds of confused notions about our duties and responsibilities in the premises. That our victories have devolved upon us certain duties as to the people of the conquered islands, I readily admit. But are they the only duties we have to perform, or have they suddenly become paramount to all other duties? I deny it. I deny that our duties we owe to the Cubans and the Porto Ricans, and the Filipinos, and the Tagals of the Asiatic islands absolve us from the duties to the seventy-five millions of our own people, and to their posterity. I deny that they oblige us to destroy the moral credit of our own republic by turning this loudly heralded war of liberation and humanity into a land-grabbing game and an act of criminal aggression. I deny that they compel us to aggravate our race troubles, to bring upon us the constant danger of war, and to subject our people to the galling burden of increasing armaments. If we have rescued those unfortunate daughters of Spain, the colonies, from the tyranny of their cruel father, I deny that we are therefore in honor bound to marry any of the girls, or to take them all into our household, where they may disturb and demoralize our whole family. I deny that the liberation of those Spanish dependencies morally constrains us to do anything that would put our highest mission to solve the great problem of democratic government in jeopardy, or that would otherwise endanger the vital interests of the republic. Whatever our duties to them may be, our duties to our own country and people stand first; and from this standpoint we have, as sane men and patriotic citizens, to regard our obligation to take care of the future of those islands and their people.

They fought for deliverance from Spanish oppression, and we helped them to obtain that deliverance. That deliverance they understood to mean independence. I repeat the question whether anybody can tell me why the declaration of Congress that the Cubans *of right ought to be* free and independent should not apply to all of them? Their independence, therefore, would be the natural and rightful outcome. This is the solution of the problem first to be taken in view.

It is objected that they are not capable of independent government. They may answer that this is their affair and that they are at least entitled to a trial. I frankly admit that, if they are given that trial, their conduct in governing themselves will be far from perfect. Well, the conduct of no people is perfect, not even our own. They may try to revenge themselves upon their tories in their Revolutionary War. But we, too, threw our tories into hideous dungeons during our Revolutionary War, and persecuted and drove them away after its close. They may have bloody civil broils. But we, too, have had our Civil War which cost hundreds and thousands of lives and devastated one-half of our land; and now we have in horrible abundance the killings by lynch law, and our battles at Virden. They may have troubles with their wild tribes. So had we, and we treated our wild tribes in a manner not to be proud of. They may have corruption and rapacity in their government, but Havana and Ponce may get municipal administration almost as good as New York has under Tammany rule; and Manila may secure a city council not much less virtuous than that of Chicago.

I say these things not in a spirit of levity, well understanding the difference; but I say them seriously to remind you that, when we speak of the government those islands should have, we cannot reasonably set up standards which are not reached even by the most civilized people, and which in those regions could not be reached, even if we ourselves conducted their government with our best available statesmanship. Our attention is in these days frequently called to the admirable and in many respects successful administrative machinery introduced by Great Britain in India. But it must not be forgotten that this machinery was evolved from a century of rapine, corruption, disastrous blunders, savage struggles, and murderous revolts, and that even now many wise men in England gravely doubt in their hearts whether it was best for their country to undertake the conquest of India at all, and are troubled by gloomy forebodings of a calamitous catastrophe that may some day engulf that splendid fabric of Asiatic dominion.

No, we cannot expect that the Porto Ricans, the Cubans, and the Filipinos will maintain orderly governments in Anglo-Saxon fashion. But they may succeed in establishing a tolerable order of things in their own fashion, as Mexico, after many decades of turbulent disorder, succeeded at last, under Porfirio Diaz, in having a strong and orderly government of her kind, not, indeed, such a government as we would tolerate in this Union, but a government answering Mexican character and interests, and respectable in its relations with the outside world.

This will become all the more possible if, without annexing and ruling those people, we simply put them on their feet, and then give them the benefit of that humanitarian spirit which, as we claim, led us into the war for the liberation of Cuba. To this end we should keep our troops on the islands only until their people have constructed governments and organized forces of their own for the maintenance of order. Our military occupation should not be kept up as long as possible, but should be withdrawn as soon as possible.

The Philippines may, as Belgium and Switzerland are in Europe, be covered by a guarantee of neutrality on the part of the powers most interested in that region,—an agreement which the diplomacy of the United States should not find it difficult to obtain. This would secure them against foreign aggression. As to the independent republics of Porto Rico and Cuba, our government might lend its good offices to unite them with San Domingo and Hayti in a confederacy of the Antilles, to give them a more respectable international standing. Stipulations should be agreed upon with them as to open ports and the freedom of business enterprise within their borders, affording all possible commercial facilities. Missionary effort in the largest sense, as to the development of popular education and of other civilizing agencies, as well as abundant charity in case of need, will on our part not be wanting, and all this will help to mitigate their disorderly tendencies and to steady their governments.

Thus we shall be their best friends without being their foreign rulers. We shall have done our duty to them, to ourselves, and to the world. However imperfect their governments may still remain, they will at least be their own, and they will not with their disorders and corruptions contaminate our institutions, the integrity of which is not only to ourselves, but to liberty-loving mankind, the most important concern of all. We may then await the result with generous patience,—with the same patience with which for many years we witnessed the revolutionary disorders of Mexico on our very borders, without any thought of taking her government into our own hands.

Ask yourselves whether a policy like this will not raise the American people to a level of moral greatness never before attained! If this democracy, after all the intoxication of triumph in war, conscientiously remembers its professions and pledges, and soberly reflects on its duties to itself and others, and then deliberately resists the temptation of conquest, it will achieve the grandest triumph of the democratic idea that history knows of. It will give the government of, for, and by the people a prestige it never before possessed. It will render the cause of civilization throughout the world a service without parallel. It will put its detractors to shame, and its voice will be heard in the council of nations with more sincere respect and more deference than ever. The American people, having given proof of their strength and also of their honesty and wisdom, will stand infinitely mightier before the world than any number of subjugated vassals could make them. Are not here our best interests both moral and material? Is not this genuine glory? Is not this true patriotism? . . .

34

Militarist Psychology and the Philippines

William James Expresses Horror at His Nation's Policy

William James (1842-1910) ranks with the greatest psychologists of all time, and is generally regarded as the greatest American in the field. A graduate of the Harvard medical school, he taught physiology at Harvard, then psychology, finally philosophy. When the United States Army launched its effort to suppress the Filipino insurrection led by Emilio Aquinaldo (an insurrection that had cleared much of the Philippines of Spanish authority before American troops arrived), James wrote the following public letter to a Boston newspaper. The line of argument advanced here culminated in his brilliant pamphlet of 1910, *The Moral Equivalent of War*. In reading this letter, note (1) James's explanation of American indifference to the war for the suppression of Philippine independence; (2) his estimate concerning the leader of the Philippine independence movement; (3) his judgment of American policy in the Philippines and the bases for that judgment; (4) his prophecy concerning the results of our mission in the Islands; and (5) James's prescription for correcting the situation. See also Ralph Barton Perry, *The Thought and Character of William James* (1935).

William James, "To the Editor of the *Transcript*," Boston *Evening Transcript*, March 1, 1899, p. 16.

To THE EDITOR OF THE *Transcript:*

An observer who should judge solely by the sort
of evidence which the newspapers present might easily suppose
that the American people felt little concern about the per-
formances of our Government in the Philippine Islands, and
were practically indifferent to their moral aspects. The cannon
of our gunboats at Manila and the ratification of the treaty
have sent even the most vehement anti-imperialist journals
temporarily to cover, and the bugbear of copperheadism has
reduced the freest tongues for a while to silence. The excitement
of battle, this time as always, has produced its cowing and
disorganizing effect upon the opposition.

But it would be dangerous for the Administration to trust
to these impressions. I will not say that I have been amazed, for
I fully expected it; but I have been cheered and encouraged at
the almost unanimous dismay and horror which I find individuals express in private conversation over the turn which things
are taking. "A national infamy" is the comment on the case which
I hear most commonly uttered. The fires of indignation are
momentarily "banked," but they are anything but "out." They
seem merely to be awaiting the properly concerted and organized signal to burst forth with far more vehemence than ever,
as imperialism and the idol of a national destiny, based on
martial excitement and mere "bigness," keep revealing their
corrupting inwardness more and more unmistakably. The process of education has been too short for the older American
nature not to feel the shock. We gave the fighting instinct and
the passion of mastery their outing; we let them have the day
to themselves, and temporarily committed our fortunes to their
leading last spring, because we thought that, being harnessed
in a cause which promised to be that of freedom, the results
were fairly safe, and we could resume our permanent ideals
and character when the fighting fit was done. We now see how
we reckoned without our host. We see by the vividest of examples what an absolute savage and pirate the passion of military
conquest always is, and how the only safeguard against the

crimes to which it will infallibly drag the nation that gives way to it is to keep it chained for ever; is never to let it get its start. In the European nations it is kept chained by a greater mutual fear than they have ever before felt for one another. Here it should have been kept chained by a native wisdom nourished assiduously for a century on opposite ideals. And we can appreciate now that wisdom in those of us who, with our national Executive at their head, worked so desperately to keep it chained last spring.

But since then, Executive and all, we have been swept away by the overmastering flood. And now what it has swept us into is an adventure that in sober seriousness and definite English speech must be described as literally piratical. Our treatment of the Aguinaldo movement at Manila and at Iloilo is piracy positive and absolute, and the American people appear as pirates pure and simple, as day by day the real facts of the situation are coming to the light.

What was only vaguely apprehended is now clear with a definiteness that is startling indeed. Here was a people towards whom we felt no ill-will, against whom we had not even a slanderous rumor to bring; a people for whose tenacious struggle against their Spanish oppressors we have for years spoken (so far as we spoke of them at all) with nothing but admiration and sympathy. Here was a leader who as the Spanish lies about him, on which we were fed so long, drop off, and as the truth gets more and more known, appears as an exceptionally fine specimen of the patriot and national hero; not only daring, but honest; not only a fighter, but a governor and organizer of extraordinary power. Here were the precious beginnings of an indigenous national life, with which, if we had any responsibilities to these islands at all, it was our first duty to have squared ourselves. Aguinaldo's movement was, and evidently deserved to be, an ideal popular movement, which as far as it had had time to exist was showing itself "fit" to survive and likely to become a healthy piece of national self-development. It was all we had to build on, at any rate, so far—if we had any desire not to succeed to the Spaniards' inheritance of native execration.

And what did our Administration do? So far as the facts have leaked out, it issued instructions to the commanders on the ground simply to freeze Aguinaldo out, as a dangerous rival, with whom all compromising entanglement was sedulously to be avoided by the great Yankee business concern. We were not to "recognize" him, we were to deny him all account of our intentions; and in general to refuse any account of our intentions to anybody, except to declare in abstract terms their "benevolence," until the inhabitants, without a pledge of any sort from us, should turn over their country into our hands. Our President's bouffé-proclamation was the only thing vouchsafed; "We are here for your own good; therefore unconditionally surrender to our tender mercies, or we'll blow you into kingdom come."

Our own people meanwhile were vaguely uneasy, for the inhuman callousness and insult shown at Paris and Washington to the officially delegated mouthpieces of the wants and claims of the Filipinos seems simply abominable from any moral point of view. But there must be reasons of state, we assumed, and good ones. Aguinaldo is evidently a pure adventurer "on the make," a blackmailer, sure in the end to betray our confidence, or our Government wouldn't treat him so, for our President is essentially methodistical and moral. Mr. McKinley must be in an intolerably perplexing situation, and we must not criticise him too soon. We assumed this, I say, though all the while there was a horribly suspicious look about the performance. On its face it reeked of the infernal adroitness of the great department store, which has reached perfect expertness in the art of killing silently and with no public squealing or commotion the neighboring small concern.

But that small concern, Aguinaldo, apparently not having the proper American business education, and being uninstructed on the irresistible character of our Republican party combine, neither offered to sell out nor to give up. So the Administration had to show its hand without disguise. It did so at last. We are now openly engaged in crushing out the sacredest thing in this great human world—the attempt of a people long enslaved to attain to the possession of itself, to organize its laws and government, to be free to follow its internal destinies according to its own ideals. War, said Moltke, aims at destruction, and at nothing else. And splendidly are we carrying out war's ideal. We are destroying the lives of these islanders by the thousand, their villages and their cities; for surely it is we who are solely responsible for all the incidental burnings that our operations entail. But these destructions are the smallest part of our sins. We are destroying down to the root every germ of a healthy national life in these unfortunate people, and we are surely helping to destroy for one generation at least their faith in God and man. No life shall you have, we say, except as a gift from our philanthropy after your unconditional submission to our will. So as they seem to be "slow pay" in the matter of submission, our yellow journals have abundant time in which to raise new monuments of capitals to the victories of Old Glory, and in which to extol the unrestrainable eagerness of our brave soldiers to rush into battles that remind them so much of rabbit hunts on Western plains.

It is horrible, simply horrible. Surely there cannot be many born and bred Americans who, when they look at the bare fact of what we are doing, the fact taken all by itself, do not feel this, and do not blush with burning shame at the unspeakable meanness and ignominy of the trick?

Why, then, do we go on? First, the war fever; and then the pride which always refuses to back down when under fire. But these are passions that interfere with the reasonable settlement of any affair; and in this affair we have to deal with a factor altogether peculiar with our belief, namely, in a national destiny which must be "big" at any cost, and which for some inscrutable reason it has become infamous for us to disbelieve in or refuse. We are to be missionaries of civilization, and to bear the white man's burden, painful as it often is. We must sow our ideals, plant our order, impose our God. The individual lives are nothing. Our duty and our destiny call, and civilization must go on.

Could there be a more damning indictment of that whole bloated idol termed "modern civilization" than this amounts to? Civilization is, then, the big, hollow, resounding, corrupting, sophisticating, confusing torrent of mere brutal momentum and irrationality that brings forth fruits like this! It is safe to say that one Christian missionary, whether primitive, Protestant or Catholic, of the original missionary type, one Buddhist or Mohammedan of a genuine saintly sort, one ethical reformer or philanthropist, or one disciple of Tolstoi would do more real good in these islands than our whole army and navy can possibly effect with our whole civilization at their back. He could build up realities, in however small a degree; we can only destroy the inner realities; and indeed destroy in a year more of them than a generation can make good.

It is by their moral fruits exclusively that these benighted brown people, "half-devil and half-child" as they are, are condemned to judge a civilization. Ours is already execrated by them forever for its hideous fruits.

Shall it not in so far forth be execrated by ourselves? Shall the unsophisticated verdict upon its hideousness which the plain moral sense pronounces avail nothing to stem the torrent of mere empty "bigness" in our destiny, before which it is said we must all knock under, swallowing our higher sentiments with a gulp? The issue is perfectly plain at last. We are cold-bloodedly, wantonly and abominably destroying the soul of a people who never did us an atom of harm in their lives. It is bald, brutal piracy, impossible to dish up any longer in the cold pot-grease of President McKinley's cant at the recent Boston banquet—surely as shamefully evasive a speech, considering the right of the public to know definite facts, as can often have fallen even from a professional politician's lips. The worst of our imperialists is that they do not themselves know where sincerity ends and insecurity begins. Their state of consciousness is so new, so mixed of primitively human passions and, in political circles, of calculations that are anything but primitively human; so at variance, moreover, with their former mental habits; and so empty of definite data and contents; that they face various ways at once, and their portraits should be taken with a squint. One reads the President's speech with a strange feeling—as if the very words were squinting on the page.

The impotence of the private individual, with imperialism under full headway as it is, is deplorable indeed. But every American has a voice or a pen, and may use it. So, impelled by my own sense of duty, I write these present words. One by one we shall creep from cover, and the opposition will organize itself. If the Filipinos hold out long enough, there was a good chance (the canting game being already pretty well played out, and the piracy having to show itself hence-forward naked) of the older American beliefs and sentiments coming to their rights again, and of the Administration being terrified into a conciliatory policy towards the native government.

The programme for the opposition should, it seems to me, be radical. The infamy and iniquity of a war of conquest must stop. A "protectorate," of course, if they will have it, though after this they would probably rather welcome any European Power; and as regards the inner state of the island, freedom, "fit" or "unfit," that is, home rule without humbugging phrases, and whatever anarchy may go with it until the Filipinos learn from each other, not from us, how to govern themselves. Mr. Adams's programme—which anyone may have by writing to Mr. Erving Winslow, Anti-Imperialist League, Washington, D.C. —seems to contain the only hopeful key to the situation. Until the opposition newspapers seriously begin, and the mass meet-ings are held, let every American who still wishes his country to possess its ancient soul—soul a thousand times more dear than ever, now that it seems in danger of perdition—do what little he can in the way of open speech and writing, and above all let him give his representatives and senators in Washington a posi-tive piece of his mind.

35

The Open Door in China

John Hay Instructs
American Ambassadors in Europe

China after 1890 was a sick empire, easy prey to any of the industrial powers. Russia in 1892 began building the Trans-Siberian
Railway, which would greatly increase her weight in the Far East.
Japan, after a whirlwind war against China in 1894-1895, seized the
Liaotung Peninsula and Port Arthur—only to be forced to return
them by the intervention of Germany, France, and Russia. Then in
1898 Germany grabbed Kiaochow; Russia took Port Arthur; Britain
extracted a lease of Weihaiwei; France snatched Kwangchowan.
These events alarmed the United States, for many Americans had
long had a romantic attachment to China, and many others had
economic hopes tied to her. China was taking large quantities of
American cotton goods and American kerosene; American bankers
and promoters such as J. P. Morgan were considering big ventures
there. These anxieties led to the Open Door Notes sent by Secretary
of State John Hay to all the interested powers. The first note was
published by the government under the heading, "Correspondence
Concerning American Commercial Rights in China." In reading this
dispatch, note (1) Hay's description of conditions that might be
prejudicial to American interests in China; (2) his proposal to the
British government; (3) the specific disclaimers which he proposed
that the powers make; and (4) the reasons given for thinking that
success might attend his efforts. See the two fine monographs by
Charles S. Campbell, Jr., *Special Business Interests and the Open
Door Policy* (1951) and *Anglo-American Understanding, 1898-1903*
(1957); also A. T. Mahan, *The Problem of Asia and Its Effect upon
International Politics* (1900).

Great Britain.

Mr. Hay to Mr. Choate.

DEPARTMENT OF STATE,

Washington, September 6, 1899.

SIR: THE GOVERNMENT OF HER BRITANNIC MAJESTY has declared that is policy and its very traditions precluded it from using any privileges which might be granted it in China as a weapon for excluding commercial rivals, and that freedom of trade for Great Britain in that Empire meant freedom of trade for all the world alike. While conceding by formal agreements, first with Germany and then with Russia, the possession of "spheres of influence or interest" in China in which they are to enjoy special rights and privileges, more especially in respect of railroads and mining enterprises, Her Britannic Majesty's Government has therefore sought to maintain at the same time what is called the "open-door" policy, to insure to the commerce of the world in China equality of treatment within said "spheres" for commerce and navigation. This latter policy is alike urgently demanded by the British mercantile communities and by those of the United States, as it is justly held by them to be the only one which will improve existing conditions, enable them to maintain their positions in the markets of China, and extend their operations in the future. While the Government of the United States will in no way commit itself to a recognition of exclusive rights of any power within or control over any portion of the Chinese Empire under such agreements as have within the last year been made, it can not conceal its apprehension that under existing conditions there is a possibility, even a probability, of complications arising between the treaty powers which may imperil the rights to the United States under our treaties with China.

John Hay to Joseph H. Choate, September 6, 1899, *Papers Relating to the Foreign Relations of the United States . . . , 1899* (Washington, D.C.: Government Printing Office, 1901), pp. 131-133; John Hay to Charles V. Herdliska, July 3, 1900, *Papers Relating to the Foreign Relations of the United States . . . , 1900* (Washington, D.C.: Government Printing Office, 1901) p. 299.

This Government is animated by a sincere desire that the interests of our citizens may not be prejudiced through exclusive treatment by any of the controlling powers within their so-called "spheres of interest" in China, and hopes also to retain there an open market for the commerce of the world, remove dangerous sources of international irritation, and hasten thereby united or concerted action of the powers at Pekin in favor of the administrative reforms so urgently needed for strengthening the Imperial Government and maintaining the integrity of China in which the whole western world is alike concerned. It believes that such a result may be greatly assisted by a declaration by the various powers claiming "spheres of interest" in China of their intentions as regards treatment of foreign trade therein. The present moment seems a particularly opportune one for informing Her Britannic Majesty's Government of the desire of the United States to see it make a formal declaration and to lend its support in obtaining similar declarations from the various powers claiming "spheres of influence" in China, to the effect that each in its respective spheres of interest or influence—

First. Will in no wise interfere with any treaty port or any vested interest within any so-called "sphere of interest" or leased territory it may have in China.

Second. That the Chinese treaty tariff of the time being shall apply to all merchandise landed or shipped to all such ports as are within said "sphere of interest" (unless they be "free ports"), no matter to what nationality it may belong, and that duties so leviable shall be collected by the Chinese Government.

Third. That it will levy no higher harbor dues on vessels of another nationality frequenting any port in such "sphere" than shall be levied on vessels of its own nationality, and no higher railroad charges over lines built, controlled, or operated within its "sphere" on merchandise belonging to citizens or subjects of other nationalities transported through such "sphere" than shall be levied on similar merchandise belonging to its own nationals transported over equal distances.

The recent ukase of His Majesty the Emperor of Russia, declaring the port of Ta-lien-wan open to the merchant ships of all nations during the whole of the lease under which it is to be held by Russia, removing as it does all uncertainty as to the liberal and conciliatory policy of that power, together with the assurances given this Government by Russia, justifies the expectation that His Majesty will cooperate in such an understanding as is here proposed, and our ambassador at the court of St. Petersburg has been instructed accordingly to submit the propositions above detailed to His Imperial Majesty, and ask their early consideration. Copy of my instruction to Mr. Tower is herewith inclosed for your confidential information.

The action of Germany in declaring the port of Kiaochao a "free port," and the aid the Imperial Government has given China in the establishment there of a Chinese custom-house, coupled with the oral assurance conveyed the United States by Germany that our interests within its "sphere" would in no wise be affected by its occupation of this portion of the province of Shang-tung, tend to show that little opposition may be anticipated from that power to the desired declaration.

The interests of Japan, the next most interested power in the trade of China, will be so clearly served by the proposed arrangement, and the declaration of its statesmen within the last year are so entirely in line with the views here expressed, that its hearty cooperation is confidently counted on.

You will, at as early date as practicable, submit the considerations to Her Britannic Majesty's principal secretary of state for foreign affairs and request their immediate consideration.

I inclose herewith a copy of the instruction sent to our ambassador at Berlin bearing on the above subject.

Austria-Hungary.

Mr. Hay to Mr. Herdliska.
DEPARTMENT OF STATE,

Washington, July 3, 1900.

In this critical posture of affairs in China it is deemed appropriate to define the attitude of the United States as far as present circumstances permit this to be done. We adhere to the policy initiated by us in 1857, of peace with the Chinese nation, of furtherance of lawful commerce, and of protection of lives and property of our citizens by all means guaranteed under extraterritorial treaty rights and by the law of nations. If wrong be done to our citizens we propose to hold the responsible authors to the uttermost accountability. We regard the condition at

Pekin as one of virtual anarchy, whereby power and responsibility are practically devolved upon the local provincial authorities. So long as they are not in overt collusion with rebellion and use their power to protect foreign life and property we regard them as representing the Chinese people, with whom we seek to remain in peace and friendship. The purpose of the President is, as it has been heretofore, to act concurrently with the other powers, first, in opening up communication with Pekin and rescuing the American officials, missionaries, and other Americans who are in danger; secondly, in affording all possible protection everywhere in China to American life and property; thirdly, in guarding and protecting all legitimate American interests; and fourthly, in aiding to prevent a spread of the disorders to the other provinces of the Empire and a recurrence of such disasters. It is, of course, too early to forecast the means of attaining this last result; but the policy of the Government of the United States is to seek a solution which may bring about permanent safety and peace to China, preserve Chinese territorial and administrative entity, protect all rights guaranteed to friendly powers by treaty and international law, and safeguard for the world the principle of equal and impartial trade with all parts of the Chinese Empire.

You will communicate the purport of this instruction to the minister for foreign affairs.

36

The American Threat and Europe's Alternatives

Brooks Adams Warns His Country to Reduce the Tariff or Increase Armaments

Tariff reciprocity—that is, reduction of American duties on imports coming from countries that gave equivalent concessions on our products—had been a pressing issue as early as the negotiations on the McKinley Act in 1890. The Dingley Tariff Act of 1897, which raised rates generally even above the McKinley Act, gave the President power to make reciprocal concessions to other nations. Meanwhile the American surplus of exports over imports was climbing steadily, to reach $500 million a year. The implications of this situation are analyzed in the following essay by Brooks Adams (1848-1927). Like his better-known older brother, historian Henry Adams, Brooks Adams was concerned to derive "fixed social laws from the facts of history." Thus although he presumably is writing here about the alternatives to tariff reciprocity by the United States, he in fact tries to analyze changes in the world balance of power since the sixteenth century. Note in passing the reference to the bounties paid by France and Germany on exports of beet sugar, which broke the world price of sugar, ruined the producers of cane sugar in the Caribbean, did much to force the Cuban revolution of 1895, and thus helped bring about the Spanish-American War. In reading this article, note (1) Adams' use of economic determinism; (2) the ways he used history; (3) illustrations of "fixed social laws" which he derived from history; (4) Adams' estimate of the world situation at the end of the nineteenth century; (5) the place of the United States in that situation; (6) the choices he saw facing Europe and how each of those involved the United States; and (7) the lessons for the United States that Adams drew from his reading of history. See Howard K. Beale's careful *Theodore Roosevelt and the Rise of America to World Power* (1956) and Brooks Adams, *America's Economic Supremacy* (1900).

Brooks Adams, "Reciprocity or the Alternative," *Atlantic Monthly*, vol. 88 (August 1901), pp. 145-155.

Each year society inclines to accept more unreservedly the theory that war is only an extreme phase of economic competition; and if this postulate be correct, it follows that international competition, if carried far enough, must end in war. An examination of history tends to confirm this view; and, thus stated, the doctrine concerns Americans, as the present policy of the United States is to force a struggle for subsistence, of singular intensity, upon Europe.

If a stable economic equilibrium could be maintained, so that not only nations, but individuals, should preserve a fixed relation to each other, war might cease. War persists because civilization is always in movement, the energy and direction of the movement depending largely on the exhaustion of old, and the discovery of new mines.

In the last century, the iron and coal of Europe not only sufficed for domestic needs, but formed the basis of her wealth by enabling the continent to build up a manufacturing supremacy. That supremacy is already passing away, and in this century European iron and coal seem likely to be largely superseded by American, since the latter are even now sold at a lower price. Clearly, no such fundamental shifting of values as this change would cause could take place without profound social and political disturbances. Before, however, attempting to deal with the future it is always safer to return to the past; and especially so in this instance, since the phenomena developed in the last great fermentation which precipitated the long wars of the seventeenth and eighteenth centuries closely resemble those occurring now. Far off as the reign of Louis XIV. may seem, France then trod the pathway which the whole continent of Europe is to-day treading, and the United States must be prepared to reckon with all the difficulties and dangers which beset that pathway's end.

In the sixteenth century the world's manufactures and commerce centred in Flanders, and the financial capital of Flanders was Antwerp. At Antwerp the famous house of the Fuggers reached its zenith between 1525 and 1560, and the chief business of the Fuggers was to finance the Spanish Empire. Unfortunately for Antwerp and the Fuggers, the Spaniards broke down under the weight they bore, exchange went against the peninsula, and in 1557 the kingdom became insolvent. Funds had to be obtained, and finally his poverty drove Philip into that radical policy which ended in the revolt of the Netherlands, the sack of Antwerp, and the migration of the seat of international exchanges to Amsterdam. From 1610 onward Amsterdam rose steadily in opulence, while France almost contemporaneously, under Richelieu, entered upon a period of centralization, which ended in 1653, with the collapse of the Fronde. Mazarin died in 1661. Louis XIV. then began his active life, and France soon saw her greatest epoch. Never before or since has France so nearly succeeded in establishing a complete ascendency over the world as in the third quarter of the seventeenth century. Louis XIV. was, without comparison, the first potentate of the age; his army was the largest and the best organized, his generals were the most renowned; his navy, though perhaps not the most numerous, yielded to none in quality; his court was the most magnificent, and his capital the most materially and intellectually brilliant. All the world admired and imitated Paris. On the one hand, Molière, Racine, La Fontaine, Bossuet, Fénelon, and many others raised letters and science to an eminence elsewhere sought in vain; on the other, France ruled in fashion even more absolutely than in literature or in arms. As Macaulay has observed: "Her authority was supreme in all matters of good breeding, from a duel to a minuet. She determined how a gentleman's coat must be cut, how long his peruke must be; whether his heels must be high or low, and whether the lace on his hat must be broad or narrow. In literature she gave law to the world. The fame of her great writers filled Europe."

Nevertheless, brilliant as had been her success elsewhere, in one department France betrayed weakness. Her administrative system had been constructed rather on a military than on an economic basis, and though consolidated in the sense that in war the nation obeyed a single will, in commerce she remained almost mediæval. The king occasionally exercised an arbitrary power over his subjects, but on many matters vital to their interests he was, in practice, helpless. The French have been called volatile, but the foundation of their character is a conservatism which has hampered them throughout their history; and long after the great fiefs had been welded into a martial mass called a monarchy, they remained, for fiscal purposes, foreign communities. In 1664 Colbert proposed to abolish all internal tariffs, and Pierre Clément, Colbert's biographer, has thus described the customs which then prevailed:—

"The provinces called the 'five great farms' assented. Others who refused, because of their persistence in isolating themselves, were designated under the name of 'foreign provinces.' Lastly, they gave the name of 'provinces reputed foreign' to a final category. The districts comprised in this category were, in reality, completely assimilated to foreign countries, with which they traded freely without paying any duties. For the same reason, the merchandise they sent into other portions of the kingdom was considered as coming from abroad, and that which they bought paid, on entering their territory, the same duty as if brought from abroad."

Trade languished, for the tariff of Languedoc had no more relation to that of Provence than either had to that of Spain; and even the provincial tariffs were trifling beside the rates and tolls of towns and baronies. Thirty dues were collected between Lyons and Arles, and Lyons herself taxed a bale of silk three times before it could be used. Merchants complained that the city closed the river. Nevertheless, in spite of conservatism, no people has ever loved lucre better than the French, and this yearning for wealth became incarnate in the great minister of finance of Louis XIV.

Jean Baptiste Colbert, the son of a draper of Rheims, was born in 1619, in humble circumstances. Little is known of his youth, but at twenty he took service as a clerk in the War Department, and in 1651 he passed into the employment of Mazarin. There he prospered, and soon after 1657 had risen high enough to dream of destroying Fouquet.

The farming of the direct taxes formed, perhaps, the most noxious part of a decaying system, and it was in the collection and disbursement of taxes that Fouquet ran riot. Louis himself afterward averred that the "way in which receipts and expenses were handled passed belief." Subject to little or no supervision, Fouquet appropriated vast sums. His famous palace of Vaux is said to have cost 9,000,000 livres, and all agreed that it outshone St. Germain or Fontainebleau. France dreamed of becoming the centre of European industries, and Colbert conceived his mission to be the realization of this dream. To attain his end, he proposed to build up manufactures by bounties and grants of privileges; but he also comprehended that to make industries really profitable he must reduce waste. Under Louis XIV. Fouquet embodied the principle of waste: therefore Colbert attacked Fouquet, and rose upon his ruin. When, however, Colbert had attained to power he paused. He improved methods of accounting, but he abstained from cutting out the sore. He did so because, when on an eminence, he saw that existing customs went to the root of contemporary life, and that the reorganization of the administration meant the reorganization of society, or, in other words, a revolution. Hence he paused, yet he could not stand still and maintain himself.

International competition cannot be permanently carried on on a great scale by bounties; for bounties mean producing at a loss. Bounties may be useful as a weapon of attack, but they cannot, in the long run, bring in money from abroad; for they simply transfer the property of one citizen to another by means of a tax. One nation can gain from another only by cheaper production. If a certain process costs more than another, the assumption of a portion of the cost by the state cannot make the transaction profitable to the community at large, though it may be to the recipient of the grant. The Continental sugar bounties, for example, have doubtless been successful in enfeebling England by ruining her colonies, and they have also enriched the makers of beet sugar, but they have never, probably, been lucrative to France or Germany.

Like any other corporation, a nation can run at a loss as long as its own savings last, or as long as it can borrow from others; and now accumulations are so large that a country like Russia can maintain itself long on loans. In the seventeenth century accumulations were comparatively slender, and Colbert came quickly to the parting of the ways. He understood that to simplify the internal organization of the kingdom sufficiently to put it upon a footing of competitive equality with Holland or England would involve the reconstruction of society; yet to continue manufacturing on the existing basis, which entailed a loss, could only be made possible by means of loans, for the people were sinking under taxation. Colbert judged that he could not borrow safely upon the necessary scale, and thus the minister, very early in his career, found himself forced to make the choice which, under such conditions, must always, sooner or later, be made, between insolvency, revolution, and war. If left undisturbed, the mechanism which operates cheapest will in the end supplant all others; and this fundamental truth Colbert learned to his cost. In three years after he had entered upon his task he had broken down. In 1664 he formulated a scheme, part of which was a liberal tariff, and part the simplification of internal fiscal usages. He dared not press his reform, and as waste continued, his whole policy fell, and with it fell his industrial system. The cost of production remained higher in France than in Holland,—therefore commercial exchanges went against the kingdom; and in 1667, to correct exchanges and prevent a drain of specie, Colbert resorted to a prohibitive tariff, or, in the words of his biographer, tried the experiment of "selling without buying."

This course struck at the life of Holland. Holland being the distributing centre of Europe, her prosperity depended on keeping open the avenues of trade. If she allowed foreign countries to be closed against her, while her market remained free, she might be suffocated by the bounty-fed exports of France. Germany has recently suffocated the West Indies by identical methods. The Dutch understood the situation perfectly, and Van Beuningen thus explained his views in a letter to John de Witt: "Since the French exclude all the manufactures of the United Provinces, means must be found, as complaints are useless, to prevent them from filling the country with theirs, and thus draw from us our quick capital."

Colbert pondered the crisis long and anxiously, and deliberately decided that it would be cheapest to cut the knot by war. In his letters Colbert discussed the situation in all its bearings, and dilated upon his disappointments and mortifications. In 1669 he lamented the stagnation of French commerce. He estimated that out of the 20,000 ships doing the traffic of the world, the Dutch owned 15,000 or 16,000, and the French 500 or 600, at most. The final blow, which is said to have almost broken his heart, came in 1670, when, just as the French East India Company admitted itself to be practically insolvent, the Dutch Company divided forty per cent. From that moment Colbert recognized peaceful competition as impossible, and nerved himself for war. In May, 1672, Turenne crossed the frontier at the head of a great army, and the campaign opened which is the point of departure for all subsequent European history down to Waterloo.

Nor was the action of Colbert exceptional. On the contrary, he obeyed a natural law. Every animal when cornered will fight, and every nation always has fought and always will fight when sufficiently pressed, each choosing those weapons which it deems aptest. The French chose arms, and in this case they were justified by the apparent probabilities of a conflict.

If it be conceded that war is a form of economic competition, war must be regarded as a speculation; a hazardous one, it is true, but one deserving to be tried, where the chance of gain outweighs the risk of loss. To Colbert it seemed, in 1672, that he risked little, and might win much.

His deadliest enemy lay before him, rich and defenseless. There could be no doubt as to the value of the spoil, should Louis prevail. Amsterdam was opulent. As late as the time of Adam Smith, the Bank of Amsterdam held the position occupied by the Bank of England during the last century, while the commerce of the country exceeded that of all the other nations combined. Furthermore, if Holland was rich, she was peaceful. The navy still retained its energy, but the population had become urban, and not only was the army small, but of questionable courage. Lastly, the Dutch were divided among themselves, and torn between the Orange and the De Witt factions.

Conversely, Louis held France as a military unit. His will met with no opposition. His organization far surpassed any then existing. Turenne and Condé had no equals on the field of battle, and every peasant in the kingdom could be called into the ranks. The nobles served from choice. No error could be greater than to attribute the Dutch war to the ambition of Louvois or the arrogance of the king. The campaign was Colbert's campaign. He conducted it as a speculation to save the money already invested in trade, and to place France where she could profitably invest more. He calculated on operations lasting a few weeks or months; he doubted not of final success. Nor at first was resistance attempted. The Dutch troops fled or surrendered; the towns opened their gates. In June it seemed that Amsterdam must fall. Scandal even asserted that nothing saved Amsterdam but the jealousy of Louvois, who feared that an immediate peace might exalt Colbert too far. Colbert, on his side, felt the victory won, and in those days of triumph laid bare the recesses of his heart. In a memorandum submitted to the king he explained the use to be made of victory. The paper may be read in Colbert's Letters and Memoirs, but in substance he proposed to confiscate the best of the Dutch commerce, and to exclude the Dutch from the Mediterranean. Nevertheless, France did not triumph. In July William of Orange became stadtholder, opened the dikes and laid the country under water. Six years later Colbert purchased peace, not only by the surrender of the tariff on which he had staked his hopes, but by accepting a provision in the treaty of Nimeguen stipulating that in future freedom of commerce between the two countries should not be abridged.

Thus Colbert failed, and having failed he fell. Louvois succeeded him, as he had succeeded Mazarin and Fouquet; but the preponderance of Louvois meant that France must travel straight to her predestined goal. France failed in 1672, when relatively strongest, because she lacked the flexibility to enable her to shed an obsolete social system. She only succeeded in doing so, after a convulsion, a century later, when it was too late. Had she been able to accomplish in 1670 some portion of what she accomplished between 1789 and 1793, London might not have become the seat of empire during the nineteenth century. Under Louis XIV. French weakness lay in a defective organization which caused waste. That waste made the drain of war insupportable. Had France possessed an economic endurance relatively as great as the endurance of Holland, she would, presumably, in 1672, have absorbed the United Provinces. In that case, resistance by the rest of Europe to Louis would have been difficult. No Dutch stadtholder could have been crowned in England, and no coalition could have been formed such as that which William of Orange afterward devoted his life to cementing. William's league survived him, and lasted for twenty-five years. It proved profitable. It crushed France and humbled Louis, who, old and broken, sued for peace after the awful fields of Blenheim and Malplaquet. Two years subsequent to the treaty of Utrecht Louis died, and under his successor the monarchy plunged onward toward its doom. At last the monarchy fell, not because it was cruel or oppressive, but because it represented, in the main, a mass of mediæval usages which had hardened into a shell, incompatible with the exigencies of modern life. Under it, a social movement of equal velocity to that which prevailed elsewhere could not be maintained. What Frenchmen craved in 1789 was, not an ideal which we now call "liberty," and which consists in certain political conventions, but an administrative system which would put them on economic equality with their neighbors. De Tocqueville dwelt on this phenomenon forty-five years ago: "Something worthy of remark is that, among all the ideas and sentiments which have prepared the Revolution, the idea and the taste for public liberty, properly so called, presented themselves the last, as they were the first to disappear."

The foregoing history illustrates the cost at which a new equilibrium is reached, when an old equilibrium has been destroyed. From Colbert's tariff of 1667 to Waterloo is a period of nearly one hundred and fifty years, almost half of which was consumed in furious wars. The bane of France was the conservatism which caused her to act too late; for in 1790, when she readjusted her society, she profited comparatively little thereby. Meanwhile, England had so developed her minerals that in 1800 she undersold France as easily as Holland had undersold her in 1672, and with the same result. Unable to compete by peaceful means, Napoleon resorted to arms, and, like Colbert, sought to starve his rival into submission by excluding her from his dominions, which then comprised most of Europe. He failed as Colbert had failed, and peace followed his fall; but the repose which succeeded Waterloo lasted less than sixty years.

In 1870 another era opened with the consolidation of Germany. The causes of disturbance then set in motion developed acute symptoms in 1890, and now, perhaps, no permanent tranquillity can be attained until the position which America shall henceforward occupy be determined.

Previous to 1890 America had remained chiefly agricultural, buying largely of European manufactures, and paying therefor, in part, in evidences of debt. Her own industries, like those of France under Louis XIV., were then organized on too costly a basis for international competition, and were mostly maintained by a system of bounties under the form of a tariff. After 1870, the economic disturbance in Europe, caused by the rise of Germany, gradually created a stringency in Great Britain; a liquidation of the English loans in America began, and in 1890 this liquidation assumed proportions which culminated in panic. One method of measuring the pressure to which the United States was subjected during a series of years, and to gauge the change of relations between the eastern and the western continent wrought thereby, is to compare the average yearly payments made on balance by America to foreigners from a date antecedent to the catastrophe of 1893 to the present time.

If three quinquennial periods be taken, beginning with 1887, the first will fall substantially before the crisis of the Baring failure. From 1887 to 1891 the average annual excess of exports over imports amounted to about $44,400,000, a sum certainly not more than sufficient to pay interest due abroad and other like charges. After the failure of the Barings creditors grew pressing, and the balance rose, between 1892 and 1896, to $185,400,000. In 1896 the United States reached the lowest point in her recent history. Her position then somewhat resembled that of France when Colbert adopted his policy of "selling without buying." The cost of production being too high, Americans could not export manufactures; agricultural supplies alone proved insufficient to yield the sum demanded of her; and the country, in that single year, had to part with $78,880,000 in gold. General insolvency seemed imminent. When confronted, in 1667, with stagnating commerce and failing industries, Colbert proclaimed his prohibitive tariff, and finding that this expedient did not correct exchanges, he invaded Holland; but he did not cut the evil he combated at the root, by reorganizing France. In 1897 the United States followed the precedent set by Colbert, so far as the tariff was concerned; but Americans, suppler than Frenchmen, did not go to war. They adopted a more effective method of routing the foe. They readjusted their entire system of industry and transportation, bringing the cost of production of the chief articles of modern commerce below the European level. No success has ever been more sudden or more startling. Between 1897 and 1901 the average excess of American exports over imports has risen to $510,000,000 yearly. The amount tends to increase, and it tends to increase for excellent reasons. Just now America can undersell Europe in agricultural products; she can likewise undersell Europe in minerals as raw material; she can also undersell Europe in most branches of manufactured iron and steel, besides many minor classes of wares. On the present basis, there seems no reason to doubt that, as time goes on, America will drive Europe more and more from neutral markets, and will, if she makes the effort, flood Europe herself with goods at prices with which Europeans cannot compete.

A moment's consideration will disclose the gravity of the situation. Whatever may have been, or may still be, the extent of America's foreign indebtedness, it is certain that, at the present rate of redemption, it must be soon extinguished. Then the time will come when the whole vast burden of payment for American exports will fall upon the annual earnings of foreign nations, at the moment when those earnings are cut down by the competition of the very goods for which they must pay.

The inversion of all that has heretofore existed has been so sudden and complete that society has somewhat lost its bearings; nevertheless, the feeling of Europe is apprehension, and that feeling is not without rational foundation. Should the movement of the next decade correspond to the movement of the last, Europe will, at its close, stand face to face with ruin. It is safe to assume, therefore, that Europe will not allow present conditions to remain unchanged, any more than France did in 1667, or than America did in 1896.

Three avenues seem open by which relief may be obtained. First, Europe may reorganize herself upon a scale to correspond with the organization of the United States; but this solution appears doubtful, in view of the decentralization of the continent. Second, the United States may be induced to abandon something of her advantages, and ameliorate the situation of Europe by commercial reciprocity. In other words, the United States may prefer to follow somewhat the same policy which Cobden advocated, as opposed to the policy of Colbert and Napoleon. Lastly, Europe may attack the United States, and attempt to break her down by arms.

In plain English, Europe finds herself in an *impasse*. She is pressed on every hand. Her soil, never rich, has been tilled until its culture costs more than that of newer land. Hence each country must choose between two alternatives: the farmers may be abandoned to their fate, as in the United Kingdom; or they may be protected, as in France and Germany. If the farmers should be abandoned, the military population will disappear, as it has disappeared in Great Britain, and food will have to be bought abroad. If the farmers should be protected, the rest of the country must pay higher for its bread and meat. In either case, the loss will correspond to the sum represented by the inferiority of the European soil, and the higher price it bears, as compared with the soil of Argentina or Nebraska.

Prior to 1897, while Europe still held a substantial monopoly in manufactures, this deterioration of agriculture, if not viewed with pleasure, might be contemplated with equanimity. Not so since 1897, when the industrial revolution in North America has brought European mines to a condition of relative exhaustion, and European workshops to a position of relative inferiority. Assuming that a satisfactory social readjustment offers, just now, insuperable difficulties, Europeans see but one method of obtaining relief, should America retain her tariff: that method is to develop regions abroad containing mines capable of vying with those of Alabama, Pennsylvania, and Lake Superior. And it is precisely here that Europe finds herself propelled toward a collision with the United States, because the United States, for her own protection, has devised a mechanism which holds her rival as in a vise.

America's attack is based not only on her superior resources and her more perfect administration, but on her tariff. To make their gigantic industrial system lucrative, Americans have comprehended that it must be worked at the highest velocity and at its full capacity, and they have taken their measures accord-

ingly. To guard against a check they rely on a practically prohibitive tariff, by which they hope to maintain the home market
at a reasonable level; and with the profit thus obtained they
expect to make good any loss which may accrue from forcing
their surplus upon foreigners at prices with which these cannot
cope. No wonder the European regards America as a dangerous
and relentless foe; and the fact that Europe has forced on
America these measures as a means of self-defense signifies nothing. The European sees in America a competitor who, while
refusing to buy, throws her wares on every market, and who,
while she drives the peasant from his land, reduces the profits
of industry which support the wage-earners of the town. Most
ominous of all, he marks a rapidly growing power, which, while
it undersells his mines, closes to him every region of the wide
earth where he might find minerals adapted to his needs. Lying
like a colossus across the western continent, with her ports on
either ocean, with China opposite and South America at her feet,
the United States bars European expansion. South America and
China are held to be the only accessible regions which certainly
contain the iron, coal, and copper which Europe seeks; and the
United States is determined that, if she can prevent it, South
America and China shall not be used as bases for hostile competition. Regarding South America her declarations are explicit,
and during the last twelve months her actions in Asia have
spoken more emphatically than words.

Moreover, the German considers the theory of the "open door"
a mockery. The German avers that no man knows so well as
the American that China can never be developed until it is
administered by western methods, and that it is for this reason
that America opposes partition. To make Asia pay, the country
must be handled as a whole,—as America is handled, though
not perhaps on so extensive a scale. At all events, in each province the mining, transportation, manufactures, police, and taxation must be controlled by Europeans. To attempt to turn Shansi
into a Pennsylvania under Chinese rule would mean ruin.

Thus the continent of Europe finds itself pressed somewhat
as Colbert found France pressed in 1667, and accordingly Europeans are restive. Evidently, unless all human experience is at
fault, that restiveness will grow. Men cannot foresee the future,

—they can only reason about it by reference to the past; and as they can never know all the forces in operation, their inferences must contain more or less of error. For example, this year competition appears to be approaching, in intensity, the point of danger; and yet next year an abundant supply of gold may raise prices, and thereby allay friction for an indefinite period. Yet, speaking generally and without limit of time, the great question of American economic supremacy remains to be settled; and as long as Europe continues armed, that question will not be settled peacefully upon America's own terms as America is now organized. There must be compromise or war, or else America must be so strong that war is deemed too hazardous to be attempted.

A compromise is a bargain, each side giving as little as it can; but doubtless the United States could make arrangements which would meet the emergency. The policy of England has always been to make such arrangements; and in this she has differed from France. Free trade as an economic dogma, applicable to all conditions of national life, has been exploded; but free trade as a form of insurance against hostile coalitions has worked well. England has found free trade cheaper than to arm; she would certainly find it more advantageous than to fight. No coalition has ever been formed against Great Britain since she became great; for evidently no one will plunge into hostilities, where little is to be made by war, and much by peace. Prussia has long maintained great armaments, and has sometimes made concessions, and sometimes used force. On the whole, Prussia has fared better than any other Continental state. Policy is a matter of judgment.

Americans are apt to reckon on their geographical position as in itself an insurance against war risks, on the principle that, like the tortoise, they are invulnerable if they withdraw within their shell. Such was the case formerly, but is not the case now. On the contrary, in European eyes, America offers the fairest prize to plunder that has been known since the sack of Rome, and, according to European standards, she is almost as unprotected as was Holland before Louis XIV.

First of all, America is valuable not only for what she has herself, but for what she keeps from others; for even without her islands the United States now closes South America and China. Were she defeated, these two vast territories would lie open to division. But more than this, Continental Europeans apprehend that were the United States crushed on the sea, were her islands taken from her, were she shut up within her own borders, all the rest of the world, save the British Empire, would fall to them, and that they might exclude American products at their will. They believe that American society would not stand the strain of the dislocation of the industrial system incident to the interruption of exports, and that disturbances would ensue which would remove all fear of American supremacy. Also, Continental statesmen are not lacking who conceive that England might see more profit in helping to divide the lion's skin than in binding up his wounds. Nor must it ever be forgotten that, with Great Britain, the success of the European or the American continent is only a choice of evils. America is her most dangerous competitor save Germany and Russia. Great Britain, therefore, at present, holds to America, as the lesser peril; but should, at a given moment, the weight in the other scale of the balance preponderate, England would shift to the side of our antagonist.

Assuming, for the moment, for the sake of argument, that the United States is determined to yield nothing, but is resolved to push all her advantages to the uttermost, it is clear that an attack upon her would be profitable, if it could be made with reasonable hope of success. Europe believes that it could be made with such hope, provided a coalition could be opportunely formed. In this Europeans may be wrong; but they judge after their own standards, and possibly they may be right.

America has an army of less than 100,000 men, with a short supply of officers, and no reserves either of soldiers or of material. At the mere rumor of war 100,000 men would have to leave the country to garrison Cuba, Porto Rico, the canal, the Philippines, and Hawaii. More ought to go, if more could be obtained. But to send 100,000 men abroad would strip the Union bare. Even the ports would be defended by militia, and no reinforcements would be at hand to supply the waste in the tropics. Such garrisons could hardly stand against the overwhelming mass of troops which could be concentrated against them.

The navy is even feebler, in proportion to the task which would be required of it. The United States has 520,000 tons of warships, built or building. France and Germany have 1,162,000, and France, Germany, and Russia have 1,731,000.

Americans, furthermore, are disposed to assume that no coalition could ever be formed against them. Judging by the past, nothing can be more certain than that coalitions both can and will be formed against them, if they so behave as to make such ventures worth the cost and risk. Combinations always have been made, under such conditions, and probably always will continue to be made. To be opulent, unarmed, and aggressive is to put a premium upon them. An arrangement of this character was, in fact, contemplated in 1898, and is generally believed to have been abandoned only through uncertainty as to the neutrality of England.

Suppose an alliance of two or more powers, of which France were to be one: they would possess an admirable base in the West Indies, in Martinique or Guadeloupe, and also convenient bases in Asia. No station on the whole Asiatic coast is more commanding than Port Arthur, held by Russia. Fleets, therefore, of any size could be concentrated and supplied close to the seat of war, and Europeans compute that ships could be concentrated against us at the least in the ratio of two to one.

Our rivals believe that a couple of defeats secured by overwhelming numbers would settle the war; for ironclads cannot be built in less than two or three years, and they calculate that two or three years of isolation, resulting from the loss of control of the sea, would produce enough domestic unrest to enforce acceptance of their terms. Those terms, they assume, would suffice to insure their future safety.

Such possibilities have not yet been maturely considered in the United States, because the change in the position occupied by the country is recent. Men do not immediately divest themselves of their old prejudices. Nevertheless, Americans are inclined to believe, and with reason, that their country is becoming the modern seat of empire. If this be so, they must accept the dangers and the cost of greatness with its advantages. All situations have their drawbacks.

From 1815 to the Boer war England claimed to be the financial capital of the world, and that claim was admitted. England, consequently, paid heavily to insure herself against attack. She not only maintained a navy supposed to be equal to that of any combination which could probably be formed against her, but, adopting free trade, she bought from all. France proceeded on the opposite theory; and yet, although France has kept up vast armies, she has been thrice disastrously defeated, twice actually conquered, and has never attained her end.

If a country would live in peace, experience has demonstrated that she must not be too grasping; for excessive greed makes her overthrow a benefit to all, and competitors act accordingly. On the other hand, certain races have felt themselves adapted to win victory in battle, and have prospered; if the American people, after due deliberation, feel aggression to be for their best interest, there is little to be urged by way of precedent against the logic of their decision.

Men inclining to this attitude can point to history, and insist that no radical readjustment of the world's economic equilibrium has ever been unaccompanied by war; and that if war must come, the United States may well face it now. To abandon any advantage would be weakness. The United States is young, strong, rich, and energetic, with an enormous military population. No permanent tranquillity can be hoped for until her supremacy is acknowledged: therefore the course which will enforce that acknowledgment soonest is the cheapest. America is as likely now as she will ever be to emerge victorious from any conflict into which she may enter.

To such reasoning it might be objected that war has proved too uncertain to be hazarded save in extremity, and the failure of the British speculation in the Transvaal might be cited as a warning. But such an argument would savor of an expression of personal opinion on a question of expediency, and this article is confined to an attempt to draw deductions as to fixed social laws from the facts of history.

No one can deny that certain nations have made war profitable: therefore profitable wars will probably occur in the future. Nevertheless, such nations have succeeded because they were military nations; that is to say, because they made war a business, and waged it better and cheaper than their rivals. In other words, they devoted their energies to fighting, and maintained fleets and armies as we maintain railroads and factories. To conduct hostilities as amateurs is futile, as the English have discovered.

If Americans are determined to reject reciprocity in all its forms, to insist on their advantages, to concede nothing to the adversary; if, having driven in the knife, they mean to turn it in the wound, they should recognize that they are provoking reprisals in every form, and accept the situation with its limitations. To carry out an aggressive policy in some security, the United States needs 300,000 trained men whom she can put in the field in twenty days, with an ample reserve of officers and of material. She needs well-fortified coasts and colonies, and an effective transport service. More especially, she needs a navy. Judging by the example of England, who has always done her best to make her friendship of value, 100 battleships and armored cruisers, equipped and ready for sea, would hardly suffice.

In a word, the experience of ages has demonstrated that alternatives are presented to aspiring nations in regard to the payment they will make for their prize. The one is the alternative of Cobden, the other that of Colbert. There is no middle course. Destruction has awaited the gambler who backs his luck; the braggart who would be at once rich, aggressive, and unarmed. Such a man or such a nation puts a premium on spoliation. It is only necessary to reflect upon the fate of France in 1870, to accept this inference as true. America enjoys no immunity from natural laws. She can pay for what she takes, or she can fight for it, but she cannot have the earth for nothing. Sooner or later the inexorable tribute will be exacted from her as it has been exacted from every predominant community, from the days of the grandeur of Babylon to those of the glory of London; for, since time began, no race has won for itself supremacy without paying a price in gold or blood to other races as ambitious and almost as powerful as itself.